MW01502919

The New England Beach Guide

by Ellen M. Ruggles

Every effort has been made to ensure the accuracy of the information provided. However, to avoid disappointment it is best to call ahead to confirm times, fees, etc.

The New England Beach Guide
by Ellen M. Ruggles
edited by Andrea Brox and Beverly J. Wood
cover design by Carin Willis
illustrations by Suzanne Goguen Will
Pleasant Street Press
Lexington, Massachusetts

ISBN No. 0-9636123-2-8
Copyright © 1996 Ellen Ruggles
Printed in the United States of America

No part of this book may be reproduced in any form without the written permission of the publisher except for brief quotations contained in critical articles or reviews.
For information address
Pleasant Street Press
1644 Massachusetts Avenue, Suite 40
Lexington, MA 02173

Ruggles, Ellen M., 1949-
    The New England beach guide / by Ellen M. Ruggles.
        p.   cm.
    Includes index.
    ISBN 0-9636123-2-8
    1. New England—Guidebooks.   2. Bathing beaches—New England-
    -Guidebooks.   I. Title.
    F2.3.R84   1996
    917.404'43—dc20

With deep gratitude I dedicate this book to family: To my husband Steve, who kept the home fires burning; my children Jane and Timothy, who frequently left one beach before they were quite ready, in order to find the next; and my parents, Elinor and Irving McDowell, who often served as my chauffeurs and map readers -- even on bleak rainy days.

A big thank you also goes out to other family members and friends, who graciously shared their knowledge with me, and to Andrea Brox whose skill and wisdom helped pull this project together.

In *Gift from the Sea*, Anne Morrow Lindbergh writes, "There are other beaches to explore. There are more shells to find. This is only the beginning."

TABLE OF CONTENTS

Introduction
page vi

Beach Basics
page vii

Things You Should Know
page xii

Maine
page 15

New Hampshire
page 59

Massachusetts -- North Shore
page 71

Massachusetts -- Boston and Beyond
page 102

Massachusetts -- South Shore
page 115

Massachusetts -- Cape Cod
page 142

Massachusetts -- Martha's Vineyard
page 225

Massachusetts -- Nantucket
page 240

Rhode Island
page 248

Connecticut
page 294

Quick Reference Index
page 324

Ellen's Picks
page 327

General Index
page 328

Acknowledgements
page 335

INTRODUCTION

New England has more than 66,000 square miles of coastline.
And while many of those miles are composed of rocky cliffs
that meet the open sea, more than 500 beaches grace these
shores. From broad swaths of sand and dune along lower Cape
Cod to quiet coves carved into Maine's rough-hewn coast,
there is a beach for virtually every taste. Even Rhode Island,
the smallest state in the U.S., has more than 100 beaches.

With so many to choose from, there is no way to find the
perfect beach for yourself, unless, of course, you visit every
one.

To wit we present *The New England Beach Guide*. The only
book of its kind, this personally-researched guide provides
information on more than 400 beaches with public access
along the New England coast.

Is the water warm or cold? Are there tidal pools to explore or
rocks to climb? What about restrooms and a snack bar? *The
New England Beach Guide* answers all these questions and
many more. Each listing includes a detailed description of the
beach's appearance, sand quality, services, parking, directions,
even the kind of people the beach attracts.

This book is a labor of love that took author, Ellen Ruggles,
years to compile. She visited every beach, walked every
shoreline, and froze her toes testing the waters on more than a
few occasions. It is dedicated to all the beach lovers who adore
the feel of salt on their skin, sun on their faces, and who smile
at the thought of getting sand in their sandwiches.

Andrea Brox
Publisher
Pleasant Street Press

BEACH BASICS

Access: Although the right to walk along the beach -- any beach -- seems as if it should be God-given, the New England shoreline is not accessible to all. In fact, Maine and Massachusetts are two of only three states in the nation that allow the shoreline (to the low-tide line) to be privately owned. And while Maine has more than 2,500 miles of coastline -- more than any other state in the nation -- only 3.5 percent of that, or a little more than 80 miles, is under public ownership.

Massachusetts is a bit more egalitarian: About 25 percent of its shoreline is publicly owned. But only about 10 percent of that truly offers public access, according to the Massachusetts Department of Environmental Management. (Comparatively, about 50 percent of California beachfront, and nearly 100 percent of Hawaii beachfront, is accessible.)

The reason? Colonial-era laws allowed beachfront ownership. Their intention was to encourage oceanfront property owners to build marine facilities that were crucial to the economic vitality of a growing nation. In the 17th century, the public's right to a day at the beach was of little concern.

In Rhode Island, New Hampshire, and Connecticut, beachfront is more accessible. Only .1 mile of New Hampshire's 17-mile open coastline is privately owned. The public has the right to stroll all beaches anywhere along the coast up to the high-tide line, which is usually marked by the trail of seaweed that rings the shore. Still, lolling on sandy beaches *above* the high-tide mark -- which is usually where everyone wants to sit -- can be off limits. And even access to beaches ostensibly open to the public is often limited.

Dunes: The great hills of sand along the beach, known as dunes, protect land from eroding during ocean storms. Because of their fragility and ecological significance, it's important to avoid treading on these treasures. Always use designated boardwalks or clear-cut paths for beach access. If you must see dunes up close, visit the Province Lands Visitors Center, Race Point Road, Provincetown, MA, 508-487-1256.

Litter: Shoreline trash is quite literally a hefty problem. In 1994 (the most recent year for which data is available), more than 55 tons of debris were collected from New England beaches. Besides a preponderance of cigarette butts and plastic bags, beach refuse included such unusual items as typewriters, bowling balls, car stereos, and toilet seats. This massive beach sweep, conducted in 35 states, was organized by Coastal Cleanup, an annual volunteer effort spearheaded by the Center for Marine Conservation.

If you'd like to participate in your local cleanup effort, contact the Center for Marine Conservation, 1725 DeSales St. NW, Washington, D.C. 20036, 202-429-5609.

Both Rhode Island and New Hampshire are trying to limit debris by encouraging state park visitors to "carry in-carry out." They provide trash bags at all fee booths. In fact, in 1989, New Hampshire became the first state in the nation to eliminate all beach trash barrels.

You can help eliminate garbage by planning ahead. Bring as few throw away items as possible. Don't take anything breakable, such as glass. And if you don't take your trash home, be sure to use designated waste and recycling bins.

Nude sunbathing: Not that this point needs reiterating, but New England is *not* St. Tropez. Nude and seminude sunbathing is discouraged. Although there is no law banning nudity on most federal land, there may overriding local laws that prohibit you from sunning "au naturel." In fact, nudity is banned on all land within the Cape Cod National Seashore. In general, however, nude is not equated with lewd, and most law enforcement officials try to avoid citations and arrests. This is not to say, however, that you shouldn't choose your beaches carefully. Following are some recommendations from the Naturist Society, whose book, *Lee Baxandall's World Guide to Nude Beaches and Resorts,* is the nude sunbathers' Bible.

Lucy Vincent Beach, Chilmark, Martha's Vineyard, MA. This is one of the few beaches that's actually zoned for nude use.

Miacomet Beach, Nantucket, MA. Although there are several beaches on Nantucket that nude bathers favor, this is considered the most social locale. Miacomet is a secluded stretch of sand between Cisco and Madaket beaches and is not listed separately in *The New England Beach Guide*.

Truro Beach, Truro, MA. Truro is technically within the National Seashore, but it has been a famous spot for nude sunbathers for more than 30 years.

North Lighthouse Beach (aka Sandy Point), Block Island, RI. Actually it's a virtually deserted section south of this beach that is recommended for nude sunbathing.

Pests: Among the most annoying, but relatively harmless, beach pests are *green heads*. Besides their sonic buzz, these flies have a nasty sting. They breed primarily in marshes. Unfortunately, in late July and early August, they plague some of the most beautiful beaches along the New England seashore, among them Crane's Beach in Ipswich, Massachusetts.

A far more serious pest is the *deer tick*, which can carry the Lyme disease bacteria. These ticks are found along the New England coast, and typically breed in tall grasses. The best way to avoid these ticks is to avoid high beach grass. But it's always a good idea, after a day at the beach, to check for ticks. Deer ticks are about the size of a pinhead and are thus, difficult to spot. Although not all tick bites leave marks, a round red circle, sometimes resembling a bull's-eye, is typical. If you have a tick or what you think is a tick bite, call your doctor.

While deer ticks pose a more likely threat to beachgoers, the shark is far more feared. And despite the fact that Hollywood would have you believe otherwise, *man-eating sharks* along the New England coast are rare. The more common variety is the plankton-eating "sand shark." Although they can grow up to 8 feet in length, sand sharks are considered innocuous and are not known to bother humans. But they are still best avoided.

Jellyfish are far less frightening, but they do pack a burning sting. They can be hard to see in water because they are opaque, but quite obvious when washed ashore. Be cautious approaching all jellyfish. Even after they beach and die, a jellyfish's stinging cells remain active for several hours. If you do get stung, washing the area with a cloth soaked in alcohol, vinegar, or witch hazel can help ease the pain.

Pollution: Like litter, pollution is no stranger to the New England beachfront. Storm water runoff, sewage, boating waste, and agricultural runoff are the primary culprits.

Boston Harbor -- which is home to some 20 beaches -- is the most notoriously polluted body of water in the region. Until 1991, solid matter from the region's sewage, or sludge, was dumped untreated into the harbor. Fortunately, recent efforts to clean up the harbor have been successful. Levels of toxic lead and silver in the sediment have dropped by 50 percent since 1977, according to the U.S. Geological Survey.

Still pollution in Boston Harbor and at beaches around New England continues to exist. In fact, polluted waters closed New England beaches 238 times in 1994, according to the Natural Resources Defense Council. (This is the most recent year for which figures are available.)

While this number is alarming, the truth is our waters may be far more polluted than we know. Connecticut is the only state that practices vigorous monitoring. Massachusetts, Rhode Island, Maine, and New Hampshire have far more limited testing and reporting programs.

Following are a sampling of some popular New England beaches that were closed for a day or more during 1994:

Massachusetts
Pegotty, Situate
Salem, Salem
Donavon's, Winthrop
Tenean, Boston
Wollaston, Boston
Malibu, Boston
King's, Boston
Lynn, Lynn
Nahant, Nahant
Lovells Island, Boston
Pleasure Bay, South
   Boston
Carson, Boston
Savin Hill, Boston
Short, Revere

Constitution, Boston
Nantasket, Nantasket
Sea Street, Barnstable
Keyes, Barnstable
Glendon, Dennis

Connecticut
Darien County, Darien
Seaside Park, Bridgeport
Pleasure, Bridgeport
Ocean, New London
Waterford, Waterford
West Haven (entire
   shoreline)

Bradley Point West to
  South Street, West
  Haven
Byram, Greenwich
Greenwich Point,
  Greenwich
Sherwood Island State,
  Sherwood
Burying Hill, Westport
Jennings, Fairfield

Penfield, Fairfield
South Pine Creek,
  Fairfield
Sasco, Fairfield

Maine
East End, Portland

Red Tide: Tiny organisms that sometimes multiply out of
control in warm, nutrient-filled water produce poisons that
create the infamous "red tide." These poisons, which affect
clams, mussels, quahogs, oysters, whelks, and snails, can kill
humans who eat the infected shellfish. Red Tide, however,
does not affect lobsters, shrimp, crabs, finfish, or periwinkles.

Sunbathing: More than 800,000 cases of skin cancer are
discovered each year, according to the American Cancer
Society. While most of those are curable, it is foolish not to
take precautions when spending time in the sun. The sun's
rays are strongest between 10:00 a.m. and 3:00 p.m. Even on
cloudy days 80 percent of the sun's burning rays get through.
Staying in the ocean doesn't offer much protection as the sun's
rays extend three feet into the water. Sunscreens, preferably
those with a SPF of 15 or higher, are essential for protecting
the skin. Evidence suggests there's a link between severe
childhood sunburns and adult melanoma, therefore it's
particularly important that children are protected.

THINGS YOU SHOULD KNOW

Season: You can walk on most beaches any time of the day, any day of the year. However, if a beach has facilities, such as restrooms, snack bars, and lifeguards, the "season" refers to the period that the beach has these facilities available. The most typical season is from Memorial Day through Labor Day.

Fees: If the listing only includes fees for nonresidents, assume that parking and beach use is free to residents.

Facilities: Many beaches have lifeguards in season. However, don't assume that all town beaches have lifeguards. If we don't list a lifeguard in the facilities section, assume that you must swim at your own risk.

Hours: Hours listed reflect the hours that the facilities are available to beachgoers. If facility hours are different from regular beach hours, it is noted. Also, a few beaches lock parking lot gates after hours. This too, is noted.

Order of Listings: Beaches are not listed alphabetically, but rather from south to north. One exception is Cape Cod. Here, listings begin on the Upper Cape, then go down the Atlantic side to Provincetown, and back up the bay side. However, in some cases, towns have beaches on both the bay and ocean sides of the Cape.

Parking: Some beaches included in this book have parking available for town residents only. However, virtually all beaches -- with the exception of those in Greenwich, Connecticut -- are open to the public. That is, anyone is free to come via foot or bike. In some cases, parking is available at nearby beaches, in town, or on streets. In other cases, car access is virtually impossible. However, whenever there are alternative parking options, we identify them.

Phone Numbers: Not all beaches have their own phone numbers. For those that do not, we list a local chamber of commerce number or one for the town offices.

Rules/Regulations: Virtually all beaches are governed by some local ordinances. These most typically include no alcohol, animals, and fires. Often, however, there are many more. In a few instances, we list "None posted" in the rules/regulations section. This means there were no signs at the beach and town officials were not available to provide guidelines. When visiting these beaches, it is always best to play it safe. In other words, be on your best behavior.

Sunglasses: 👓 The sunglasses icon you'll see preceding some of the listings is <u>not</u> a reminder to bring your shades, although it's always a good idea. Rather, it identifies the beach as one of "Ellen's Picks". These are the author's favorite beaches. The selections are entirely subjective and based on visceral reaction rather than any quantifiable criteria. But after visiting more than 400 beaches, the author ought to know a good place to plunk an umbrella when she sees one.

MAINE

View from Sand Beach, Mount Desert Island

Californians may be shocked, but Maine has more miles of coastline than any other state in the nation. All told, there are 2,500 miles of shore between Kittery and Eastport. Sounds impossible, but remember the most distinctive feature of Maine's coast is its jagged profile -- full of coves and inlets. Just as surprising is the fact that of those miles, only 80 are publicly owned. Maine is one of three states in the nation (the others are Massachusetts and Virginia) to allow beachfront to be privately owned.

That said, Maine's publicly accessible coast packs plenty of personality. However, many of its beaches are not those of a sun worshipper's dream. Most are rough-hewn, with rocks, cliffs, and bracingly cold water. Their charm is unique. Once it gets you, no benign, flat expanse of sand will ever do again.

Fort Foster Park
Pocohontas Road
Kittery, ME 03904
207-439-3800

Season: Memorial Day - Labor Day, and weekends through September
Hours: 10:00 a.m. - 8:00 p.m.

Parking: Lots
Fees: $2 per car plus $1 per adult and $.50 for children under 12
Sand: Soft with stones
Crowd: Families
Facilities: Restrooms, picnic areas, pavilion, nature trails, ball field
Rules/Regulations: No alcohol

Directions: From Route 1 to Route 103. Turn right onto Chauncey Creek Road, then right onto Pocohontas Road. After the bridge, turn right and follow to the end of the road.

This municipal park is a virtual secret. Fort Foster was a military post in the early 1900s. After it closed in 1948, the town of Kittery purchased it for recreation. Three beaches are surrounded by hills, woods, and trails. Both Fort Foster beach, near a long pier on the Piscataqua River, and Whaleback Beach, which faces the ocean, have a mixture of soft sand, stone and rock outcroppings. They have calm waters and are great beaches for lounging. Windsurfing is permitted at Whaleback Beach. On the northern side, Rocky Beach is popular with scuba divers.

"A good family beach."
          Judy Smart, Kittery Point, ME

Sea Point and Crescent Beach

Seapoint Road
Kittery, ME 03904
207-439-7545

Season: Year-round
Hours: 10:00 a.m. - 5:00 p.m.
Parking: Small lot a short walk away; resident-stickers required for a few spaces right at the beach
Fees: None
Sand: Soft with rocks
Crowd: Mixed
Facilities: None
Rules/Regulations: No alcohol, animals, open fires

Directions: Route 1 to Route 103. Turn right onto Chauncey Road and right again onto Sea Point Road. Follow to the end.

These two beaches sit on either side of a protective rocky point. Both are medium-size and have soft sand. A great spot for timid swimmers -- the water drops off gradually and there is hardly any undertow. Windsurfing is permitted at the east end.

"It's quiet, with only the sound of the water lapping the shore."
Joe Donnelly, Somersworth, NH

York Harbor Beach

Harbor Beach Road
York Harbor, ME 03911
207-363-4422

Season: Memorial Day - Labor Day
Hours: None
Parking: Limited at beach, nearby roadside parking
Fees: None
Sand: Sand with stone
Crowd: Mixed
Facilities: Lifeguard, portable restrooms
Rules/Regulations: No alcohol, animals, balls, fires
Directions: From Route 1A to York Street, then right onto Harbor Beach Road.

Flanked on either side by rocky banks, this is a medium-size, but shallow beach. Although parts are covered with smooth sand, the upper end has lots of pebbles. Surfers should note that boards are allowed only in designated areas.

"It's small enough so I can keep track of my kids."
Nancy Richard, York, ME

Special Notes: Need to stretch your legs? Head back on 1A to Route 103 S and walk over the length of Wiggly Bridge to an inlet and the lovely Stedman Woods wildlife preserve.

Small fish swim in schools to promote survival. When swimming together and in synchronization they can look like one "big" fish to a potential predator.

Long Sands Beach
Route 1A
York, ME 03910
207-363-4422

Season: Memorial Day - Labor Day
Hours: None posted
Parking: Roadside meters
Fees: $.25 for 30 minutes, 8-hour maximum
Sand: Soft
Crowd: Mixed
Facilities: Lifeguard, restrooms, restaurants, snack bars
Rules/Regulations: No alcohol, animals, balls, fires; surfing permitted in designated areas.
Directions: Off Route 1A, north of York Harbor.

This sandy, 2-mile open stretch lies just south of the picturesque Nubble Lighthouse on Cape Neddick. Unfortunately, much of the beach is covered at high tide. There's still room to spread a blanket, but things can get crowded. Both floats and surfboards are available for rent.

Special Notes: The York trolley makes hourly stops along the coast from Harmon Park in York Harbor to all of the beaches and Nubble Lighthouse. Call the York Chamber of Commerce (207-363-4422) for a schedule.

Short Sands Beach
Route 1A
York, ME 03910
207-363-4422

Season: Memorial Day - Labor Day
Hours: None posted
Parking: Lot
Fees: $.25 for 30 minutes, 8-hour maximum
Sand: Soft with stones
Crowd: Mixed
Facilities: Lifeguard, restrooms, playground, basketball court, arcades, snack bars and restaurants
Rules/Regulations: No alcohol, animals, balls, fires

Directions: Along Route 1A, in downtown York Beach.

This .25-mile long beach is next to the Fun-O-Rama arcade and Ellis Park. Although there is some surf, its protected location in Cape Neddick Harbor provides gentle waters. There is, however, some undertow. That aside, it's a great spot for kids who love the proximity to the arcade.

"There seems to be fewer people and more beach than at Long Sands. And the arcade is here."
Amy Goldstein, Billerica, MA

Special Notes: Salt water taffy lovers shouldn't miss the Goldrenrod. It's been making this gooey confection for 100 years. In addition to 12 flavors of taffy, it sells other candies as well as 135 flavors (serving 24 at a time) of its own award-winning ice cream.

Passaconaway Beach
aka **Cape Neddick Beach**
Shore Road
York, ME 03909
207-363-4422

Season: Year-round
Hours: None posted
Parking: Limited roadside
Fees: None
Sand: Sand and stones
Crowd: Mixed
Facilities: None
Rules/Regulations: No fires without a permit

Directions: From Route 1A to Shore Road by the bridge.

This is a small beach near where the Cape Neddick River enters the sea. When the tide goes out, some great tidal pools emerge -- perfect for kids. Also, the view toward the ocean and Nubble Lighthouse is charming.

"We enjoy it here because there are not too many people."
James Brown, Eliot, ME

Little Beach
Israel Head Road
Ogunquit, ME 03907
207-646-5533

Season: Year-round
Hours: None posted
Parking: Limited roadside; lots at a distance
Fees: $4 per car at lots
Sand: Soft
Crowd: Mixed
Facilities: None
Rules/Regulations: No alcohol, animals, glass

Directions: From Route 1 (Main Street) turn right onto Shore Road and left up Israel Head Road to a small, short-term parking area by a lighthouse.

Midway along the rocky shoreline footpath known as Marginal Way -- it extends from Perkins Cove into Ogunquit Village -- you'll find a series of diminutive beaches. Separated by rocky outcroppings, they are known collectively as "Little Beach." People love this ocean trail, which can be walked in under a half hour. But take your time and enjoy watching the surfers, body boarders, swimmers, and birds.

"There is plenty of space to walk and play at low tide. High tide can chase you off the beach and onto the rocks or even into the parking lot."
David Kreed, Manchester, NH

Special Notes: Ogunquit has a trolley service that ferries people from beach parking lots to in-town attractions. It's $.50 per ride, and operates between mid May and Columbus Day weekend.

Ogunquit Beach
Beach Street
Ogunquit, ME 03907
207-646-5533

Season: Memorial Day - Labor Day
Hours: 7:30 a.m. - 4:30 p.m.

Parking: Lot; also a few 30-minute spots at beach
Fees: $2 per hour
Sand: Super soft
Crowd: Mixed
Facilities: Lifeguard, restrooms, bath house, shaded benches, restaurants, shops; chair, umbrella, float, and surfboard rental
Rules/Regulations: No alcohol, animals, glass

Directions: From Route 1 (Main Street), turn right onto Beach Street.

A perennial favorite, this 3-mile stretch has magnificent fine, white sand. The drop is gentle into the ocean, except near the sand bar where it's quite sharp. Both surf and undertow are strong along the ocean side of the beach. The water along the Ogunquit River, just behind the dunes, is warmer and gentler.

"Ogunquit is a wonderful, busy place. The trolley is the only way to go."
      Donna Williams, New Boston, NH

Special Notes: The Family Fun Run takes place on the beach at the end of June. It's sponsored by the Ogunquit Recreation Department. For information call 207-646-3032.

Footbridge Beach
Ocean Street
Ogunquit, ME 03907
207-646-5533

Season: Memorial Day- Labor Day
Hours: 7:30 a.m. - 4:30 p.m.
Parking: Lot; some 15-minute spots along the roadside
Fees: $6 per car
Sand: Super soft
Crowd: Families
Facilities: Lifeguard, restrooms, snack bar
Rules/Regulations: No alcohol, animals, glass

Directions: From Route 1 to the end of Ocean Street.

This northern section of Ogunquit Beach, which runs to the Wells town line, gets its name from the footbridge that crosses the Ogunquit River. (It allows pedestrians to get from the parking lot to the beach.) It has the same wonderful surf and sand as Ogunquit Beach, but not the rental facilities or the crowds that go with it.

Wells Beach
Atlantic Avenue
Wells, ME 04090
207-646-2451

Season: Memorial Day - Labor Day
Hours: 5:00 a.m. - 11:00 p.m.
Parking: Lots
Fees: Residents, $6 per car; nonresidents, $7 per car
Sand: Super soft
Crowd: Mixed
Facilities: Lifeguard, restrooms, snack bar, benches (facilities 9:00 a.m. - 5:00 p.m.)
Rules/Regulations: No alcohol, balls, fires, glass, in-line skates, skateboards

Directions: From Route 1 to Mile Road. Turn left at Atlantic Avenue to reach parking lot at the end.

This popular long, barrier beach is backed by many cottages and homes. It has wonderful, fine sand and moderate surf. Waves break over sand bars, and there is a gradual drop-off and virtually no undertow. Rocky outcroppings in the central beach area form an interesting natural sculpture. At the northern end you can walk the jetty and enjoy views of Drakes Island Beach. A view machine near the sea wall will give you a close-up look.

Drakes Island Beach
Drakes Island Road
Wells, ME 04090
207-646-2451

Season: Memorial Day - Labor Day
Hours: 5:00 a.m. - 11:00 p.m.
Parking: Lots
Fees: $7 per car; $4 per car after 12:00 p.m.

Sand: Super soft
Crowd: Mixed
Facilities: Lifeguard, restrooms (facilities 9:00 a.m. - 5:00 p.m.)
Rules/Regulations: No alcohol, balls, fires, glass

Directions: From Route 1 to Drakes Island Road (there is one lot here that's a short walk to the beach). For additional parking, turn right onto Island Beach Road and follow to the end, where there is a second lot.

This gently curving beach is 2 miles long. The jetty on the southern end is a good spot to watch boats entering and leaving the harbor. The sand is delightfully fine and the ambiance, decidedly uncommercial. Although cottages dot the beach front, it is typically uncrowded.

"Our family has been coming here for years. It's very relaxing."
Leonard Osborne, Rensselaer, NY

Laudholm Beach
Laudholm Farm Road
Wells, ME 04090
207-646-1555

Season: Year-round
Hours: 8:00 a.m. - 5:00 p.m.; visitors center is open weekdays from 10:00 a.m. - 4:00 p.m., and between May 1 and October 31 it's also open weekends 12:00 p.m. - 4:00 p.m.
Parking: Lot
Fees: $5 per car
Sand: Soft
Crowd: Mixed
Facilities: Restrooms, visitor center, picnic tables
Rules/Regulations: No animals, bicycles, grills, smoking

Directions: Route 1 to Laudholm Farm Road. Left at fork, right into entrance.

North of and adjacent to Drakes Island Beach is this undeveloped shorefront. Part of the Wells National Estuarine Research Reserve, there are nature trails through the woods, fields, and marshes which lead to the beach. Swimming, however, is not encouraged.

"Laudholm is a great place to visit for anyone who loves nature."
Margaret Battey, Goffstown, NH

Parsons and Crescent Surf Beaches
Kennebunk, ME 04043
207-967-0857

Season: Mid June - mid September
Hours: 8:00 a.m. - 6:00 p.m.
Parking: Small lot
Fees: None
Sand: Super soft with some rocks
Crowd: Mixed
Facilities: None
Rules/Regulations: No animals, floats, surfboards

Directions: From Route 9 to Parsons Beach Road, which is an unmarked, narrow, and tree-lined private lane across from Brown Street.

These two adjacent beaches are on private land just north of the Rachel Carson Wildlife Refuge and are accessed by the same road. A sign at the entrance pathway asks visitors to "observe and enjoy wildlife, bird life, marine life in their natural habitats." We should be grateful to the owners for allowing public access to this gorgeous beach area. The mouth of the Mousam River, now on the north side of Parsons Beach, used to separate these beaches: A straighter channel was cut in 1846 to improve shipping.

"I like the seaweed and snails."
Melody Harris, Harrisburg, PA

Mother's Beach
Beach Avenue
Kennebunk, ME 04043
207-967-0857

Season: Mid June - mid September
Hours: 8:00 a.m. - 6:00 p.m.
Parking: Lot; sticker required

Fees: Nonresidents, $5 per day per car, $15 per week, $30 per season
Sand: Soft with stones
Crowd: Families
Facilities: Lifeguard
Rules/Regulations: No alcohol, animals, balls, Frisbees, swimming over your head

Directions: From Route 9 to Sea Road to Beach Avenue.

This is a small and quiet sandy beach in a residential area. It's the southern-most of the three beaches that compose what is often collectively called, Kennebunk Beach. (The other two beaches are Middle and Gooch's. Descriptions follow.)

"It's called Mother's Beach because mothers can easily keep track of their children."
      Judy Linehan, Pittsfield, MA

Special Notes: Stickers are required for most beach parking. They are available weekdays at the Town Hall (207-985-3675) or weekends at the Police Station (207-985-6121). It is also possible to park in town and take one of the privately operated trolleys.

Middle Beach
Beach Avenue
Kennebunk, ME 04043
207-967-0857

Season: Mid June - mid September
Hours: 8:00 a.m. - 6:00 p.m.
Parking: Limited roadside; sticker required
Fees: Nonresidents, $5 per day per car, $15 per week, $30 per season
Sand: Soft with stones
Crowd: Mixed
Facilities: None
Rules/Regulations: No alcohol, animals, glass
Directions: From Route 9 to Boothbay Road to Beach Avenue.

This mid-sized beach that's scattered with stones is separated from the other two parts of Kennebunk Beach by rocky outcroppings.

Gooch's Beach

Beach Avenue
Kennebunk, ME 04043
207-967-0857

Season: Mid June - mid September
Hours: 8:00 a.m. - 6:00 p.m.
Parking: Limited roadside, sticker required
Fees: Nonresidents, $5 per day per car, $15 per week, $30 per season
Sand: Super soft
Crowd: Mixed
Facilities: Lifeguard, restrooms
Rules/Regulations: No alcohol, animals, glass

Directions: From Route 9 to Beach Avenue.

Located at the mouth of the Kennebunk River, this 1.5-mile-long, crescent-shaped stretch, is the largest of the "Kennebunk Beach" beaches. Surfers enjoy the rolling waves that break both right and left.

Colony Beach

Ocean Avenue
Kennebunkport, ME 04046
207-967-4243

Season: Year-round
Hours: 8:00 a.m. - 6:00 p.m.
Parking: Small lot
Fees: None
Sand: Soft
Crowd: Mixed
Facilities: None
Rules/Regulations: No alcohol, animals, glass

Directions: From Kennebunkport village to Ocean Avenue across from the Colony Hotel. At the mouth of the

Kennebunk River is a small beach with soft sand mixed with some stone. Although it's decidedly quiet, there is always some activity -- boats traveling down the river and people fishing off the jetty.

"Quiet, compared to the busy town."
Bob Rosene, York, ME

Cleaves Cove Beach
Turbats Creek Road
Kennebunkport, ME 04046
207-967-4243

Season: Year-round
Hours: 8:00 a.m. - 6:00 p.m.
Parking: None
Fees: None
Sand: Soft with stones and shells
Crowd: Mixed, but very sparse
Facilities: None
Rules/Regulations: No alcohol, animals, glass

Directions: From Ocean Avenue, which becomes Shore Avenue, to Turbats Creek Road. Or, from Main Street to Wildes District Road, turn right onto Turbats Creek Road.

This mini beach, at the end of a year-round neighborhood road, is picturesque. Unfortunately, there's little sand for lounging. However, at low tide you can walk across to Vaughn's Island Preserve, a 40-acre island. Don't forget to allow time to return.

Goose Rocks Beach
Goose Rocks Road
Kennebunkport, ME 04046
207-967-4243

Season: Mid June - mid September
Hours: 8:00 a.m. - 6:00 p.m.
Parking: Limited roadside, sticker required; no trolley service
Fees: Residents, $3 per season per car; nonresidents, $5 per day per car, $30 per season

Sand: Soft
Crowd: Mixed
Facilities: Lifeguard
Rules/Regulations: None posted

Directions: From Route 9 turn onto Goose Rocks Road.

Located on Goosefare Bay, this 2-mile long, house-lined beach is great for children. There is some surf but no undertow, and a very gentle drop-off into the water. Small tidal pools form at low tide. A salt marsh is a favorite spot for birders. The islands visible in the bay are, from south to north, West Goose Rocks, East Goose Rocks, and Timber Island.

"I swam here once with a sea lion."
        Toni Krause, Arundel, ME

Fortune Rocks Beach
Fortune Rocks Road
Biddeford, ME 04005
207-282-1567

Season: Memorial Day - Labor Day
Hours: Sunrise - sunset
Parking: Limited roadside, sticker required
Fees: Nonresidents, $50 per car for seasonal sticker; no day passes available
Sand: Soft
Crowd: Mixed
Facilities: None
Rules/Regulations: No alcohol

Directions: From Route 9 to Fortune Rocks Road.

The surf during incoming tides is fine for surfing. It's steep, hollow, and breaks right. The beach drops off gently but there is some undertow. Huge rocks and broken concrete pieces form a sea wall.

Special Notes: To obtain a pass, call 207-284-9307.

Biddeford Pool Beach
Biddeford, ME 04005
207-282-1567

Season: Memorial Day - Labor Day
Hours: 9:00 a.m. - 5:00 p.m.
Parking: Lot, sticker required
Fees: Nonresidents, $50 per car for seasonal pass; no day passes available
Sand: Soft
Crowd: Mixed
Facilities: Lifeguard, restrooms, bath house, bicycle rack
Rules/Regulations: No alcohol, unrestrained animals

Directions: From Route 9/208 to Route 208, bear left at the intersection, and right across from Hatties restaurant.

Take the boardwalks over protected dunes to an ample sandy beach. As the name suggests, there are tidal pools to explore. Surfing is allowed in designated areas. Ball playing is also permitted, but at the waterline only. Recently dedicated as the Gilbert R. Boucher Memorial Park, improvements may be forthcoming.

"I love the waves, and the hard sand is just right for walking."
Albertine LaBelle, Biddeford, ME

Hills Beach
Hills Beach Road
Biddeford, ME 04005
207-282-1567

Season: Year-round
Hours: None posted
Parking: Limited roadside; sticker required
Fees Nonresidents, $50 per car for seasonal pass; no day passes available
Sand: Grainy
Crowd: Families
Facilities: None
Rules/Regulations: No alcohol

Directions: From Route 9/208 (Pool Street) to Hills Beach Road at the University of New England. The beach is across from Bufflehead Restaurant.

The section of town called Hills Beach is a protected point. The waters are calm and at low tide the outgoing sea water leaves behind Maine's largest tidal basin – it's about a mile wide. The main beach area is a sandy spot across from Bufflehead Restaurant, although there is limited access between some of the small beachside homes. While it is possible to walk to the small Monument Island at low tide, the seagulls have claimed it for their own.

"The water is warm here. And it is quiet."
Chris Hunter, Hanson, MA

Camp Ellis Beach
Surf Street
Saco, ME 04072
207-282-1567

Season: Year-round
Hours: 6:00 a.m. - 10:00 p.m.
Parking: Lot
Fees: $5 per car
Sand: Coarse
Crowd: Mixed
Facilities: None, but restaurants and shops nearby
Rules/Regulations: No alcohol, unrestrained animals, surfing, jet skis near beach

Directions: From Route 9 to Camp Ellis Village.

South of the Old Orchard Beach amusement area is the charmingly old-fashioned Camp Ellis neighborhood. This fishing village, which runs along the mouth of the Saco River, has several beaches that are separated from the river by a long, protective breakwater. Beach erosion is a problem here: Witness the rubber barriers on the sand and the S.O.S. (Save Our Shores) fundraising signs.

Ferry Beach State Park

Route 9
Saco, ME 04072
207-283-0067

Season: Memorial Day - September 30
Hours: 9:00 a.m. - sunset; gates lock at 8:00 p.m.
Parking: Lot
Fees: $2 per adult, $.50 per child ages 5-11; no charge for children under 5 and seniors over 65 (Family season passes to all Maine State Parks cost $40 per family and $20 per individual.)
Sand: Coarse
Crowd: Families
Facilities: Lifeguard, restrooms, bath house, picnic tables, trails
Rules/Regulations: No alcohol, animals, fires, floats ("boogie boards" are okay), face masks/snorkel equipment

Directions: Off Route 9 between Camp Ellis and Old Orchard Beach.

The sandy, family-oriented beach is within a 117-acre preserve situated between the Old Orchard Beach amusements and the Saco River. A wide path takes you from the parking lot and under Route 9 to a boardwalk through the dunes. The water drops gradually into the sea. Waders will find that they can walk *way* out. There are many walking trails in the preserve, and leashed dogs and bicycles are welcome on them. Be sure to ask attendants about, and look for, the stand of tupelo trees, an uncommon species in this latitude.

"A nice family beach. It's a placid part of the ocean with not many waves."
Tom O'Donnell, Westbrook, ME

Bay View Beach

Bay View Road
Saco, ME 04072
207-283-0067

Season: Memorial Day - Labor Day

Hours: 6:00 a.m. - 10:00 p.m.
Parking: Roadside and lots
Fees: None
Sand: Coarse
Crowd: Mixed
Facilities: Lifeguard, portable restrooms
Rules/Regulations: No alcohol, unrestrained pets, surfing, jet skis near beach

Directions: From Route 9 to Bay View Road.

A narrow roadway by a religious community takes you to this small beach which is actually part of Old Orchard Beach. (Old Orchard Beach is 7 miles long.)

Ocean Park
Temple Avenue
Old Orchard, ME 04064
207-934-9068

Season: Year-round
Hours: 6:00 a.m. - 10:00 p.m.
Parking: Lot, roadside
Fees: None
Sand: Coarse
Crowd: Families
Facilities: Lifeguard, restaurants, shops
Rules/Regulations: No alcohol, animals, fires, floats ("boogie" boards" are okay), snorkels

Directions: From Route 1 to Route 5 (Saco Avenue). Turn right onto Temple Avenue to Ocean Park.

This section of Old Orchard Beach was founded in 1881 as a religious enclave. Today, the area is overseen by the Ocean Park Association and protective covenants have prevented the neighborhood from changing too much. As a result, it's a somewhat exclusive, quiet area. A boardwalk over dunes leads to the narrow beach, which is maintained by the town. It's also accessible from various locations along the road.

Special Notes: Concerts are held Sunday evenings. Educational, cultural, and religious programs are also sponsored by the Ocean Park Association. Call 207-934-9068.

Old Orchard Beach
East Grand Avenue
Old Orchard, ME 04064
207-934-2500

Season: Memorial Day - mid September
Hours: 9:00 a.m. - 10:00 p.m.
Parking: Lots
Fees: $5 per car
Sand: Coarse
Crowd: Mixed
Facilities: Lifeguard, restrooms ($.25 fee at the Chamber of Commerce facility, free at the two public facilities), bath house, bicycle rack, public telephones; restaurants/take out food, shops nearby
Rules/Regulations: No alcohol, animals, fires, floats ("boogie" boards" are okay), snorkels

Directions: From Route 1 to Route 5 (Saco Avenue); or Route 98 (Cascade Road) to Route 9 (East Grand Avenue).

Don't look for the apple orchards for which this beach was named. They're long gone. What has remained, however, is Old Orchard's reputation as a summer resort: People have been vacationing here since the late 1800s. The greater Old Orchard Beach shoreline is 7 miles long. But people primarily congregate near the arcades, snack bars, and amusements, which proliferate on a 3.5-mile stretch. On its northern side is a 475-foot pier that holds the beach's major attraction, Palace Playground. While the surf is generally gentle, there's a designated surfing area. For a while this area was rowdy, but police have been cracking down to prevent public drinking and raucous behavior. Trolley service is available for $1. Children under 12 must be accompanied by an adult.

Special Notes: There are fireworks every Thursday night. Also, the popular "Beach Olympics" are held in mid August. Events include volleyball, bubble-gum blowing, and sand-castle building. Proceeds benefit Maine's Special Olympics program. Call 800-365-9386 or 207-934-2500.

The ocean gets its blue color from light scattering among the water molecules.

Pine Point Beach
Pine Point Road
Scarborough, ME 04074
207-883-7778

Season: Memorial Day - Labor Day
Hours: 9:00 a.m. - 4:00 p.m.; lot closes at 9:00 p.m.
Parking: Lot
Fees: $5 per car
Sand: Soft
Crowd: Mixed
Facilities: Restrooms, showers, fishing, boat ramp
Rules/Regulations: No alcohol, dogs

Directions: From Route 1 to Route 9, left on Pine Point Road to the end.

This is a quiet and beautiful mile-long sand spit at the northern tip of Old Orchard Beach. However, it is strikingly different from the "honky tonk" arcade area to the south and much less crowded. Strong tides attract lots of surfers.

"A nice beach, and within a half-hour of almost everything."
A. Murphy, Scarborough, ME

Special Notes: For ice cream, head to Beals Ice Cream stand, which is several miles from the beach on routes 9 & 1, on the left.

Ferry Beach and Western Beach
Black Point Road
Scarborough, ME 04074
207-883-7778

Season: Memorial Day - Labor Day
Hours: 9:00 a.m. - 4:00 p.m.; lot closes at 9:00 p.m.
Parking: Lot
Fees: $5 per car
Sand: Soft
Crowd: Mixed
Facilities: Portable restrooms, benches, boat ramp
Rules/Regulations: No alcohol, animals

Directions: From Route 1 to Route 77 and straight onto Black Point Road. Just past the entrance to Scarborough Beach Park (it's on the left), look for Ferry Road on the right and a sign for a public boat launch.

Adjacent to the exclusive Prouts Neck neighborhood, these two beaches are accessed from the same parking area. Ferry Beach is sheltered from ocean winds and surf by Prouts Neck. It overlooks Pine Point Beach. The sand is great for castle building, though a bit mushy underfoot in the water. On the other side of the neck, at the entrance to the Scarborough River, is a long, narrow strip known as Western Beach. It's close to a golf course, so beware of errant balls.

Special Notes: Another way to explore the shore is to visit the Scarborough Marsh Nature Center, Maine's largest salt marsh. The Maine Audubon Society's Nature Center has maps to its trails, canoe rentals, and tours. Call 207-883-5100.

Scarborough Beach Park
Black Point Road
Scarborough, ME 04074
207-883-2416

Season: Memorial Day - Labor Day
Hours: 9:00 a.m. - 8:00 p.m.
Parking: Limited lot
Fees: $2.50 per adult; $1.50 for seniors 65 and over; $1 for children 5-11; no charge for children under 5
Sand: Soft
Crowd: Families
Facilities: Lifeguard, restrooms, bath house, fishing, picnic tables
Rules/Regulations: No animals

Directions: From Route 1 to Route 77 to Black Point Road.

Sandy and shallow, this 1.5-mile half barrier beach is backed by dunes and a saltwater marsh. Gate attendants will tell you its the best beach around and that it actually has pretty warm water -- for Maine. Water temperature can hit 70° because the beach is located on a shallow tidal flat. Early in the season you might see baby seals. This is also a popular area for surfing with little worry about undertow.

Higgins Beach

Ocean Avenue
Scarborough, ME 04074
207-883-2416

Season: Mid May - mid October
Hours: 9:00 a.m. - 5:00 p.m.
Parking: No roadside parking, but locals typically open their yards and driveways to beachgoers
Fees: $4 per car at most private lots
Sand: Soft
Crowd: Families
Facilities: Groceries nearby
Rules/Regulations: No alcohol, animals; surfing is permitted before 10:00 a.m. and after 5:00 p.m.

Directions: From Route 1/9 to Route 207, left onto Route 77 and right onto Ocean Avenue at Higgins Beach Market Vegetable Station.

This .5-mile long beach is quiet because of limited public parking and lack of facilities. The town office reports that an enormous number of $25 tickets are dispensed to people who try to park along the roadsides, keeping the police quite busy all summer. The beach is adjacent to Scarborough State Beach. Pools form at low tide and surfers enjoy the steady waves during incoming tides. You'll find rocks and sand and some strong surf. While we don't recommend littering, a young local girl wrote a letter, popped it into a bottle, and tossed it out to sea from this beach. Thirteen years later it was retrieved in Ireland.

Crescent Beach State Park

Route 77
Cape Elizabeth, ME 04107
207-767-3625

Season: Memorial Day - end of September
Hours: 9:00 a.m. - sunset; gates locked at 8:00 p.m.
Parking: Lot
Fees: $2.50 for adults; $.50 for children 5-11; no charge for children under 5 and seniors 65 and over
Sand: Soft with stones

Crowd: Families
Facilities: Lifeguard, restrooms, bath house, snack bar, picnic tables, fishing, playground, bicycle rack
Rules/Regulations: No alcohol, animals, open fires, floats, face masks/snorkel equipment

Directions: From Route 1/9 to Route 207, left onto Route 77 to the park.

The beach lies within a 243-acre park on Shell Cove and has views of Richmond Island. Stones dot this shore -- the western section is covered -- which is not quite a mile long. A great spot for young families, the beach is protected by the cove and the surf is gentle.

Willard Beach
Preble Street
Portland, ME 04104
207-772-5800

Season: Memorial Day - Labor Day
Hours: 9:00 a.m. - sunset
Parking: Lot (Southern Maine Technical College)
Fees: None
Sand: Soft
Crowd: Families
Facilities: Lifeguard, restrooms
Rules/Regulations: No alcohol, animals, glass

Directions: From Route 1 in South Portland, turn right onto Broadway (just beyond where Route 9 departs to the left). Cross Route 77, still on Broadway and turn right onto Pickett Street. This brings you to the college parking lot. The beach is on Preble Street.

Located at historic Fort Preble (Spring Point Museum is housed here now) and Southern Maine Technical College, families enjoy the gentle surf. The sandy beach wraps around to the entrance of Portland Harbor where there are great views of the harbor and of the famous Portland Head Light, Maine's oldest lighthouse.

"Fine beach for sunbathing and swimming."
Linda Libby, Gorham, ME

Special Notes: Spring Point Museum specializes in local seafaring history and has interesting changing exhibits, such as "Merchants and Shipbuilding, 1865 to 1900" for the 1996 summer season. It's open 1:00 p.m. - 4:00 p.m. Wednesday through Sunday from Memorial Day through the end of October. Call 207-799-6337.

East End Beach
Eastern Promenade
Portland, ME 04104
207-772-5800

Season: Year-round
Hours: 9:00 a.m. - sunset
Parking: Lot
Fees: None
Sand: Coarse with stones and broken shells
Crowd: Mixed
Facilities: Restrooms, picnic tables, benches, boat launch
Rules/Regulations: No alcohol, animals, glass, floats, fishing, unaccompanied children under 12

Directions: From Route 1 to Route 1A to the Eastern Promenade.

Located below the grassy heights of Fort Allen Park in Portland harbor, this is a popular family beach. At the time of our visit swimming was not allowed due to pollution. However, people were strolling along the shore searching for beach glass.

Special Notes: The Annual Cumberland Craft Show is held at the nearby Cumberland Fairground the second weekend in August. There are over 350 exhibitors and plenty of free parking. Admission for everyone over 12 is $2. Call United Maine Craftsmen, 207-621-2818.

Winslow Memorial Park
Staples Point Road
Freeport, ME 04032
207-865-4198

Season: Memorial Day - end of September
Hours: 8:00 a.m. - sunset
Parking: Lot
Fees: $1.50 per person
Sand: Coarse
Crowd: Families
Facilities: Restrooms, picnic tables, playground, campground, boat launch
Rules/Regulations: No alcohol, animals, floats

Directions: From Route 1 to South Freeport Road to Staples Point Road.

The view is great from this small, sandy beach. The water is calm and, by Maine standards, quite warm. There's a raft to swim to, but you may have to share it with a couple dozen seagulls. Also, at low tide the shoreline is unpleasantly mucky.

"This is where I come to get my peace."
Laura Doyle, Freeport, ME

Special Notes: If you wonder why protecting the dunes is so important, visit The Desert of Maine, the site of an old farm where the topsoil was lost. Call 207-865-6962.

Wolfe's Neck State Park
Wolfe's Neck Road
Freeport, ME 04032
207-865-4465

Season: Memorial Day - Labor Day
Hours: 9:00 a.m. - sunset
Parking: Lot
Fees: $2 per person
Sand: None
Crowd: Mixed
Facilities: Restrooms, picnic table
Rules/Regulations: No alcohol, animals, open fires

Directions: From Route 1 to Bow Street (across from L.L. Bean), to Flying Point Road, right onto Wolfe's Neck Road (on the left after Burnett Road), to the park entrance on the left.

When bargain shopping starts to bore you, head over to this wonderfully peaceful park. Hard to imagine it's such a short distance from frantic downtown Freeport. There are lots of trails from which to explore: Wolfe's Neck encompasses 233 acres. The Casco Bay Trail leads walkers by a rocky shoreline which is grand for strong swimmers at high tide. (Those entering the water should remember that there are no lifeguards.) Further along is a small pocket beach, also good for cooling off -- but again only at high tide. The water at low tide is too shallow for any real swimming.

Thomas Point Beach

Meadow Road
Brunswick, ME 04011
207-725-6009

Season: Memorial Day - Labor Day
Hours: 9:00 a.m. - sunset
Parking: Lot; special lot for motorcycles
Fees: $2.50 per adult; $2.00 for children under 12
Sand: Soft with stones
Crowd: Families
Facilities: Lifeguard, restrooms, outside showers, snack bar and ice cream shop, 500 picnic tables, playground, arcade, softball fields, volleyball courts, camping, laundry, grandstand
Rules/Regulations: No alcohol, animals

Directions: From Route 1, Cooks Corner/Route 24 exit. Continue straight at the lights (Route 24) for about 2.5 miles. Turn left onto Board Road, then left onto Meadow Road. Watch for the brick house and large totem pole at the park entrance on the right.

Forty-two acres of grass and trees along the New Meadows River make up this privately owned and operated facility. This is a tidal river, so there is no surf or undertow, which makes it especially great for young children. The only drawback is that the beach gets a bit muddy at low tide. A popular locale for camping, company picnics, and special events, it seems as if there is always something going on here.

Special Notes: The owners of Thomas Point host a number of interesting events throughout the summer, from a concert by the Portland Symphony and fireworks around the 4th of July.

Other events include the Maine Festival, held the first weekend in August (this is billed as a four-day celebration of creativity); the Highland Games, held the third Saturday in August; and the Bluegrass Festival on Labor Day weekend. Call 207-729-8346.

Seawall and Small Point Beaches
Route 209
Phippsburg, ME 04562
207-389-2653

Season: Year-round
Hours: Sunrise - sunset
Parking: Lot
Fees: None
Sand: Soft with stones
Crowd: Mixed
Facilities: None
Rules/Regulations: None posted

Directions: From end of Route 216, off Route 209 to a private dirt road.

The Bates-Morse Mountain Conservation Group (which owns these beaches) is protective of the area because it's been abused in the past. It's an important nesting spot for piping plovers and least terns (so named because they're the smallest species of tern). The conservation group will restrict access if visitors don't respect the wildlife and local residents. From the parking lot, it's a half-hour, 2-mile walk through pitch pine woods around Morse Mountain to this large, pristine barrier spit beach. The area, which extends from the Sprague to the Morse rivers and out to Seawall Beach, looks out to the Heron Islands. Rocky headlands are to the northeast, as well as a salt marsh, dunes, and tidal systems. The drop into the water is gentle and the surf is usually calm. But swimmers should be aware of occasional undertow.

"This beach is pristine. It has tidal pools and intact dunes."
Patsy Hennin, Bath, ME

Popham Beach State Park
Route 209
Phippsburg, ME 04562
207-389-1335

Season: April 15 - October 30
Hours: 9:00 a.m. - sunset
Parking: Lot and roadside
Fees: $2.50 for adults; $.50 for children 5-11; no charge for children under 5 and seniors 65 and over
Sand: Soft
Crowd: Families
Facilities: Lifeguard, restrooms, bath house, picnic tables, grills, fishing
Rules/Regulations: No alcohol, animals, open fires, floats, face masks/snorkel equipment

Directions: From Route 1 in Bath, follow Route 209 to the park (15 miles from Bath).

Located within a 529-acre state park is this wonderfully spacious, pristine 4.5-mile-long beach at the mouth of the Kennebec River. The sand is fine, and the surf is gentle. At low tide, climb the rocky hill (known as Fox Island) or walk out to a sand bar and look to Seguin Lighthouse. (Keep the incoming tide in mind.) Some areas have strong rip tides and deep drops. Warmer tidal pools sometimes form. Fisherman take note: Striper is plentiful.

Half Mile Beach
at Reid State Park
Seguinland Road
Georgetown, ME 04548
207-371-2303

Season: Year-round
Hours: 9:00 a.m. - sunset
Parking: Lot
Fees: $2.50 for adults; $.50 for children 5-11; no charge for children under 5 and seniors over 65

Sand: Soft
Crowd: Families
Facilities: Lifeguard, restrooms, bath house, snack bar, picnic tables, grills
Rules/Regulations: No alcohol, animals, floats, face masks/snorkel equipment
Directions: From Route 1 to Route 127, right onto Seguinland Road. Once inside the park, bear right to Todd's Point.

There are two beaches at the popular Reid State Park. This is the smaller one, but every bit as wonderful as its larger neighbor. Its sandy banks stretch from the southern end of the beach to a rocky point which becomes an island when the tide is in. Like Singing Beach in Massachusetts, the sand sings when you scuff your heels.

Mile Beach at Reid State Park
Seguinland Road
Georgetown, ME 04548
207-371-2303

Season: Year-round
Hours: 9:00 a.m. - sunset
Parking: Lot
Fees: $2.50 for adults; $.50 for children ages 5-11; no charge for children under 5 or and seniors over 65
Sand: Coarse
Crowd: Families
Facilities: Lifeguard, restrooms, bath house, snack bar, grills, picnic tables, viewing machines
Rules/Regulations: No alcohol, animals, open fires, floats, face masks/snorkel equipment

Directions: From Route 1 to Route 127. Turn right onto Seguinland Road. After the park entrance, turn left to Griffith Head.

This large, sandy barrier spit beach in 766-acre Reid State Park is a half mile longer than its name. The ocean water is cold and the surf is strong. Low dunes stand between the beach and a salt water lagoon. A boardwalk takes you across the length of the dunes. Water temperature in the lagoon, which is held by a dam from Tuesday through Sunday, can reach an extraordinary 80 degrees on August weekends (except during the lunar high tide period).

Pemaquid Beach Park
Bristol, ME 04539
207-677-27545

Season: Memorial Day - Labor Day
Hours: 9:00 a.m. - 5:00 p.m.
Parking: Lot
Fees: $1 per person
Sand: Soft
Crowd: Mixed
Facilities: Bath house, restrooms, picnic tables, grills, first aid, telephones
Rules/Regulations: No alcohol, animals, glass

Directions: From Route 1 to Route 129/130. At the fork, bear left, staying on Route 130. Turn right at Hanna's Harbor to beach.

Boat lovers will enjoy the scene at this sandy beach located on John's Bay. The drop into the water is gradual and there's no undertow. To the right are some rocks for exploring.

Special Notes: If a lobster roll is essential to your beach-going experience, head to Shaw's Fish and Lobster Wharf. It's open daily for lunch and dinner in summer, and is on Route 32 in New Harbor. Call 207-677-2200.

Birch Point State Park
aka **Lucia Beach**
Ballyhac Road
Owls Head, ME 04854
207-594-7434

Season: Year-round
Hours: 9:00 a.m. - sunset
Parking: Lot
Fees: None
Sand: Soft
Crowd: Mixed

Facilities: Restrooms, picnic tables, grills
Rules/Regulations: No alcohol, animals, open fires, floats, face masks/snorkel equipment

Directions: From Route 73 in South Thomaston, to Ballyhac Road, to the park entrance on the left.

Gray sand covers this secluded and undeveloped pocket beach. With rocky headlands, a fresh water marsh, and views of the Muscle Ridge Islands, beach scenery doesn't get much better. This is strictly for people who like things rustic. Don't let the fact that this is a state facility fool you -- there are few amenities here.

Crescent Beach
Crescent Beach Road
Owls Head, ME 04854
207-594-7434

Season: Memorial Day - end of September
Hours: Sunrise - sunset
Parking: Limited roadside
Fees: None
Sand: Soft with rocks
Crowd: Mixed
Facilities: None
Rules/Regulations: None posted

Directions: From Route 1 in Rockland, south on Route 73 to Dublin Road, then left onto Ash Point Road, right onto South Shore Road, and right onto Crescent Beach Road.

Although there's public access to the shore, there are no facilities, not even parking. The beach area is scenic, but definitely has the forbidding feeling of being private property.

Owls Head Light Beaches
Lighthouse Road
Owls Head, ME 04854
207- 594-7434

Season: Year-round
Hours: Sunrise - sunset
Parking: Lot
Fees: None
Sand: Soft with stones
Crowd: Mixed
Facilities: Restrooms, picnic tables, grills
Rules/Regulations: No alcohol, unrestrained animals

Directions: From Route 1 to Route 73, North Shore Drive to Main Street, and left onto Lighthouse Road.

Several small, rocky cove beaches can be found on either side of the point at Owls Head. Access to them is not always easy, but if you are seeking a classic northern Maine beach with cold water, rugged rocky cliffs, evergreens, and lobster boats working the waters, here it is. You can also walk a gravel trail to visit the nearby lighthouse which is staffed by the Coast Guard.

Special Notes: Many modes of transportation, from early Harley Davidson motorcycles to horse-drawn carriages, are on display at the Owls Head Transportation Museum. It has an international reputation for its collection of pioneer aircraft. Call 207-594-4418.

Sandy Beach Park
Ocean Street
Rockland, ME 04841
207-594-8431

Season: Year-round
Hours: None posted
Parking: Lot
Fees: None
Sand: Soft with stones
Crowd: Mixed
Facilities: Benches
Rules/Regulations: None posted

Directions: From Route 1 to Route 73 to Ocean Street.

Just south of the harbor is a small grassy park with a little beach. Not really a place to spend the day, it's nonetheless a great spot to relax and enjoy the view, which includes the Fox Islands and Camden's Mount Battie.

Special Notes: For the inveterate bargain hunter, Rockland is also known for its state prison store. Inmate handiwork, from furniture to toys, is sold at rock bottom prices. Open daily 9:00 a.m. - 6:00 p.m. Call 207-354-2535.

Rockland Point Beach
at Marie H. Reed Memorial Park
Samoset Road
Rockland, ME 04841
207-594-8431

Season: Year-round
Hours: Sunrise - sunset
Parking: Roadside
Fees: None
Sand: Soft with stones
Crowd: Mixed
Facilities: Restrooms, benches
Rules/Regulations: None posted

Directions: From Route 1 to Waldo Road (there's a traffic light here), right onto Samoset Road to the end.

This beach's most notable landmark is its mile-long stone breakwater that reaches into the bay. At the end is a historic lighthouse. It takes about an hour to stroll round trip: Be careful maneuvering around the mackerel fishermen. The beach, which is near the parking area, is protected by this great jetty.

Special Notes: The Annual Maine Lobster Festival is held at Harbor Park in Rockland the first weekend in August. It received national attention recently when actress and vegetarian Mary Tyler Moore placed an ad in the local paper the week before the festival, beseeching people *not* to eat lobster. Her plea apparently fell on deaf ears. The event was a big success -- as usual. There's also a pancake breakfast each morning, lobster activities, boat tours, boat rides, crafts, games (such as the lobster crate race), music, and other entertainment. Call 207-596-0376.

Walker Park

Elm Street
Rockport, ME 04841
207-236-9648

Season: Year-round
Hours: None posted
Parking: Lot
Fees: None
Sand: Soft with rocks
Crowd: Families
Facilities: Portable restrooms, benches, playground, picnic tables (some covered), grills
Rules/Regulations: No unleashed dogs (leash must be no longer than 8 feet), feeding the ducks

Directions: From Route 1 to Pascal Avenue (at Hoboken Gardens), and right onto Elm Street.

At the base of a small, grassy, shaded playground park is a small rocky beach. It's a great spot to picnic, or take a breather if you're exploring downtown Rockport.

Special Notes: For a picnic lunch, head to the Market Basket, located on the corner of routes 1 and 90 in a barn-red building. Known by locals and discovered by sleuthing tourists, the store offers specialty foods and homemade breads. Call 207-236-4371.

Laite Memorial Park

Bayview Street
Camden, ME 04843
207-236-3438

Season: Year-round
Hours: 6:00 a.m. - 10:00 p.m.
Parking: Lot
Fees: None
Sand: Soft with rocks
Crowd: Mixed
Facilities: Restrooms, picnic tables, grills, swings, raft in water
Rules/Regulations: No alcohol, animals on beach (okay on grassy area)

Directions: Route 1 to Bayview Street in the center of town. The park is a short distance out of town, on the left.

As the Camden Hills rise above the harbor, so Laite Memorial Park rises above the beach. This is a lovely shaded, grassy park, with picnic tables all around. Even though there's a steep path up from the beach to the park and parking lot, the footing is sure. There are views of the harbor and Mount. Battie. At low tide the water extends out beyond the raft.

Camden Hills State Park

Route 1
Camden, ME 04843
207-236-3109

Season: May 15 - October 15
Hours: 9:00 a.m. - sunset
Parking: Lot
Fees: $2 for adults, $.50 for children 5-11; no charge for children under 5 and seniors over 65
Sand: None, mostly rocky ledge
Crowd: Mixed
Facilities: Restrooms, picnic tables, grills, camping
Rules/Regulations: No alcohol, unrestrained animals

Directions: On Route 1, just north of downtown Camden.

While there is no swimming beach here, this 5,474-acre state park offers a wonderful opportunity to explore the rugged Maine coastline. A stone-lined trail leads down from the parking lot to the coast, where there are accessible rock ledges and a tremendous view. For a different perspective, cross Route 1 and climb (by car on a toll road or by footpath) Mount Battie: It offers an outstanding panorama too.

> In 1848, workmen in Charlotte, Vermont -- over 150 miles from the nearest ocean -- uncovered a whale skeleton. It belonged to a species not extinct, but one still very much alive. These remains provided conclusive evidence that the Champlain Valley, as well as coastal sections of Maine and New Hampshire, were under water until fairly recent times.

Lincolnville Beach
Route 1
Lincolnville, ME 04849
207- 763-3555

Season: Year-round
Hours: None posted
Parking: Lot
Fees: None
Sand: Soft
Crowd: Mixed
Facilities: Picnic tables
Rules/Regulations: No animals

Directions: At the intersection of routes 1 and 173.

Beside the dock for the Islesboro ferry and along the side of the highway is a pleasant beach. It's not a place where you'd spend the day sunning – the traffic from Route 1 is too intense in summer – but it's a nice place to stop for lunch.

Special Notes: The Lobster Pound Restaurant next to this beach is wildly popular. It offers eat-in or take-out. Order some steamed clams and chowder, sit at one of the picnic tables near the beach, and enjoy the view.

Ducktrap Beach
FR (fire road) 22
Northport, ME 04849
207-338-3819

Season: Year-round
Hours: Sunrise - sunset
Parking: Lot
Fees: None
Sand: Soft, but very rocky with shells and sand dollars
Crowd: Mixed
Facilities: None
Rules/Regulations: No alcohol

Directions: Off Route 1 just north of Lincolnville Beach, turn onto FR 22, across from Whitney Road (Duck Trap Decoys gallery sign) and go to the end.

This stony beach would probably be beautiful anytime. But when we arrived here early one morning when the fog was still sitting low and the fog horn rang clear, the scene was unforgettable. The parking lot sits above the beach. To its left is a small flow of water which extends into a rocky bay. At low tide there are some sandy areas.

"It's very quiet and peaceful with beautiful scenery."
Linda Coates, Albion, ME

Special Notes: Stories on tape enhance any auto trip. And Northport just happens to be home to Audio Bookshelf. Its titles include many that will hold special interest for Maine travelers, including *Andre*, the story of Maine's world-famous seal; *Lost! On a Mountain in Maine*, by Donn Fender, a true story of a 12-year-old boy's ordeal when he was lost for nine days on Mount Katahdin (this is great for young listeners); and *Time of Wonder*, by Robert McCloskey, about the islands and rocky shores of Penobscot Bay. Call 800-234-1713.

Rocky Beach at City Park
Northport Avenue
Belfast, ME 04915
207-338-3370

Season: Spring - fall
Hours: Sunrise - 10:00 p.m.
Parking: Lot
Fees: None
Sand: None; rocks
Crowd: Mixed
Facilities: Restrooms, playground, tennis and basketball courts, picnic tables, grills, large gazebo on the waterfront, in-ground pool, showers, golf
Rules/Regulations: No alcohol

Directions: Route 1 to the Route 1 By-pass to Northport Avenue to Belfast City Park.

A local treasure, this 15-acre park offers something for everyone. The view of Searsport and Penobscot Bay, with its bevy of lobster boats and traps, is truly picturesque. The beach area is rocky and has no sand, but is fun to explore.

"My daughters like to look for starfish and sea urchins."
   Sherry Raven, Knox, ME

Special Notes: The Annual Belfast Bay Festival is held for five days around the second weekend in July. It includes a 2-hour parade, 10K foot race, chicken barbecue, rides, sidewalk sales, concerts, crafts, and fireworks. Call 207-338-5900.

Sandy Point Beach
Sandy Point, ME 04972
207-567-3408

Season: Year-round
Hours: Sunrise to sunset
Parking: Lot
Fees: None
Sand: Coarse with stones
Crowd: Mixed
Facilities: Restrooms nearby (return the way you came in, take your first left and you'll find public facilities)
Rules/Regulations: No alcohol

Directions: From Route 1 turn onto an unnamed, narrow road across from the Rocky Ridge Motel and follow to the end.

Sandy Point sits between Stockton Springs and Bucksport and is wonderfully undeveloped. There are several small sandy areas. A large rotting pier reminds visitors of how things change with time. If you walk to your right, beyond the fields, you'll encounter some of Maine's famous rocks.

"I like to climb the rocks, but the water's cold."
   Carl Keicher, Sandy Point, ME

Special Notes: There are many forts in the area, but the most interesting is Fort Knox. Located in nearby Prospect, it was used during both the Civil and Spanish-American wars. Don't forget to check out the underground passageways. Fees are $2 per person; no charge for children under 12. Call 207-469-7719.

Fort Point State Park

Fort Point Road
Stockton Springs, ME 04981
207-596-2253

Season: Memorial Day - Labor Day
Hours: 9:00 a.m. - sunset
Parking: Lot
Fees: $1 for adults; free for children under 12 and seniors 65 and over
Sand: Rocky
Crowd: Mixed
Facilities: Restrooms, fishing, picnic tables, grills
Rules/Regulations: No alcohol, unrestrained animals, open fires, floats
Directions: From Route 1 to Cape Road. At fork, turn left onto East Cape Road and then left onto Fort Point Road.

Although not a swimming beach park, this 154-acre historic site sits on an ocean peninsula near the mouth of the Penobscot River. The fort is gone and only the foundation remains, but there's a museum where you'll learn the history of the hand-pulled bell warning, along with other local events. The pebbly beach is full of colorful rocks and some shells.

"I like the variety here -- big fields, lots of paths, and what a wonderful view of the water."
Heather Frederick, Northport, ME

Sand Beach

Loop Road
Mount Desert Island, ME 04660
207-288-3338

Season: Year-round
Hours: Sunrise - sunset
Parking: Lot
Fees: Entrance fee to the park, $5 per car, is good for a week; $2 per person without a vehicle
Sand: Coarse
Crowd: Mixed
Facilities: Lifeguard, restrooms, picnic tables
Rules/Regulations: No alcohol

Directions: Beach is within Acadia National Park, on the Ocean Drive section of Loop Road, just beyond the Entrance Station. From Bar Harbor, take Schooner Head Road to the trail at the end.

It's surprising to find this beautiful sandy beach among such great rock. Tucked into Newport Cove, the sand is coarse enough for the shell and rock particles to be discernible. Pick up a handful -- it's different from what you see at most beaches. The beach drops gently into *very* chilly water. Surf is moderate and steady and hits the beach with determination.

Special Notes: If you're ready for a hike, a path leads from here to Otter Cliffs, 107 feet above the sea.

Seal Harbor Beach
Route 3
Mount Desert Island, ME 04675
207-288-3338

Season: Year-round
Hours: Sunrise - sunset
Parking: Lot
Fees: Entrance fee to the park, $5 per car, is good for a week; $2 per person without a vehicle
Sand: Coarse
Crowd: Mixed
Facilities: Restrooms, two wooden rafts usable at high tide, restaurants nearby
Rules/Regulations: No alcohol

Directions: From routes 102/198, turn left onto Route 198, then right onto routes 3/198 to Seal Harbor at the Stanley Brook Entrance to Acadia National Park.

This rock and sand beach drops gently into the calm -- but very cold -- waters. (It's been said the warmest swimming around is in Somesville, at the end of Somes Sound, near the intersection of routes 198 and 102.) Little Cranberry Island is visible from here.

Lamoine Beach at Lamoine State Park
Route 184
Lamoine, ME 04605
207-667-4778

Season: May 15 - October 15
Hours: 9:00 a.m. - sunset
Parking: Lot
Fees: $2 for adults; no charge for children under 12 and seniors over 65
Sand: Rocky
Crowd: Mixed
Facilities: Restrooms, picnic tables (some shaded), grills, boat launch, playground, fishing, volleyball
Rules/Regulations: No alcohol, animals, open fires, floats, face masks/snorkel equipment

Directions: Take Route 1 to near the end of Route 184.

Sensational views of Mount Desert Island make this beach unforgettable. Located along the Mount Desert Narrows, boat activity is in close proximity. The beach has both rock and shells and a stone pier to climb out to for a different perspective. Above the beach is a long, grassy park.

Marlboro Beach
Seal Point Road
Lamoine, ME 04605
207-667-2242

Season: Year-round
Hours: Sunrise - sunset
Parking: Lot
Fees: None
Sand: Stones
Crowd: Mixed
Facilities: None
Rules/Regulations: No alcohol

Directions: From Route 1 to Route 184 and left onto Route 204. Just beyond Marlboro Road (with a homemade sign that reads "This is Marlboro Country") turn right onto the narrow Seal Point Road and go to end.

The large piece of sweeping coastline has views across Raccoon Cove to the great hills of Mount Desert Island. The beach is primitive and stony.

Sea Beach
at Roque Bluffs State Park
Roque Bluffs Road
Roque Bluffs, ME 04654
207-255-3475

Season: May 15 - September 30
Hours: 9:00 a.m. - 1/2 hour before sunset
Parking: Lots
Fees: $1 for adults (honor system); no charge for children under 12
Sand: Coarse
Crowd: Mixed
Facilities: Restrooms, bath house, picnic tables, grills, playground, fishing
Rules/Regulations: No alcohol, open fires

Directions: From Route 1 in Jonesboro or Machias to Roque Bluffs Road, to Roque Bluffs.

Well off the beaten track, Roque Bluff State Park's 300 acres on Englishman Bay are a pleasant surprise. Even though this park was opened in 1977, this sand and pebble beach remains primarily undeveloped and has gorgeous open views out to Roque Island. Low dunes with beach grass hide the narrow, quiet road from view and add to the sense of being far away. Pond Beach, with warmer fresh water is across the road and is stocked with brown trout.

"It's lovely, and so are the cliffs nearby, though I'm told they're eroding."
Elaine Emery, Orrington, ME

Special Notes: History buffs should check out the Ruggles House in Columbia Falls (off Route 1), which is a restored 1818 Federal-style home. Special features include hand-carved interiors and a flying staircase. Open July 1 - October 15. Call 207-483-4637.

Jasper Beach
Starboard Road
Machias, ME 04654
207-255-6621

Season: Year-round
Hours: Sunrise - sunset
Parking: Lot
Fees: None
Sand: Rocks
Crowd: Mixed
Facilities: None
Rules/Regulations: No alcohol

Directions: From Route 1 to Route 92 (Elm Street), to Machias Road which becomes Starboard Road, left at the bottom of a hill onto a dirt road to the end.

There is no sand -- just a large, long, and surprisingly lovely pile of fist-size rocks. The rocks are mostly jasper (a type of quartz and hence the name), polished from the force of the sea. The water is clear and cold and you probably won't want to swim. But do bring binoculars and see if you can spot eagles nesting. Also check out the group of towers you spotted on the way here. There are 26 of them: They stand 800+ feet tall, and they are part of the Navy's communication system.

Special Notes: The Annual Machias Blueberry festival is held mid August. In addition to lots of blueberries, there are races, crafts, and entertainment. Call 207-255-3524.

South Lubec Beach
South Lubec Road
Lubec, ME 04652
207-733-4522

Season: Year-round
Hours: None posted
Parking: Lot

Fees: None
Sand: Soft with rocks
Facilities: None
Rules/Regulations: No alcohol

Directions: From Route 1 in Whiting to Route 189. Turn right onto South Lubec Road. Look for parking just beyond the medical center.

This open beach extends for miles along the Lubec Channel. The Bay of Fundy's influence causes 30-foot tidal changes here. The great mud flats are popular with clammers. The beach is also an artist's dream, with splendid views of Campobello Island, the Bay of Fundy, and far off, Grand Manaan Island.

"This is one of the world's foremost bird-watching beaches. There are flocks of sandpipers."
    Connie Harter-Bagley, East Machias, ME

Carrying Place Cove
South Lubec Road
Lubec, Me 04652
207-255-3005

Season: Year-round
Hours: Sunrise - sunset
Parking: Roadside
Fees: None
Sand: Coarse
Facilities: None
Rules/Regulations: No alcohol, walking on the bogs

Directions: From Route 1 in Whiting to Route 189. Turn right onto South Lubec Road to the end.

This beach is part of the West Quoddy Head State Park. However, it's not near the park's parking lot. The hike along the coastline of rocky cliffs and grassy points to the beach is several miles long -- and beautiful. Those less ambitious could park along the road and reach the beach more directly.

NEW HAMPSHIRE

Hampton Central State Beach, Hampton

New Hampshire has just 17 miles of oceanfront. Yet those few miles are a microcosm of New England's waterfront: rocky coastline and sandy beach; row-house-style cottages and elegant estates; quiet nature centers and noisy arcades.

A portion of the coast is state-operated beach, some is community-maintained. By far, New Hampshire's most popular beach is Hampton Central State Beach. While aficionados may not agree with the label "honky-tonk," the myriad of fried dough stands, T-shirt shops, and pinball arcades give the place an undeniable amusement-park ambiance. It may not suit every taste, but the place is a sight and is at least worth a visit, if only for its beautiful -- but usually crowded -- sandy beach.

By auto, I-95 provides access to New Hampshire's seacoast. From I-95, beachgoers can take Route 1A, which runs parallel to the coast. Average summer water temperatures are 55-65 degrees.

If you'd like information on things to do and places to stay, contact: Seacoast Council on Tourism, 100 Market St., Portsmouth, NH 03801, 603-436-7678 or 800-221-5623.

Seabrook Beach

Ocean Drive
Seabrook, NH 03874
603-926-8717

Season: Year-round
Hours: Sunrise - 1:00 a.m.
Parking: None at the beach except for a few handicapped spaces; a parking lot on Route 1A is about a 5-minute walk away
Fees: None
Sand: Coarse
Crowd: Families
Facilities: None
Rules/Regulations: No alcohol, animals, open fires, glass, or surfing

Directions: From Route 1A, turn east onto Hooksett Street at the lights. Turn down any one of the small side streets that lead to Ocean Drive. Ocean Drive runs parallel to the beach.

This long, open, sandy stretch is the state's southernmost beach. A thin line of grassy dunes, currently undergoing restoration, separates the beach from the highway and clusters of oceanside cottages. To the north, the dunes block a large, dense neighborhood. Despite the thick settlement that surrounds it, Seabrook Beach is relatively quiet. Not a big spot for day trippers, it's frequented primarily by local residents and renters.

"Great waves, and the beach is nice for walking."
Theresa Starkey, Raleigh, NC

Hampton State Beach

Route 1A
Hampton, NH 03842
603-926-8717

Season: Memorial Day - Labor Day
Hours: 9:00 a.m. - 6:00 p.m.
Parking: Large lot
Fees: $5 per car weekdays, $8 per car weekends and holidays
Sand: Soft

Crowd: Families
Facilities: Lifeguard, restrooms, first aid, snack bar, picnic tables/pavilion, volleyball, fishing, boat launch, RV camping
Rules/Regulations: No alcohol, animals

Directions: On Route 1A just north of the Hampton River bridge and south of the arcade area.

More than 200,000 people come to this beach area (which includes Hampton Beach and North Beach) on peak-season weekends, and there's room to hold them all. For RVs, there's a small state campground with a public beach located near the Hampton Harbor Inlet. The main 2,800-foot stretch of beach is comprised of sand, some smooth stones, and protected dunes. The water drops gradually, so it's nice for young bathers.

"It's very clean. We enjoy the soft sand and dunes and the jetty nearby."
        Charry MacDonald, New Boston, NH

Hampton Central State Beach
Route 1A
Hampton, NH 03842
603-926-8717

Season: Memorial Day - Labor Day
Hours: 9:00 a.m. - midnight
Parking: Roadside meters, parking lots nearby
Fees: Meters are $.25/15 minutes (8-hour limit); lots are $5/day
Sand: Soft
Crowd: Teens
Facilities: Lifeguards, restrooms, bath house, pavilion, playground (enclosed)
Rules/Regulations: No alcohol, animals, glass, fires

Directions: On Route 1A between M Street and Great Boars Head.

If you've got a hankering for honky tonk, Hampton Central State Beach is the place to go. Pinball arcades, fried dough vendors, cotton candy stands, waterslides, and T-shirt shops line the main thoroughfare. Everywhere you look are people --

walking, sitting, driving, biking, and in-line skating. Rental homes and motel units abound. Despite this controlled (and sometimes not so controlled) chaos, the beach is surprisingly well-maintained: It's groomed daily, usually before dawn. And the sand is whisper soft.

"I enjoy this beach because it is NOISY!"
Tim McDowell, Stoneham, MA

Special Notes: In season, concerts are held at The Sea Shell, a state-owned amphitheater and bandstand located at the beach's midpoint. Also, there are fireworks every Wednesday at 9:30 p.m.

North Beach State Park
Route 1A
Hampton, NH 03842
603-926-8717

Season: Memorial Day - Labor Day
Hours: 9:00 a.m. - 6:00 p.m.
Parking: Meters
Fees: $.25/15 minutes (8-hour limit)
Sand: Soft with stones
Crowd: Families
Facilities: Lifeguards, restrooms
Rules/Regulations: No alcohol, animals, fires, glass

Directions: On Route 1A between Great Boars Head and 19th Street.

If you're looking for a giant swath of sand, this may not be the beach for you. Although sandy at low tide, at high tide, water reaches the rocks at the sea wall's base. Far quieter than the central beach, it's a good spot if you're looking for solitude. The northern end is particularly quiet, but by no means desolate. Route 1A is just behind the sea wall. The waters around Great Boars Head are popular with surfers.

"It's a fun place to bring the family."
Gloria Ashley, VT

Bicentennial Park
Route 1A
Hampton, NH 03842
603-926-8717

Season: Year-round
Hours: 5:00 a.m. - 2:00 a.m.
Parking: A small lot for residents and a few meters for nonresidents.
Fees: $.25/15 minutes
Sand: Soft
Crowd: Families
Facilities: Picnic tables, benches
Rules/Regulations: No alcohol

Directions: On Route 1A, just north of North Beach (near High Street).

This community-maintained beach has an unusual setup. There's a spacious, flat, sandy area for sunbathing that's level with the sea wall. Stairs, on either end, lead to the actual beach (there isn't any at high tide). At low tide, there's a mixture of sand, rocks, and seaweed -- a great spot if you like examining sea life.

"We've always come to this area, ever since the children were little and we lived in Massachusetts."
Eunice Harrington, Hampton, NH

North Side Park
Route 1A
Hampton, NH 03842
603-926-8717

Season: Year-round
Hours: 7:00 a.m. - 10:00 p.m.
Parking: Small lot, permit required
Fees: None
Sand: Soft with stones
Crowd: Mixed
Facilities: Benches
Rules/Regulations: None posted

Directions: From Route 1A, turn east onto a small lane called Ancient Highway Road, just north of North Beach and Bicentennial Park.

A short walk on a stone-lined boardwalk that's surrounded by low dunes brings you to a small, sandy beach. Although it's lined with cottages, the place has a private feel.

"It's private, and in the evening, at low tide, it is a perfect place for my dog to run."
Priscilla MacInnish, Hampton, NH

North Hampton Beach
Route 1A
North Hampton, NH 03862
603-926-8717

Season: Memorial Day - Labor Day
Hours: 7:00 a.m. - midnight
Parking: Roadside meters
Fees: $.25/15 minutes (8-hour limit)
Sand: Soft
Crowd: Mixed
Facilities: Lifeguard, restrooms
Rules/Regulations: No animals, floats

Directions: On Route 1A, just south of Little Boars Head.

This little beach is about 1,000-feet long, has soft, gray sand, and is bounded by a stone sea wall. The north view offers a glimpse of New Hampshire's finest seaside estates.

"It seems to change as the day progresses, and it is very peaceful."
Cary Short, Amesbury, MA

Bass Beach
Route 1A
Rye, NH 03870
603-926-8717

Season: Year-round
Hours: Sunrise - midnight

Parking: Limited roadside
Fees: None
Sand: Soft with stones
Crowd: Mixed (virtually nonexistent)
Facilities: None
Rules/Regulations: No alcohol, animals, glass

Directions: On Route 1A, North Hampton/Rye line.

We almost missed this small gravel beach, sometimes call Rye on the Rocks. It is bordered by Fox Hill to the south and a natural jetty to the north. A rock sea wall protects the road at high tide and provides a sense of privacy.

"So beautiful -- my favorite place to surf."
Robbin Levin, Rye Beach, NH

Sawyers Beach
Route 1A
Rye, NH 03870
603-926-8717

Season: Year-round
Hours: Sunrise - midnight
Parking: Roadside, permit required
Fees: None
Sand: Pebbly
Crowd: Mixed
Facilities: None

Directions: Route 1A, near Sea Road.

This beach, typical of many small New Hampshire beaches (and almost identical to Foss Beach), is perfect for those seeking a bit of quiet. It's got a high sea wall, which provides a good screen from the road.

Sea water is so salty it takes more water from you than you get from it. Volume for volume it has three times as much salt as human blood.

Jenness State Beach
Route 1A
Rye, NH 03870
603-926-8717

Season: Memorial Day - Labor Day
Hours: 9:00 a.m.- 5:00 p.m. (bathrooms open until 8:00 p.m.)
Parking: Meters
Fees: $.25/15 minutes (8-hour limit)
Sand: Soft
Crowd: Families
Facilities: Lifeguard, restrooms
Rules/Regulations: No alcohol, animals, fires, glass

Directions: On Route 1A, across from Eel Pond.

A pleasant sandy beach, not too big, not too small. There are nice views of Hampton to the south and the Isles of Shoals to the east.

"It doesn't seem as crowded as other nearby state beaches."
Polly Martel, Goffstown, NH

Cable Road Beach
Cable Road
Rye, NH 03870
603-926-8717

Season: Year-round
Hours: Sunrise - midnight
Parking: Small lot, permit required
Fees: None
Sand: Soft
Crowd: Families
Facilities: Lifeguard, portable restrooms

Directions: From Route 1A, look for Cable Road and/or Old Beach Road. There are a few little paths, between homes, leading to the beach.

This beach is virtually unknown to tourists and is frequented almost exclusively by summer rental tenants in nearby cottages. It's tiny, but a good spot to escape the Hampton crowds.

Ragged Neck State Park
Route 1A
Rye, NH 03870
603-436-1552

Season: Memorial Day - Columbus Day
Hours: 9:00 a.m. -5:00 p.m.
Parking: Lot
Fees: $2.50/adults (July and August); no charge for children 12 and under and NH seniors 65 and over
Sand: Mostly rocks
Crowd: Families
Facilities: Restrooms
Rules/Regulations: No alcohol, animals, glass

Directions: On Route 1A at the sharp bend in the road near Rye Harbor.

This park has wonderful views of beach, sea, and harbor. The grassy area is edged with picnic tables. On the right, just inside a 200-ft. jetty, is a rock-strewn beach -- not a great place for swimming. For a quarter, an optical viewing machine will bring into focus the boats in Rye Harbor and the Isles of Shoals, a chain of nine islands sitting six miles offshore.

Foss Beach
Route 1A
Rye, NH 03870
603-926-8717

Season: Year-round
Hours: Sunrise - midnight
Sand: Soft with stones
Crowd: Mixed
Facilities: None
Parking: Roadside, permit required
Fees: None

Directions: On Route 1A, just north of Ragged Neck Point.

Walk along the boardwalk to this lovely crescent-shaped beach of gray sand, round stones, and pebbles.

"It's a real pretty beach ...and peaceful."
Jim Kane, Washington, DC

Wallis Sands Beach
Route 1A
Rye, NH 03870
603-926-8717

Season: Year-round
Hours: Sunrise - midnight
Parking: Small lot, permit required; some free parallel parking on Route 1A near the entrance
Fees: None
Sand: Soft
Crowd: Mixed
Facilities: Lifeguard, restrooms, snack bars

Directions: On Route 1A between Jenness State Beach and Wallis Sands State Park.

You have to have good eyes to spot the small opening for this sandy stretch of beach. It lies just south of the Wallis Sands State Beach. It's mid-sized and pleasant, with a mix of cottages and low-key restaurants in view across the street on Route 1A.

Special Note: Veggie burgers, chicken fingers, and onion rings are specials at Levi's Beachside Grille, a small place with great beach atmosphere (but no seafood) right at the entranceway to the beach.

Wallis Sands State Park
Route 1A
Rye, NH 03870
603-436-9404

Season: Memorial Day - Labor Day,
Hours: 8:00 a.m. - 6:00 p.m. (facilities), gate closes at 8:00 p.m.
Parking: Lot

Fees: $5 per car weekdays, $8 weekends and holidays
Sand: Soft
Crowd: Families
Facilities: Lifeguard, restrooms, snack bar, picnic tables, fishing (from the jetty)
Rules/Regulations: No alcohol, animals, glass, fires, floats

Directions: On Route 1A, two miles south of Odiorne Point State Park.

Although it's only 700 feet long and just 150 feet wide at high tide, Wallis Sands State Park is a favorite. A jetty to the south and rocks to the north give the place a rugged beauty. There's good swimming and a grassy area for those who don't like sand on their towels.

"It hasn't the noise or the fried dough of Happy Hampton, which is why we like it."
       Joseph McQuaid, Manchester, NH

Odiorne Point State Park
Ocean Boulevard
Rye, NH 03870
603-436-7406

Season: Year-round
Hours: 8:00 a.m. - 8:00 p.m. in summer
Parking: Lot
Fees: $2.50/adult; no charge for children 12 and under and NH seniors 65 and over
Sand: Mostly rocky
Crowd: Mixed
Facilities: Visitor center with interpretive nature programs, picnic tables (bring your own grill), restrooms, boat launch, bicycle paths
Rules/Regulations: No alcohol, animals, glass, swimming

Directions: From Route 1 turn onto Elwyn Road. Continue straight at the intersection of Route 1A (This is also known as Pioneer Road. Pioneer turns into Ocean Boulevard.) Parking is on the left. Watch for signs to the main entrance.

This 137-acre nature preserve is the site of the first New Hampshire European settlement, and more recently, a World

War II military base. History buffs will admire the earth-covered bunkers used during the war. No swimming is allowed, but the rocky coastline is fun to explore.

New Castle Beach

Wentworth Road
New Castle, NH 03854
603-431-6710/436-1992

Season: Mid May - mid September
Hours: 9:00 a.m. - 9:00 p.m.
Parking: Lot
Fees: $2.50/adults; no charge for children under 16 and seniors 65 and over
Sand: Both soft and very coarse
Crowd: Families
Facilities: Restrooms, picnic tables, boat launch, grills, playground, volleyball nets
Rules/Regulations: No alcohol, dogs, open fires

Directions: Take Route 1A to Route 1B, Wentworth Road.

More than a beach, this is a delightful grassy park with a playground, nature trail, and sports facilities. The beach area looks across the bay to a lighthouse, Coast Guard facility, and Fort Constitution Historic Site.

"The beach is cozy, quiet, and scenic. There is a corner for everyone."
      Lucy Therien, Portsmouth, NH

Special Note: The Ice House on Route 1B is a good stop for ice cream. Call 603-431-3086.

THE NORTH SHORE, MASSACHUSETTS

Annisquam Lighthouse near Wingaersheek Beach, Gloucester

The Massachusetts North Shore extends from Revere all the way north to Salisbury, at the New Hampshire border. Beaches range from urban coves barely beyond earshot of busy streets, to quiet enclaves that feel little touched by time and humanity. A few stretches have amusement rides, arcades, and air redolent of cotton candy and fried dough.

The major access roads to the north are I-95 and Route 1, both of which run inland. The coast is better served by the eastern portion of Route 128, which ends in Gloucester and Route 1A.

Public transportation is another option, and the Massachusetts Bay Transit Authority (MBTA) (617-722-3200) runs all the way to Cape Ann. The Cape Ann region (Gloucester, Rockport) has the Cape Ann Transport Authority (CATA), and buses stop at many of the beaches (508-283-7916) and tourist attractions.

Black Rock Beach
Nahant Road
Nahant, MA 01908
617-598-6286

Season: Year-round
Hours: None posted
Parking: None
Fees: None
Sand: Coarse with gravel-like consistency
Crowd: Mixed; extremely sparse
Facilities: None
Rules/Regulations: None posted

Directions: From Route 1A to Lynnway, right on Nahant Road, just as you enter "Big Nahant." (Nahant has two sections known as Big Nahant and Little Nahant.)

This small beach along the Lynnway faces Lynn Harbor and has views of Revere Beach. A good spot to visit if you're biking or walking. But, with no parking or facilities, this is not a beach to spend the day.

Tudor Beach
Willow Street
Nahant, MA 01908
617-598-6286

Season: Year-round
Hours: Sunrise - sunset
Parking: None
Fees: None
Sand: Soft
Crowd: Families
Facilities: None
Rules/Regulations: None posted

Directions: From Nahant Road, right onto Summer Street, then right onto Willow. Also on the MBTA line.

Because there's no visitor parking, this is a real neighborhood beach. Yet it's also a choice spot for car-less urban dwellers. It affords great city views, and because the beach is sheltered by Nahant Harbor, the waters are calm.

The stinging cells of a dead jellyfish can be active for several hours after beaching.

Wharf Beach

Summer Street
Nahant MA 01908
617-598-6286

Season: Year-round
Hours: Sunrise - sunset
Parking: Small lot for residents
Fees: None
Sand: Soft with stones
Crowd: Mixed
Facilities: None
Rules/Regulations: None posted

Directions: From Nahant Road, turn right onto Summer Street and follow to end. Also on the MBTA bus line.

This tiny, quiet spot at Tudor Wharf is typical of many neighborhood beaches. The plus here is the harbor view and all its activity. Although the beach has a lot of stones, above the sea wall is a small patch of grass with shade trees.

"You can pick sun or shade for sitting."
Barbara Powers, Nahant, MA

Canoe Beach

Nahant Road
Nahant, MA 01908
617-598-6286

Season: Year-round
Hours: Sunrise - sunset
Parking: Lot for residents only
Fees: None
Sand: Stone
Crowd: Mixed
Facilities: None
Rules/Regulations: None posted

Directions: Near the end of Nahant Road.

To the right of this small beach is the Northeastern University Marine Science Center and to the left are rocks that are perfect for exploring. The beach itself is covered with small round stones. Cruising boats, and divers examining sea life (or perhaps searching for treasure), are both common sights.

Forty Steps Beach
Nahant Road
Nahant, MA 01908
617-598-6286

Season: Year-round
Hours: Sunrise - sunset
Parking: None
Fees: None
Sand: Coarse with stones
Crowd: Mixed, limited
Facilities: None
Rules/Regulations: None posted

Directions: At the bend in Nahant Road.

Huge cliffs and rugged red rocks form a protective barrier and provide this suburban beach with a distinctly remote feeling. It's difficult to believe you're in greater metropolitan Boston. Named for the 40 wooden steps that lead down its steep embankment, the beach is small and has a mix of sand and pebbles.

Short Beach
Nahant Road
Nahant MA 01908
617-598-6286

Season: Memorial Day - Labor Day
Hours: Sunrise - sunset
Parking: 30-minute roadside parking
Fees: None
Sand: Soft
Crowd: Families
Facilities: Outside shower, water bubbler, snack bar
Rules/Regulations: None posted

Directions: From Route 1A to the Lynnway, right onto Nahant Road; beach on the left.

Situated between Little Nahant and Big Nahant, this beach has an uncommon (for the area) feeling of privacy. Another boon are the views of Nahant Bay and of the rounded Egg Rock, which is about three miles out.

"It has nice sand and it is clean."
            Ione Hansell, Nahant, MA

Special Notes: The locals' ice cream spot is Seaside Scoops. It's directly across the street from the beach.

Nahant Beach and Long Beach
Nahant Road
Nahant, MA 01908
617-598-6286

Season: Late June - Labor Day
Hours: Sunrise - 11:00 p.m.
Parking: Lot
Fees: $2 per car
Sand: Soft
Crowd: Mixed
Facilities: Lifeguard, restrooms, bath house, boat launch, fishing, playground.
Rules/Regulations: No alcohol, animals, glass, floats, skis or grills

Directions: Rte 1A to Lynnway. Right onto Nahant Road. Also on MBTA bus line.

The 2.5-mile long, gently sloped sandy beach is operated by the Metropolitan District Commission. The stretch is popular because the MDC encourages activity: One area, by the first bath house, is designated for wind surfing, and a paved bike path runs through the low dunes.

"The water and sand are crystal clean. Parking is inexpensive and there is always room to sit on the beach."
            Lanie Levine, Swampscott, MA

Blaney Beach
Puritan Road
Swampscott, MA 01907
617-596-8854

Season: Year-round
Hours: Sunrise - sunset
Parking: 2-hour roadside parking
Fees: None
Sand: Soft
Crowd: Mixed
Facilities: None
Rules/Regulations: No alcohol, animals, floats, balls, grills, rock climbing

Directions: From Route 129 N (Humphrey Street), turn right onto Puritan Road.

This village beach by the town pier offers a sliver of sand on which to relax. Sit on the beach, benches, or grassy area and watch the colorful boats cruise the harbor.

Whales Beach
Puritan Road
Swampscott, MA 01907
617-596-8854

Season: Year-round
Hours: Sunrise - sunset
Parking: None
Fees: None
Sand: Soft
Crowd: Families
Facilities: None
Rules/Regulations: No alcohol, animals, floats, balls, grills, rock climbing, boat launching

Directions: From Route 129 N (Humphrey Street), turn right onto Puritan Road. Whales is north of Blaney Beach.

Because there is no parking, this beach is frequented almost exclusively by neighborhood families. A sea wall separates the grassy area of Johnson Park from the short sandy beach.

Phillips Beach

Longley Avenue
Swampscott, MA 01907
617-596-8854

Season: Year-round
Hours: Sunrise - sunset
Parking: None
Fees: None
Sand: Coarse
Crowd: Families
Facilities: None
Rules/Regulations: No alcohol, animals, floats, balls, grills, rock climbing, boat launching

Directions: From Route 129 (Atlantic Avenue), right onto Longley Avenue.

A boardwalk at the corner of Longley and Shepherd takes you down to this beach. Crumbling cement sea walls aren't too attractive, but the short grassy dunes behind the sandy beach are as beautiful as any on the North Shore.

Preston Beach

Atlantic Avenue
Swampscott, MA 01907
617-596-8854

Season: Year-round
Hours: 8:30 a.m. - 8:00 p.m.
Parking: Small lot
Fees: Nonresidents, $6 per car
Sand: Soft
Crowd: Mixed
Facilities: None
Rules/Regulations: No alcohol, animals, floats, balls, grills, rock climbing, boat launching

Directions: Route 129 (Atlantic Avenue) on the Swampscott/Marblehead line.

At this writing, a committee is busy raising funds to construct a park on the lawn above the sea wall of this narrow sandy beach. The rock on the left becomes an "island" at high tide.

"It's always changing. Sometimes it's all rocks, sometimes it's all sand, as it is now."
Mike Reed, Swampscott, MA

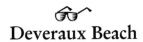

Deveraux Beach
Ocean Avenue
Marblehead, MA 01945
617-631-3350

Season: Memorial Day - Labor Day
Hours: Sunrise - sunset
Parking: Lots, for both residents (with permits) and nonresidents
Fees: Nonresidents, $3 per car weekdays, $5 weekends
Sand: Coarse
Crowd: Mixed
Facilities: Lifeguards, restrooms, bath house, snack bar, picnic tables, playground, fishing
Rules/Regulations: No alcohol, glass, animals, floats, balls, skin divers

Directions: From Route 114 or Route 129 to Ocean Avenue.

This long, ocean beach has been restored since extensive damage from the No-Name Storm of October 30, 1992, wreaked its havoc. It's one of the few beaches where water is visible from the front -- the beach faces the ocean -- and back -- Marblehead Harbor. Don't like the sun? Sit under one of the pavilions. Hungry? At Flynnies, you can eat in or on the beach.

"The children (Daniel, Corey, Brett, & Kate) now enjoy the beach my husband Daniel went to when he was a kid."
Beth Gauthier, Salem, MA

Special Notes: This town is interesting anytime, with its narrow streets, historic homes, and shops. One of the best times to visit is around the 4th of July for the Festival of the Arts.

Grace Oliver Beach
Beacon Street
Marblehead, MA 01945
617-631-3350

Season: Year-round
Hours: Sunrise - sunset
Parking: Roadside
Fees: None
Sand: Soft
Crowd: Mixed
Facilities: None
Rules/Regulations: None posted

Directions: From Route 129 (Atlantic Avenue), turn right onto Washington Street. Follow to the end. Left onto Orne Street, right onto Beacon Street, which is beyond the intersection of Norman.

Just north of Fort Sewall, this pocket-size beach is on scenic Doliber's Cove. The beach's unique aspect is its proximity to Brown Island, which people can walk to at low tide. The good-size island has trees, rocks, and sandy beaches.

"We've had lots of picnics on the island."
Laura Williams, Marblehead, MA

Forest River Park
West Street
Salem, MA 01970
508-744-0180

Season: Memorial Day - Labor Day
Hours: Sunrise- 10:00 p.m.
Parking: Lot
Fees: Nonresidents, $6 per car
Sand: Soft with shells and stones
Crowd: Family

Facilities: Lifeguard, restrooms, bath house, snack bar, playground
Rules/Regulations: No unleashed dogs

Directions: From routes. 114 and 1A in South Salem, turn onto West Street, across from Loring Avenue. Follow to the end.

There are three small beaches at this lovely, grassy, woodland park. Two of the beaches are ungroomed with a mixture of sand, stones, and shells. Another is beautifully groomed and has soft beige sand. A playground, picnic tables, and benches make this is a popular getaway for local families. There are also two large swimming pools. (They weren't filled when we visited.)

Special Notes: You can enter the circa 1630 Pioneer Village, America's oldest living history museum, from here. Hours: Mon-Sat 10:00 a.m. - 5:00 p.m., Sun 12:00 p.m. - 5:00 p.m. Adults $4; seniors 62 and over and teens 13 - 17, $3.50; children $2.50. Call 508-745-0525.

Waikiki Beach
Winter Island Road
Salem, MA 01970
508-745-9430

Season: May 1 - October 31
Hours: Restrooms locked at 7:00 p.m., gate at 10:00 p.m.
Parking: Lot
Fees: $5 per car
Sand: Coarse with crushed shells and stone
Crowd: Mixed
Facilities: Restrooms, picnic tables
Rules/Regulations: No unleashed animals

Directions: From routes 114 and 1A to Derby Street/Fort Avenue. Right onto Winter Island Road.

At Winter Island Marine Recreational Park, the beach is just a small part of this historic fort site. There are RV and tent spaces, a pier, and a restaurant. Sun worshippers will find the harbor location provides a gentle surf, but the sand is mixed with crushed shells and stone.

"I think this is the best beach in Salem."
Suzanne Borowski, Marblehead, MA

Special Notes: Salem celebrates its notable past with a week-long celebration in mid August known as Heritage Days.

Willow Beach
Fort Avenue
Salem, MA 01970
508-744-0180

Season: March - October
Hours: 8:00 a.m. - 10:00 p.m.
Parking: Lot
Fees: None
Sand: Coarse with rocks and shells
Crowd: Families
Facilities: Lifeguard, restrooms, snack bar, picnic tables, grills, rowboat rentals, fishing, arcades, amusements
Rules/Regulations: No unleashed animals

Directions: From routes 114 and 1A onto Fort Avenue to end. Enter Salem Willows Amusement Park.

This beach is smaller than nearby Dead Horse Beach, but it's much more popular because it affords easy access to the park's busy arcades and restaurants.

Dead Horse Beach
Fort Avenue
Salem, MA 01970
508-744-0180

Season: March - October
Hours: 10:00 a.m. - 11:00 p.m.
Parking: Lot
Fees: None
Sand: Coarse
Crowd: Mixed
Facilities: None
Rules/Regulations: No unleashed animals

Directions: From routes 114 and 1A onto Fort Avenue. Left at the ballpark near Salem Willows Amusement Park.

We don't know where this medium-size suburban beach got its unusual name, but we didn't see any signs of dead horses during our visit. Located in Collins Cove, the water is great for people who like things calm.

Sandy Beach
River Street
Danvers, MA 01932
508-762-0232

Season: Memorial Day - Labor Day
Hours: Sunrise - sunset
Parking: Lot
Fees: None
Sand: Muddy
Crowd: Mixed, but sparse
Facilities: Lifeguard, playground
Rules/Regulations: None posted

Directions: From Route 35 (Liberty Street) to River Street (almost to the end).

Because this is a small ocean river beach, the sand is pretty muddy at low tide. A lifeguard is on duty only for the three hours before and after high tide.

Independence Park
Lothrop Street
Beverly, MA 01915
508-921-6067

Season: None
Hours: Sunrise - sunset
Parking: Roadside
Fees: None
Sand: Soft
Crowd: Families
Facilities: None
Rules/Regulations: None posted

Directions: Route 127 (Lothrop Street) just south of Dane Street.

The open, grassy park sits on a hill above Beverly Harbor. A low sea wall separates the hillside from the shallow beach. Although it looks across to Willows Park on Salem Neck, the more imposing (albeit distant) views are of urban factories.

Dane Street Beach
Dane Street
Beverly, MA 01915
508-921-6067

Season: Year-round
Hours: Sunrise - sunset
Parking: Roadside
Fees: None
Sand: Soft
Crowd: Families
Facilities: Lifeguard, restrooms, playground, snack cart
Rules/Regulations: No alcohol, dogs

Directions: From Route 127 (Lothrop Street) at Dane Street.

This small, sandy beach in Mackerel Cove connects with Woodbury Beach at Lynch Park during low tide.

Lynch Park
Ober Road
Beverly, MA 01915
508-921-6067

Season: Year-round
Hours: 8:00 a.m. - 10:00 p.m.
Parking: Lot
Fees: Nonresidents, $5 weekdays, $10 weekends
Sand: Coarse with stones
Crowd: Families
Facilities: Lifeguard, restrooms (10:00 a.m. - dusk), playground, boat rentals, picnic tables.
Rules/Regulations: No alcohol, dogs, balls

Directions: From Route 127 to Ober Road.

Lynch Park has two beaches, Woodbury and Lynch. Woodbury, to the south, is the first beach you see as you enter the park and the sand is a bit stony. Lynch Beach has mushy sand at low tide. Both are great for children, especially those who love to look for crabs when the tide is out. Kayak rentals are available at Woodbury ($3/30 minutes). It's a perfect place for beginners to experiment because the surf is gentle. At low tide, Woodbury Beach connects with Dane Street Beach.

Special Notes: A variety of concerts are held here on Sundays throughout the summer from 6:00 p.m. - 8:00 p.m.

Rices Beach
Ober Street
Beverly, MA 01915
508-921-6067

Season: Memorial Day - Labor Day
Hours: 10:00 a.m. - 5:00 p.m.
Parking: Park at Lynch Park and walk down a dirt path
Fees: Nonresidents, $5 per car weekdays, $10 weekends
Sand: Soft with some stones
Crowd: Mixed
Facilities: Lifeguard
Rules/Regulations: None posted

Directions: From Route 127 to end of Ober Street.

Beautiful views and relative inaccessibility -- you have to park your car at Lynch Park and walk -- make this a perfect spot for those who enjoy peace and quiet.

Singing Beach
Beach Street
Manchester-by-the-Sea, MA 01944
508-526-1731

Season: Memorial Day - Labor Day
Hours: 9:00 a.m. - 5:00 p.m.

Parking: Lot for residents. Nonresidents must walk a mile from the small parking lot in town. The daily rate is $15 and benefits the local Boy Scout troup. (Note that the town is rigorous about towing cars that are parked downtown in one-hour spaces for more than the allotted time.)
Fees: $2 for nonresident walk-ins
Sand: Soft
Crowd: Mixed, but with many young singles
Facilities: Lifeguard, restrooms, snack bar, bicycle racks
Rules/Regulations: No alcohol, dogs, floats, diving off rocks, open fires; ball playing okay on the right end

Directions: From Route 127 in village to Beach Street.

Yes, the sand literally "sings" as you walk on it. (Push forward with the balls of your feet and listen.) Although just a quarter mile long, it's a gorgeous beach, with steep cliffs and rocks at both ends and a broad swath of fine sand. Many nonresidents who come here arrive via the train which runs from Boston's North Station.

Special Notes: If you're making an early trip to the beach, stop off at the Beach Street Cafe to pick up some coffee and blueberry muffins. It's right across the street from the train station. At the end of the day, head to Ben Sprague's (right next to the train station) for ice cream. This is also a great place to pick up sandwiches. If a cold beer is more in order, head straight to 7 Central on Central Street.

White Beach
Ocean Street
Manchester-by-the-Sea, MA 01944
508-526-1731

Season: Year-round
Hours: Sunrise - sunset
Parking: Residents only
Fees: None
Sand: Coarse with stones
Crowd: Mixed
Facilities: None
Rules/Regulations: None posted

Directions: From Route 127 (Summer Street) onto Ocean Street (a U-shaped road).

This small, unspoiled crescent-shaped beach sweeps gently into the water. Located in a sheltered cove, the surf is minimal.

Black Beach
Ocean Street
Manchester-by-the-Sea, MA 01944
508-526-1731

Season: Year-round
Hours: Sunrise - sunset
Parking: None
Fees: None
Sand: Very coarse
Crowd: Mixed
Facilities: None
Rules/Regulations: None posted

Directions: From Route 127, turn onto Ocean Street (a U-shaped road).

Sheltered in quiet Kettle Cove, this is a narrow neighborhood beach. Not the greatest for sunbathing -- at low tide the sand is a bit mushy.

"We can come to this beach on our boat."
Anne Hannah, Manchester-by-the-Sea, MA

Gray Beach
Shore Road
Manchester-by-the-Sea, MA 01944
508-526-1731

Season: Year-round
Hours: Sunrise - sunset
Parking: Resident lot, limited roadside spaces nearby
Fees: None
Sand: Soft
Crowd: Mixed
Facilities: Boat launch, benches, picnic table

Rules/Regulations: None posted

Directions: From Route 127 to Raymond Street or Magnolia Street to Shore Road. The beach is on the Magnolia-Gloucester border. (Magnolia is a section of Gloucester.)

This medium-size beach on Magnolia Harbor affords bathers good views of Kettle Island. To the left is the boat launch and to the far right is a trail that leads to Clark Pond.

"It's quiet, not commercial."
        Helen, Dan & Priscilla, Magnolia, MA

Cressey's Beach
Stage Fort Avenue
Gloucester, MA 01930
508-283-1601

Season: Memorial Day - Labor Day
Hours: Sunrise - sunset
Parking: Lot
Fees: $10 per car
Sand: Soft with stones
Crowd: Mixed
Facilities: Restrooms, snack bar, picnic area
Rules/Regulations: No alcohol, animals, fires, floats, glass, surfing

Directions: Off Route 127 at Stage Fort Park.

A notable feature of this narrow length of sand and stone is the smooth ledge that has a green serpent painted on it. The storm-damaged sea wall belies the fact that waters here are calm. Above the sea wall is a large, grassy field which is part of Stage Fort Park.

"If you come here alone, you'll soon have company!"
        Ann Grace Militello, Gloucester, MA

Special Notes: Hammond Castle was home to one of our nation's most prolific inventors, John Hays Hammond. (He's second only to Thomas Edison.) The castle is just down the road, off Route 127, and has a stunning collection of Roman,

Medieval, and Renaissance artifacts. It's open to visitors 9:00 a.m. - 5:00 p.m. daily. Admission is $5.50. Call 508-283-2080.

Half Moon Beach
Stage Fort Avenue
Gloucester, MA 01930
508-283-1601

Season: Memorial Day - Labor Day
Hours: Sunrise - sunset
Parking: Lot
Fees: $10 per car
Sand: Soft with stones
Crowd: Families
Facilities: Snack bar, picnic tables
Rules/Regulations: No alcohol, animals, fires, floats, glass, surfing

Directions: From Route 127 to Stage Fort Park.

Although this beach is within the park, it is tucked away in a small cove and flanked by trees, boulders, ledges, and cliffs. Views are of Ten Pound Island in Gloucester Harbor.

"It's a small, cute beach that's great for kids."
Mary Louasco, Gloucester, MA

Pavilion Beach
Western Avenue
Gloucester, MA 01930
508-283-1601

Season: Year-round
Hours: Sunrise - sunset
Parking: Roadside
Fees: None
Sand: Soft with stones
Crowd: Mixed
Facilities: Benches, coin-operated viewers
Rules/Regulations: No alcohol, animals, fires, floats, glass, surfing

Directions: On Route 127 (Western Avenue).

Located in downtown Gloucester, this beach is also known as Fisherman's Statue Beach for the famous Fisherman's Memorial there. Because it's situated right on Gloucester Harbor, beachgoers are treated to a parade of vessels -- more working ships than pleasure boats. (Note: Some locals are pushing to have a Fisherman's wife statue erected nearby.)

Special Notes: In mid August, there's an annual three-day Waterfront Festival. It includes a pancake breakfast on Saturday, arts & crafts fairs, a harbor swim competition, and a fish fry on Sunday.

If you want to pick up supplies for a beach picnic, head to Virgilio's on 29 Main Street. Call 508-283-5295. Sweet lovers might also consider a stop by Mike's Pastry and Coffee Shop, just a few doors down.

Niles Beach
Eastern Point Road
Gloucester, MA 01930
508-283-1601

Season: Memorial Day - Labor Day
Hours: Sunrise - sunset
Parking: Residents only, sticker required
Fees: None
Sand: Coarse
Crowd: Families
Facilities: Lifeguards
Rules/Regulations: No alcohol, animals, fires, floats, glass, surfing

Directions: From end of Route 128 (and 127A), East Main Street to Eastern Point Road. The beach is also a stop on the Salt Water Trolley line.

At high tide this Gloucester Harbor beach is sandy, but low tide exposes a coarse gravelly stretch. Notice the exclusive-looking neighborhood on the left (including the Beauport Museum of art and furniture). It was to have been a grand development of some 250 summer estates. But the development ran into financial difficulties and the scheme was reduced to its present size.

"You can see your children -- and Boston, too -- on a clear day."
Kathy Santuccio, Gloucester, MA

Special Notes: Take time to walk around and shop or eat at Rocky Neck Arts Colony, which you'll pass on the way to or from Niles Beach. It's the oldest colony of working artists in America.

Good Harbor Beach
Thatcher Road
Gloucester, MA 01930
508-283-1601

Season: Memorial Day - Labor Day
Hours: 9:00 a.m. - 5:00 p.m.
Parking: Lot
Fees: $15 per car
Sand: Super soft
Crowd: Mixed
Facilities: Lifeguard, restrooms, bath house, snack bars, fishing (allowed at approved times)
Rules/Regulations: No alcohol, animals, fires, floats, glass, surfing, radios, or games, such as Frisbee, above the high tide line

Directions: On Route 127A (Thatcher Road) in East Gloucester.

This popular half-mile of groomed sandy beach with low dunes can be enjoyed by all. On the right is "the Creek." Children love to swim in its placid waters or walk over the bridge that crosses it. On the left is the undeveloped Salt Island, accessible via a sand bar at low tide.

"Beautiful for its scenic view and spacious sands. Even with a powerful surf, it is practical for all."
Eileen Parisi, Gloucester, MA

Plum Cove Beach

Route 127N
Gloucester, MA 01930
508-283-1601

Season: Mid June - early September
Hours: 9:00 a.m. - 5:00 p.m.
Parking: Limited roadside
Fees: None
Sand: Coarse
Crowd: Families
Facilities: Lifeguard
Rules/Regulations: No alcohol, animals, floats, fires, surfing, glass

Directions: From Route 128 at the circle, to Route 127 N, beyond Annisquam.

Because it's in a protected cove, the water is warmer than at most Gloucester beaches. It's perfect for those who appreciate a rocky "Maine-like" atmosphere.

"I came here as a child. It is a good family beach."
David Starkey, Wake Forest, NC

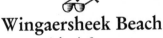

Wingaersheek Beach

Atlantic Street
Gloucester MA 01930
508-283-1601

Season: Memorial Day - Labor Day
Hours: 9:00 a.m. - 5:00 p.m.
Parking: Lot
Fees: $10 per car
Sand: Soft
Crowd: Families
Facilities: Lifeguards, restrooms, showers, snack bar, fishing
Rules/Regulations: No alcohol, animals, fires, floats, glass, surfing

Directions: From Route 128, take exit 13, Concord Street to Atlantic Street in West Gloucester.

This popular and picturesque sandy beach is about a quarter-mile long. Backed by small dunes, the water slopes gently into Ipswich Bay. Wading pools form at low tide. The water isn't too cold, and there are some rocks to climb. The salt water channel (Annisquam River) has got lots of boat traffic.

"It gets crowded (so arrive early), but still it's quiet."
Tim McDowell, Stoneham, MA

Long Beach
Rockport Road
Rockport, MA 01966
508-546-6575

Season: Memorial Day - Labor Day
Hours: 9:00 a.m. - 5:00 p.m.
Parking: Lot
Fees: $5 per car weekdays, $10 weekends and holidays
Sand: Soft
Crowd: Mixed
Facilities: Lifeguards, portable restrooms
Rules/Regulations: No alcohol, animals

Directions: From Route 127A (Thatcher Road) to Rockport Road.

This half-mile long, sandy beach is on the Rockport - Gloucester town line and looks out to Cape Ann Light and the twin lighthouses on Thatcher Island. The mixed sand and gravel beach reaches to Cape Hedge. Arrive early to find a parking spot.

"Very scenic. A great place to go swimming or to sunbathe."
Robert Handel, Rockport, MA

Pebble Beach
South Street
Rockport, MA 01966
508-546-6575

Season: Memorial Day - Labor Day
Hours: 9:00 a.m. - 5:00 p.m.
Parking: Limited roadside
Fees: None
Sand: Soft with stones
Crowd: Mixed
Facilities: Lifeguard, fishing
Rules/Regulations: None posted

Directions: From Route 127A to South Street.

This .25-mile long beach has an interesting history. The smooth, round stones found here were used in early fishing ships as ballast. Later when the ships' hulls were filled with fish, sailors tossed the stones overboard.

"All the rocks are soft and round from the water's action. I like to look out at the Twin Lights."
Steve Stamas, Milford, NH

Old Garden Beach
Ocean Avenue
Rockport MA 01966
508-546-6575

Season: Year-round
Hours: Sunrise - sunset
Parking: Lot for residents; roadside parking okay on weekdays
Fees: None
Sand: Soft with stones
Crowd: Mixed
Facilities: Lifeguard
Rules/Regulations: No dogs

Directions: From Route 127A near Bearskin Neck to Norwood Avenue to Ocean Avenue.

Maintained by volunteers, this small, sandy spot is frequented almost exclusively by residents. The beach has large, seaweed-covered boulders. Above, there is also a grassy area with benches for relaxing. The adjacent waters are popular with divers. If this is your interest, be courteous to residents: Be

quiet in the morning and store your gear behind the rocks --
out of sight.

Front Beach

Beach Street
Rockport, MA 01966
508-546-6575

Season: Memorial Day - Labor Day
Hours: 9:00 a.m. - 5:00 p.m.
Parking: Roadside meters
Fees: $.25/30 minutes, 5-hour limit
Sand: Soft with stones
Crowd: Mixed
Facilities: Lifeguard, restrooms, snack bar
Rules/Regulations: None posted

Directions: From Route 127A to Beach Street near Bearskin
Neck.

Far from being a secluded little cove, this beach is close to the
famous -- and famously crowded -- Bearskin Neck shopping
and art area. As the name might suggest, Front Beach is closer
to, or at the front of, Bearskin Neck. Thus, it's more popular
than its neighbor, Back Beach. Both share a view of Sandy
Bay.

Special Notes: If you want to head to Bearskin Neck for
lunch, locals claim that Ellen's, on T-Wharf, serves the best
lobster roll in town. If you'd prefer something with scenic
outdoor seating, head to My Place by the Sea. The seafood
salad sandwich is topnotch -- not too heavy on the mayo.

Back Beach

Beach Street
Rockport, MA 01966
508-546-6575

Season: Year-round
Hours: Sunrise - sunset
Parking: Roadside
Fees: None

Sand: Soft with stones
Crowd: Mixed
Facilities: Restrooms, benches
Rules/Regulations: None posted

Directions: From Route 127A to Beach Street near Bearskin Neck.

On the other side of Front Beach's grassy bluff, Back is quieter and less commercial because it's further from Bearskin Neck. Back Beach also affords views of Straitsmouth Light. A popular area with scuba divers, don't be surprised to see a few heads bobbing in the waves.

"My husband and son are scuba diving; I'm soaking up the sun."
Beata Lebeau, Springfield, MA

Special Notes: In July and August, the Rockport Legion Band performs weekly Sunday night concerts at the Back Beach bandstand.

Halibut Point Reservation

Gott Avenue
Rockport, MA 01966
508-546-2997

Season: Year-round
Hours: 8:00 a.m. - 8:00 p.m.
Parking: Lot
Fees: $2 per car
Sand: None
Crowd: Mixed
Facilities: Restrooms, bicycle rack
Rules/Regulations: No alcohol, unrestrained pets, bicycles, fires

Directions: On Route 127, at Gott Avenue, between Annisquam and Rockport.

This 54-acre park, with its magnificent view of Ipswich Bay, is not a beach in the traditional sense, but an oceanside experience you won't forget. (On a clear day you can see the

Isle of Shoals in New Hampshire and Mount Agamenticus in Maine.) A one-time granite quarry, visitors can explore exposed ledges, some of which drop precipitously into the ocean. Due to severe drops and undertow, swimming here is dangerous. But do enjoy the trails and rocky terrain: They're good for hiking, picnicking, sunbathing, fishing, and examining the life found in the tidal pools. Self-guided trail brochures are available at the WWII Tower Building inside the park.

"It's breathtaking to sit on the rocks, holding onto the seaweed while the cold waves sweep over you."
    Elinor McDowell, New Boston, NH

Special Notes: Imagine, a house and furnishings made from rolled newspaper! It's called the Paper House, and it was made of 100,000 newspapers in the 1920s. Located in Pigeon Cove (between Halibut Point and Front/Back Beaches) it's open daily, 10:00 a.m. - 5:00 p.m., during July and August. Adults $1; children 6-14, $.50. Call 508-546-2629.

Crane's Beach Reservation

Argilla Road
Ipswich, MA 01938
508-356-4351

Season: May 1- September 30
Hours: 8:00 a.m. - sunset
Parking: 3,000-car lot
Fees: Nonmembers: $8 per car weekdays, $14 weekends and holidays; $4 per motorcycle weekdays, $5 weekends and holidays; $2 walk-ins
Sand: Super soft
Crowd: Mixed
Facilities: Lifeguards, restrooms, bath house, snack bar, fishing
Rules/Regulations: No alcohol, dogs

Directions: From I-95/128 N, take exit 20A, Route 1A to Ipswich. Right onto Route 133 E to Northgate Road. Left on Northgate to Argilla Road. Right on Argilla.

Privately owned by the Trustees of Reservations, Crane's offers 2.6 wonderful miles of dune-backed, white sandy beach facing Ipswich Bay. Sand bars create warm, shallow swimming pools for children. A recent survey called it "the 5th best beach in the Northeast" with more than 250,000 visits annually. Boardwalks and fenced trails protect the dunes. Beware of the green-headed flies which can be bothersome in late July and early August. (Signs will be posted and repellents are sold at the beach.) A town permit is required for fishing.

"It's clean, well-preserved, and a simple, natural wonder of nature."
Raymond R. Rioux, Manchester, NH

Special Notes: Every August, Crane's has a spectacular sand "art" contest called "The Sand Blast." Competition is stiff: Artists build everything from elaborate castles to whales. Even if you don't feel particularly creative, it's fun to see. Although the Blast is usually held the third weekend of the month, call ahead to check exact dates.

Pavilion Beach
Little Neck Road
Ipswich, MA 01938
508-356-3231

Season: Memorial Day - Labor Day
Hours: 10:00 a.m. - 4:00 p.m.
Parking: Lot
Fees: $.50 per car per day
Sand: Soft with stones, some shells
Crowd: Mixed
Facilities: Lifeguard, playground nearby
Rules/Regulations: No alcohol, animals, balls in the water, fires, floats, glass

Directions: From I-95, exit 54, east on Route 133. Cross Route 1, continue on Route 133/1A. As you enter the village area where the main road bears to the right, go straight on High Street. Continue straight and then left onto East Street, and onto Jeffrey's Neck Road, to the end of Little Neck Road.

This small beach sits between Great Neck and Little Neck, and faces Plum Island State Park. Although it has no facilities -

- it's nonetheless a pleasant spot. The Ipswich Bay waters are warm and calm. Small rubber rafts can be launched from the designated area to the left of the beach.

"For those not interested in swimming, it's still a nice place to park and read the paper or eat lunch."
Elva Nelson, Ipswich, MA

Special Notes: No trip to Ipswich would be complete without stopping for fried clams – it is, after all, the place where they were invented. While most tourists flock to Woodman's, locals will tell you the best fried clams can be found at Farnham's on Route 133. Don't forget to wash down your meal with a can of locally made Twin Lights "tonic." (That's Yankee for soda.) Call 508-768-6643.

Sandy Point State Reservation
Beach Road
Newburyport, MA 01950
508-462-4481

Season: Year-round
Hours: 1/2 hour before sunrise - 8:00 p.m.
Parking: Lot
Fees: None
Sand: Soft
Crowd: Mixed
Facilities: Restrooms, fishing
Rules/Regulations: No alcohol, animals, fires, camping, cans, glass; "carry-in carry-out" trash policy

Directions: From Route 1A in Newburyport to Plum Island. Right after Bridge.

This 77-acre park is not well-known and has few amenities. Still, the small parking lot fills up quickly. The park's beach is a mile long and is at the southernmost tip of Plum Island. Surf is rough and the water is cold on the ocean side but calmer and warmer in the bay side's tidal pools.

"The sand ripples are incredible."
Marty Stein, Oakland, RI

Parker River National Wildlife Refuge

263 Northern Boulevard
Newburyport, MA 01950
508-465-5753

Season: Year-round
Hours: 1/2 hour before sunrise - 1/2 hour after sunset
Parking: Lot
Fees: $5 per car or $1 per person; free with Golden Age/Golden Access passports
Sand: Soft
Crowd: Mixed
Facilities: Restrooms
Rules/Regulations: No driving on beach 8:00 a.m. - 6:00 p.m. except between early September and late November; no tent camping

Directions: From Route 1A in Newburyport to Parker River Reservation Road. Right after Plum Island bridge.

The refuge encompasses about two-thirds of the southern portion of Plum Island. About 6.5 acres are on the barrier beach. Take the boardwalk to the beach or, when open, the trails through the refuge. You may spot seals, ducks, deer, rabbits, or birds. (More than 300 species call this refuge home.) Climb the observation towers for a bird's-eye view. Be cautious in the water because the undertow can be surprisingly strong. Also watch for green-headed flies in July and early August. A permit is required for fishing.

"We love it here in the spring and fall."
Sandi and Tom Lowery, Francestown, NH

North Plum Island Beach

261 Northern Boulevard
Newburyport, MA 01950
508-465-6680

Season: Memorial Day - Labor Day
Hours: 9:00 a.m. - 5:00 p.m.
Parking: Lot
Fees: $3 per car

Sand: Soft
Crowd: Mixed
Facilities: Lifeguards, restrooms, showers, fishing (mouth of Merrimack)
Rules/Regulations: No alcohol, pets

Directions: From Route 1A in Newburyport to Plum Island, left after bridge.

The shore of this inhabited 3-mile long section of Plum Island's barrier beach drops quickly into the water. Be sure to use extra caution near the jetty. And be aware that currents from the Merrimack River are strong. Green-headed flies can be a problem too.

Salisbury Beach State Reservation

Beach Road
Salisbury, MA 01952
508-462-4481

Season: Year-round
Hours: Sunrise - sunset
Parking: Lot
Fees: $2 per car
Sand: Soft
Crowd: Families
Facilities: Lifeguard, restrooms, bath house, fishing, boat launch, picnic tables, camping (no reservations), nature trail
Rules/Regulations: No alcohol, unrestrained pets

Directions: From I-95 to Route 110 E to Route 1A N.

The beach is several miles long, and the sand is raked clean daily. Camping facilities (on the southern side of the beach) and fishing near the jetty make this a popular vacation spot. But swimmers should be aware of undertows.

"We've been coming here for more than 19 years now. The beach is clean and supervised, and there are activities for the children."
Pauline Jobin, Manchester, NH

Salisbury Beach
Route 1A
Salisbury, MA 01952
508-465-3581

Season: Late spring - early fall
Hours: Sunrise - sunset
Parking: Lot
Fees: $3 per car
Sand: Soft
Crowd: Young
Facilities: Lifeguard, restrooms, snack bar, arcades, amusements, shops
Rules/Regulations: No alcohol, unleashed animals, in-line skating, skateboards, fires; horseback riding allowed off season
Directions: From I-95 to Route 1A.

This large, 5-mile stretch, with its amusements and concessions, is hugely popular with teens. The gently sloping shoreline makes it generally safe for families, although there is some undertow. Be sure to stick your toe in the water before you make a running dive: Salisbury has perhaps the coldest water in Massachusetts.

Special Notes: Every Friday night there are fireworks. Also, the nearby Old Burying Ground is an interesting -- albeit macabre -- place to visit: It has flat rocks, called Wolf Slabs, placed over graves that were designed to protect those buried from -- you guessed it -- hungry wolves.

BOSTON AND BEYOND, MASSACHUSETTS

Carson Beach, South Boston

Most city beaches are under the jurisdiction of the Metropolitan District Commission (MDC), which was founded in 1893 to protect and manage metropolitan Boston's open spaces. It currently operates 18 salt water beaches in addition to numerous parks, playgrounds, bicycle paths, and boating facilities. The MDC is in the midst of an ambitious "Back to the Beaches" campaign. The central idea is to improve waterfront maintenance. Efforts include acquiring sifters to remove cigarette butts and other debris, and having golf-cart-riding rangers enforce pooper scooper rules.

An integral part of beach cleanliness is the cleanliness of Boston Harbor. Until 1991, solid matter from the region's sewage was dumped untreated into the harbor. After a series of lawsuits in the early 1980s -- not to mention then Vice President Bush's claim that the harbor was the dirtiest in America -- a cleanup effort began. In 1985, The Massachusetts Water Resources Authority was created to build a $3.5 billion water treatment plant, which is now known as Deer Island. Today, the waters are abundantly cleaner: Beach closings due to high bacteria went down from 60 in 1989 to 35 in 1995. It's no surprise that since these efforts, residents are starting to come back to Boston beaches -- and yes, even swim.

Wollaston Beach

Quincy Shore Drive
Quincy, MA 02669
617-727-8865

Season July 4th weekend - Labor Day
Hours: 9:00 a.m. - sunset
Parking: Roadside
Fees: None
Sand: Soft with stones
Crowd: Mixed
Facilities: Lifeguards, restrooms, bath house, restaurants
Rules/Regulations: No alcohol, animals

Directions: From I-93 (Southeast Expressway), exit 8, to
Furnace Brook Parkway across Adams Street, then across
Hancock Street to the end. Turn left onto Quincy Shore
Drive. MBTA: Red Line to Wollaston, Wollaston
Beach/Ashmont bus #217.

Views of the Boston skyline define Wollaston as a decidedly
urban beach, albeit a pleasant one. Located within the Quincy
Shores Metropolitan District Commission Reservation, it's a
sweeping 2.3 miles long. The low sea wall here is a busy and
popular spot -- so popular, some beachgoers never make it to
the sand or water. The northern end, near an old Indian
campsite, is sandy, while the southern end, near Caddy Park
(playground), is mostly stones. Swimmers should watch for
water quality postings, especially following periods of heavy
rain.

Tenean Beach

Tenean/Conley Street
Dorchester, MA 02112
617-727-8665

Season July 4th weekend - Labor Day
Hours: 9:00 a.m. - sunset
Parking: Lot
Fees: None
Sand: Coarse with rocks
Crowd: Mixed

Facilities: Lifeguard, restrooms, benches, picnic table, playground, bicycle rack, tennis courts
Rules/Regulations: No alcohol, animals

Directions: I-93 (Southeast Expressway) exit 12, to Redfield Street, left onto Water Street, right onto Tenean Street where it joins Conley Street. By MBTA: Red Line to Fields Corner, Neponset Adams bus #20 or Quincy Center bus #210, or Red Line to North Quincy and walk back over Neponset Boulevard (not a quick trip).

In the inner reaches of Dorchester Bay, near the Neponset River and just below the Southeast Expressway, sits a small, mostly unknown but locally popular beach. The MDC manages it along with the adjacent playground and basketball court. Its best feature is a double-decker observation deck from which to view the boats in the bay, the planes in the sky, or the brightly painted Boston Gas tank to the north. Unfortunately, this area has questionable water quality, somewhat muddy sand, and an encroaching salt marsh.

Savin Hill Beach

Savin Hill Avenue
Dorchester, MA 02125
617-727-8865

Season July 4th weekend - Labor Day
Hours: 6:00 a.m. - 9:00 p.m.
Parking: Lot
Fees: None
Sand: Coarse
Crowd: Mixed
Facilities: Lifeguard, restrooms, benches (some covered), ball field and playground nearby
Rules/Regulations: No alcohol, animals

Directions: I-93 (Southeast Expressway), exit 15, east on Columbia Road, right onto Morrissey Boulevard, right before the drawbridge into parking lot. MBTA: Red Line to Savin Hill.

A salt marsh is gradually encroaching on this city beach, which shares a parking lot and MDC facilities with Malibu Beach. The bay is also home to the Dorchester Yacht Club, and sometimes boats entering or leaving must have the bridge at Morrissey Boulevard raised for them. Surf is calm, but the sand in the water can be mucky.

Malibu Beach
Morrissey Boulevard
Dorchester, MA 02125
617-727-8865

Season July 4th weekend - Labor Day
Hours: 6:00 a.m. - 9:00 p.m.
Parking: Lot
Fees: None
Sand: Coarse
Crowd: Mixed
Facilities: Lifeguard, restrooms, benches (some covered), ball field and playground nearby, public boat landing
Rules/Regulations: No alcohol, animals

Directions: I-93 (Southeast Expressway), exit 15, east on Columbia Road, right before the drawbridge into the parking lot shared with Savin Hill Beach. MBTA: Red Line to Savin Hill.

The MDC-maintained Malibu Beach is actually made up of two beaches. Malibu Inner Beach shares the bay and sandy beach area with Savin Hill Beach. Malibu Outer Beach is on the harbor side, across the road and difficult to reach from the parking lot. Plans are underway to increase facilities and services at the inner beach. The most outstanding feature here is the brightly painted Boston Gas tank looming nearby.

Carson Beach
William J. Day Boulevard
South Boston, MA 02127
617-727-8865

Season July 4th weekend - Labor Day
Hours: 6:00 a.m. - 9:00 p.m.
Parking: Lots
Fees: None
Sand: Coarse

Crowd: Mixed
Facilities: Lifeguard, restrooms, snack bar, playground, ball fields
Rules/Regulations: No alcohol, animals

Directions: I-93 (Southeast Expressway), exit 15, east onto Columbia Road, straight onto the William J. Day Boulevard. MBTA: Red Line to Andrew, City Point bus #10.

The large, sweeping MDC beach is in Old Harbor (part of Dorchester Bay), and faces Thompson Island and the Bayside Expo Center. With Columbus Park at its back, great shaded sidewalks, and a bathhouse due for renovation in 1997 (currently closed), there is the potential for a great city beach. On the down side, sewer overflows following periods of heavy rain have caused high pollution levels. Because it's within the bay and a mud flat area, the sand in the water can be mucky.

L Street Beach
at Curley Recreation Center
William J. Day Boulevard
South Boston, MA 02127
617-635-5104

Season July 4th weekend - Labor Day
Hours: 6:00 a.m. - 9:00 p.m.
Parking: Roadside
Fees: $20 - $40 annual membership dues
Sand: Coarse with shells
Crowd: Mixed
Facilities: Lifeguard, restrooms, snack bar, public boat landing; recreation center facilities include saunas, steam rooms, gymnasiums, and aerobic classes
Rules/Regulations: No alcohol, animals

Directions: From I-93 (Southeast Expressway) exit 15, east onto Columbia Road, straight onto the William J. Day Boulevard, to Columbia Road again. The bathhouse is across from the end of L Street. MBTA: Red Line to Andrew, City Point bus #10.

Who hasn't heard of this beach, where every New Year's Day the intrepid "L Street Brownies" take a winter dip. The City of Boston owns this swimming area and adjacent health club.

To provide bathers with privacy, wooden walls extend from the bathhouse into the water.

Special Notes: How did the Brownies get their name? In the early days, regular L Street beachgoers were called "brownies" because of their deep tans.

M Street Beach
William J. Day Boulevard
South Boston, MA 02127
617-727-8865

Season July 4th weekend - Labor Day
Hours: 6:00 a.m. - 9:00 p.m.
Parking: Roadside
Fees: None
Sand: Coarse with shells
Crowd: Mixed
Facilities: Lifeguard, restrooms, snack bar, benches, public boat launch
Rules/Regulations: No alcohol, animals

Directions: From I-93 (Southeast Expressway), exit 15, east on Columbia Road to William J. Boulevard where it picks up Columbia Road again, later to become William J. Day Boulevard once more.

The water here may not be as clean as other MDC-operated beaches because it's surrounded by yacht clubs. Wearing shoes is a good idea, especially at low tide, because the beach is littered with stones and mussel shells. Trucking in sand is among some proposed improvements, but it hasn't happened as of this writing.

Pleasure Bay Beach
aka Castle Island Beach
William J. Day Boulevard
South Boston, MA 02127
617-727-8865

Season July 4th weekend - Labor Day
Hours: 6:00 a.m. - 9:00 p.m.

Parking: Roadside
Fees: None
Sand: Coarse
Crowd: Mixed
Facilities: Lifeguard, restrooms, snack bar, benches, bandstand, public landing, public telephone
Rules/Regulations: No alcohol, animals

Directions: From I-93, (Southeast Expressway) exit 15, east onto Columbia Road. Straight onto the William J. Day Boulevard, past Carson Beach and joining Columbia Road again to City Point. MBTA Red Line to Andrew, City Point bus #10.

The swimming area at this beach is popular, partly because a protective causeway encloses the bay, thus limiting waves and easing pollution. In addition, a lovely park is to its back, and Castle Island to its side. Consider walking the man-made Head Island Causeway footpath to Head Island Lighthouse and then across to Castle Island and Fort Independence.

Special Notes: The Boston Harbor Association (TBHA) is a nonprofit, public interest organization committed to revitalizing Boston Harbor. TBHA is supportive of maritime industrial uses along the Boston waterfront, but has also helped make improvements to shoreline parks and beaches. Basic membership is $35 and includes a newsletter, harbor updates, and cruise discounts. TBHA may be reached at 374 Congress Street, Boston, Massachusetts 02210, 617-482-1722.

Lovells Island

Boston Harbor
Boston, MA
617-727-8865

Season July 4th weekend - Labor Day
Hours: 6:00 a.m. - 9:00 p.m.
Parking: None
Fees: None
Sand: Soft with shells and stone
Crowd: Mixed
Facilities: Lifeguard, restrooms, camping (permit required)
Rules/Regulations: No alcohol, animals, bicycles

Directions: From Long Wharf, near the Aquarium, the Hingham Ship Yard, or Lynn Heritage Park, take a ferry to Georges Island, then a free water taxi to Lovells Island. Limited docking for private boats is available at Georges Island, with off-loading only at the other harbor islands. Call Bay State Cruises for ferry fare and schedule information: 617-723-7800. Typically, the first water taxi departs for Lovells around 11:00 a.m. and departs Lovells for Georges around 3:15 p.m. on weekdays, 9:00 a.m. and 4:30 p.m. on weekends. For water taxi information call 617-727-5290.

Lovells, one of several islands in Boston Harbor, is the only one with an officially designated swimming beach and lifeguard. Because it faces east, it's not exposed to as much pollution from the city and harbor as other local beaches. Besides a sandy shoreline, Lovells -- thankfully still undeveloped -- has dunes, marshlands, and woods. History buffs will enjoy the remains of Fort Standish, a World War II base.

Special Notes: Nearby Spectacle Island may soon offer facilities at its beaches too, with Long Island (off Squantum Peninsula in Quincy via bridge) not far behind.

Constitution Beach
aka **Orient Heights Beach**
Bennington Street
East Boston, MA 02128
617-662-8370

Season July 4th weekend - Labor Day
Hours: Sunrise - sunset
Parking: Lot
Fees: None
Sand: Soft
Crowd: Mixed
Facilities: Lifeguard, restrooms, food nearby, basketball, tennis, and handball courts, playground
Rules/Regulations: No alcohol, animals

Directions: I-93 (Southeast Expressway) to the Sumner Tunnel to the Boston Expressway which soon becomes the McClellan Highway. Turn right (lights) onto Boardman Street. Straight at the lights onto Saratoga Street and immediately over the bridge turn right onto Bayswater Street and right onto Barnes Avenue to Bennington Street and into the park. MBTA: Blue Line to Orient Heights.

Tucked into the back of the bay and facing Logan International Airport, the MDC developed this beach in the 1950s. Sandy and moderately well-groomed, it affords close proximity to stores and restaurants, and is an easy walk from neighboring homes and apartments. The basketball courts and bathhouse (renovations are scheduled) are also plusses.

Simon J. Donovan's Beach
Pleasant Street
Winthrop, MA 02152
617-846-8243

Season Year-round
Hours: Sunrise - sunset
Parking: None
Fees: None
Sand: Coarse with beach grass
Crowd: Families
Facilities: None
Rules/Regulations: No alcohol, animals

Directions: I-93 (Southeast Expressway) to the Sumner Tunnel to the Boston Expressway which soon becomes the McClellan Highway. Turn right (lights) onto Boardman Street. Straight at the lights onto Saratoga Street. Continue on Saratoga to Main Street, then turn right onto Pleasant Street. The beach is across from Brookfield Road. MBTA: Blue Line to Orient Heights, Center bus.

Certainly Winthrop residents are used to the planes at Logan International Airport. However, if you can't get enough of them, this neighborhood beach is pretty close to the runways. Real junkies can bring binoculars for a closer view. The beach is located in Winthrop's inner harbor known as Crystal Cove. The water here is warmer than at Winthrop, Yirrell, or Short beaches, although it is muddy. It's in a mud flat area and has a salt marsh.

Frederick W. Yirrell, Jr. Beach
Shirley Street
Winthrop, MA 02152
617-846-8243

Season July 4th weekend - Labor Day
Hours: Sunrise - sunset
Parking: Roadside; parking is also permitted at the nearby school lot
Fees: None
Sand: Soft
Crowd: Mixed
Facilities: None; public boat landing and playground are nearby (Coughlin Playground is at the end of Bayview Avenue off Shirley Street.)
Rules/Regulations: No alcohol, animals

Directions: I-93 (Southeast Expressway) to the Sumner Tunnel to the Boston Expressway which soon becomes the McClellan Highway. Turn right (lights) onto Boardman Street. Straight at the lights onto Saratoga Street. Turn right onto Pleasant Street, which becomes Washington Avenue and right onto Shirley Street, which winds through the neighborhoods on either side of the peninsula. MBTA Blue Line to Orient Heights, Point Shirley bus.

Even though this beach is not far from the Deer Island sewage treatment facility, it's reasonably clean. A tall sea wall holds back the persistent sand from overtaking the road. The Deer Island plant looms at the southern end, in sharp contrast to the naturally formed jetty to the north.

Winthrop Beach
Winthrop Shore Drive
Winthrop, MA 02152
617-846-8243

Season July 4th weekend - Labor Day
Hours: Sunrise - sunset
Parking: Limited roadside
Fees: None
Sand: Soft
Crowd: Mixed

Facilities: Lifeguard, restrooms, snack bar, volleyball nets
Rules/Regulations: No alcohol, animals

Directions: Follow Washington Avenue to Sturges Street, then left onto Winthrop Shore Drive. MBTA: Blue Line to Orient Heights, Point Shirley or Winthrop Beach bus.

Winthrop's largest and most popular beach has a broad sea wall and clean water. Currently under MDC authority, in the late 1800s this beach anchored a summer cottage community known as "Ocean Spray." At low tide it's fun to walk out to the three stone breakwaters just offshore.

Short Beach
Winthrop Parkway
Revere, MA 02151
617-662-8370

Season: July 4th weekend - Labor Day
Hours: Sunrise - sunset
Parking: Limited roadside
Fees: None
Sand: Soft with stones
Crowd: Mixed
Facilities: Lifeguard
Rules/Regulations: No alcohol, animals

Directions: From Route 1 to Route 16 (Revere Beach Parkway), bear right at the lights. Continue straight, where the Revere Beach Parkway bears to the left, onto Winthrop Avenue and Sea Wall Parkway (also known as Winthrop Parkway) to just before Winthrop Highlands.

Unfortunately, there's little parking here and a high sea wall limits roadside water views. Across the busy street is Belle Isle Marsh Reservation, a 241-acre salt marsh preserve with trails and a 16-foot observation tower. The MDC, which controls both the beach and the Reservation, hopes to soon improve facilities, as well as access to these neighboring natural areas.

Boston isn't alone in its water quality problems. Pollution caused over 2,200 U.S. beach closings in 1994.

Revere Beach Reservation

Revere Beach Boulevard
Revere, MA 02151
617-727-8856

Season: Late June - early September
Hours: Sunrise - sunset
Parking: Roadside and lots
Fees: None
Sand: Soft
Crowd: Mixed
Facilities: Lifeguard, restrooms, bath house, snack bars,
pavilions
Rules/Regulations: No alcohol, animals

Directions: Route 1A to Revere Beach Boulevard.

This, the first public beach in the United States, recently
underwent a much-needed renovation. It no longer has the
amusements that were once its focal point. Yet it still prides
itself on accessibility: Public rail transportation brings this
extensive sandy beach within reach of many.

*"You walk Revere Beach and you visit the world -- it is very
cosmopolitan."*
Mary Hampton, Malden, MA

Special Notes: Kelly's Roast Beef is an institution on Revere
Beach. It's famous for fried fish and clams, and of course, roast
beef.

Lynn Beach

Lynn Shore Drive
Lynn, MA 01902
617-598-4000

Season: Mid June - early September
Hours: Sunrise - 11:00 p.m.
Parking: Limited roadside
Fees: Meters
Sand: Soft
Crowd: Mixed
Facilities: Lifeguard, restrooms, bath house, snack bar

Rules/Regulations: No alcohol, animals

Directions: From Rte 1A and the Lynnway, left to Lynn Shore Drive. Also on the MBTA line.

New sea walls back this sandy crescent, which sits between Nahant and King beaches. There's a grassy park with benches, which you may want to consider because the sand is extremely soft -- almost like quicksand. A sign at the beach explains that the sand problem is due to algae buried underneath.

King's Beach
Lynn Shore Drive
Lynn, MA 01902
617-598-4000

Season: Year-round
Hours: Sunrise - sunset
Parking: Limited roadside
Fees: None
Sand: Soft
Crowd: Mixed
Facilities: None
Rules/Regulations: No alcohol, animals

Directions: From Route 1A to Lynnway, left onto Lynn Shore Drive.

This sandy, medium-sized beach is bounded by Red Rock (a rocky outcropping) to the south and the Swampscott town line to the north. Low tide exposes a large, hard-packed beach. But at high tide waves roll right into the sea wall.

Special Notes: In nearby Swampscott, Dales Restaurant is good spot for ice cream and light fare. (There's a take-out window.) If you're beaching it on a Sunday, head out a little early and visit Dale's for its "Chowder Brunch," served until 2:00 p.m.

SOUTH SHORE,
MASSACHUSETTS

Horseneck Beach State Reservation, Westport

Southeastern Massachusetts' beaches may as well not exist for many travelers who are too busy making their way to the exalted Cape. To them, Nantasket -- a run-down stretch of sand that has long since seen its heyday -- is all they know of the South Shore.

And while Nantasket, now under the auspices of the Metropolitan District Commission, is in need of improvement, the South Shore has beaches that will rival any of its Cape neighbors. Among them is the Horseneck State Reservation in Westport. It offers pristine white sand and high dunes. And Duxbury Town Beach, an undeveloped barrier beach, is perhaps among the most beautiful on the Atlantic Coast. It does however offer only limited access. Nonresidents must belong to the Duxbury Bath House to gain admittance. For information call 617-837-3112, or try the Duxbury Harbor Master at 617-934-2866.

Westport Town Beach
Cherry Lane Road
Westport, MA 02790
508-636-1000

Season: Memorial Day - Labor Day
Hours: 8:00 a.m. - 9:00 p.m.
Parking: Lots, resident stickers required
Fees: Residents, $10 per season per car
Sand: Super soft
Crowd: Mixed
Facilities: Portable restrooms
Rules/Regulations: No alcohol, animals, fires, glass

Directions: From Route 6 to Route 88. After passing over the Westport River, turn right onto Cherry Webb Lane and follow to the end.

There are two town beaches in Westport, one on either side of the state reservation. This one is located where the Westport River enters the ocean. Paths from the parking lots lead through the woods and dunes to the beach. Look for Elephant Rock, out by the point.

"Across the bay are beautiful estates and turn-of-the-century beach homes."
　　　　Tracy Cavanaugh, Stow, MA

Horseneck Beach State Reservation
Route 88
Westport, MA 02790
508-636-8816

Season: Memorial Day - Labor Day
Hours: 8:00 a.m. - 5:00 p.m.
Parking: Several lots
Fees: $2 per car
Sand: Super soft
Crowd: Mixed
Facilities: Lifeguard (from 10:00 a.m. - 5:00 p.m.), restrooms, bath house, snack bar, camping
Rules/Regulations: No alcohol, pets, fires, glass,

Directions: From Route 6 to Route 88, several miles past the Westport River.

White sand dunes back this long, narrow stretch that is part of a large barrier beach system protecting the Westport River area. If the water's too rough and you'd rather walk the shoreline, stretch your legs out to Gooseberry Neck (a popular place for windsurfers). It's to the left, past the state campground. Or head to Elephant Rock to the right. This is a popular beach and the lots fill up fast on hot summer weekends. There is a parking lot at Gooseberry Neck for boaters.

Westport Town Beach
aka East Beach
East Beach Road
Westport, MA 02790
508-636-1000

Season: Year-round
Hours: Sunrise - sunset
Parking: Roadside, resident sticker required
Fees: Residents, $10 per season per car
Sand: Soft with rocks
Crowd: Mixed
Facilities: None
Rules/Regulations: No alcohol, animals, fires, glass

Directions: From Route 6 to Route 88. Follow to the end and turn left on East Beach Road.

Just beyond a neighborhood of RVs is Westport's second town beach. The grand ocean view couldn't be better: It looks into Buzzards Bay and across to the Elizabeth Islands.

Demarest Lloyd State Park
Allens Neck Road
Dartmouth, MA 02714
508-636-8816

Season: Memorial Day - Labor Day
Hours: 8:00 a.m. - 6:00 p.m.
Parking: Lot
Fees: $2 per car
Sand: Soft with stones

Crowd: Families
Facilities: Lifeguard, restrooms, bath house, shaded picnic tables, grills
Rules/Regulations: No animals on the beach

Directions: From Route 6 to Chase Road, then take Russells Mills Road to Horseneck Road. Continue straight onto Barney's Joy, then left onto Allens Neck Road.

It's a long ride to this beach, but worth it. Parents of young children feel comfortable with the calm, shallow water here, and at low tide a sand bar emerges. On the left end of the beach is an unguarded tidal pool along the marshland.

Apponagansett Park Beach
Gulf Road
Dartmouth, MA 02714
508-999-0712

Season: Memorial Day - Labor Day
Hours: 6:00 a.m. - 10:00 p.m.
Parking: Lot
Fees: $2 per car weekdays, $3 weekends
Sand: Coarse
Crowd: Families
Facilities: Lifeguard (9:00 a.m. - 5:00 p.m.), restrooms, picnic tables, playground, volleyball court
Rules/Regulations: No alcohol, animals, fishing, windsurfing

Directions: From Route 6 to Tucker Road, left onto Gulf Road. Beach is on the left just before the bridge.

The small beach at this open, grassy park is located in a scenic and sheltered salt water bay. There is no surf, and little tidal change, so the water is calm. As a result, the sand in the water can be mucky under foot.

Round Hill Beach
Ray Peck Drive
Dartmouth, MA 02714
508-999-0712

Season: Memorial Day - Labor Day
Hours: 6:00 a.m. - 10:00 p.m.
Parking: Lot
Fees: $4 per car
Sand: Soft
Crowd: Mixed
Facilities: Lifeguard (9:00 a.m. - 5:00 p.m.), restrooms
Rules/Regulations: No alcohol, animals, floats, in-line skating, skateboards, windsurfing

Directions: From Route 6 to Tucker Road, left onto Gulf Road, past Apponagansett Park, right before the bridge onto Smith Neck Road. The entrance to the beach is at the top of Ray Peck Drive.

This beach has lots of history. It was an old defense site and was the former homeport of the *Charles W. Morgan* (1841). (The *Morgan* is the only surviving whaling ship of its time and now resides at the Mystic Seaport Museum.) The restful beach faces Buzzards Bay and has views of Cuttyhunk.

"Our grandchildren love to play in the creek."
Terry Krenmayer, Dartmouth, MA

Jones Park Town Beach
St. John Street
Dartmouth, MA 02714
508-999-0712

Season: Memorial Day - Labor Day
Hours: 6:00 a.m. - 10:00 p.m.
Parking: Lot
Fees: $2 per car weekdays, $3 weekends
Sand: Coarse
Crowd: Mixed
Facilities: Lifeguard (9:00 a.m. - 5:00 p.m.), restrooms, picnic tables, playground, baseball field
Rules/Regulations: No alcohol, animals, fishing, windsurfing

Directions: From Route 6 to John F. Kennedy Memorial Highway, right onto Cove Road, left onto St. John Street, to the end.

This town beach has a neighborly, suburban feeling. The water is protected by Clark Cove. If you want to get out of the sun, head to the park area, which has plenty of shade trees.

West Beach

Rooney French Boulevard
New Bedford, MA 02741
508-979-1400

Season: Mid June - Labor Day
Hours: 10:00 a.m. - 5:30 p.m.
Parking: Roadside
Fees: None
Sand: Soft
Crowd: Families
Facilities: Lifeguard, restrooms, bath house, boat landing, snack bar
Rules/Regulations: No alcohol, floats, animals, ball playing

Directions: From Route 6 to John F. Kennedy Memorial Parkway to Rooney French Boulevard.

A restoration program is giving new life to this long, narrow stretch of beach in Clark Cove, situated directly across the street from the sweeping lawns of Hazelwood Park. On the opposite shore is Jones Park Town Beach.

Special Notes: New Bedford celebrates its place in oceanic history throughout the summer. For example, the Buzzards Bay Sailboard Classic Regatta is held the third weekend in June, the Whaling City Festival is the second weekend in July, and the Seafood Festival and Blessing of the Fleet are held the third weekend in August.

Dr. O'Toole's Memorial Beach

aka **East Beach**
Rooney French Boulevard
New Bedford, MA 02741
508-979-1400

Season: Mid June - Labor Day
Hours: 10:00 a.m. - 5:30 p.m.

Parking: Municipal lot across from beach
Fees: $1 per car
Sand: Coarse with rocks and shells
Crowd: Mixed
Facilities: Lifeguard, benches, playground
Rules/Regulations: No alcohol, floats, pets, ball playing

Directions: From Route 6 to John F. Kennedy Memorial Parkway to the east side of Rooney French Boulevard.

Large and small jetties divide this length of roadside beach, which was recently re-named for a father and son who were U.S. Navy surgeons. While it is fun to look for shells along here, as of this writing there is still too much broken glass on the beach. Hopefully, restoration and maintenance will allow visitors to enjoy New Bedford's Harbor area.

Special Notes: Visit the Whaling Museum to learn about New Bedford's role as a whaling capital. Adults $3.50; children 6-14 $2.50; seniors 59 and over $3. Call 508-997-0046.

Fort Phoenix State Beach

Green Street
Fairhaven, MA 02719
508-992-4524

Season: Memorial Day - Labor Day
Hours: 8:00 a.m. - 6:00 p.m.
Parking: Lot
Fees: $2 per car
Sand: Soft
Crowd: Families
Facilities: Lifeguard, restrooms, pavilion with picnic tables, playground, tennis courts
Rules/Regulations: No alcohol

Directions: From Route 6 to Green Street.

This long, sandy beach, popular with shell-seekers, is located at a historic site. The fort was built on the ledges of the park's western portion. There, you'll find a small lot with one-hour free parking, open from 7:00 a.m. to 8:00 p.m.

Pope's Beach

Manhattan Road
Fairhaven, MA 02719
508-979-4025

Season: Memorial Day - Labor Day
Hours: 8:00 a.m. - 4:30 p.m.
Parking: Lot
Fees: None
Sand: Coarse
Crowd: Mixed
Facilities: None
Rules/Regulations: None posted

Directions: From Route 6 to Sconticut Neck Road to Manhattan Road.

This is a tiny, no-frills, old fashioned beach -- just a small rock jetty, some ungroomed sand, dune grass, shells, and stones. The water is calm and the view expansive.

West Island Town Beach

Bass Creek Road
Fairhaven, MA 02719
508-979-4025

Season: Memorial Day - Labor Day
Hours: 10:00 a.m. - sunset
Parking: Lot, residents only
Fees: $5 per car; $2 for walk-ins; no charge for senior citizens
Sand: Soft
Crowd: Families
Facilities: Lifeguard, restrooms, outside shower
Rules/Regulations: No alcohol, unleashed animals, fires, floats

Directions: From Route 6 to Sconticut Neck Road, left onto West Island Road, across the bridge, right onto Balsam Road. Turn left onto Bass Creek Road and follow to the end.

There are two sections of beach on West Island. From the parking lot, the beach directly ahead is unguarded. The grassy path to the left, brings you to a beautiful, open beach from which only a few homes are visible. At low tide, waders can walk way out. Officially, this beach is for residents and their guests. But gratefully, this rule is rarely enforced.

"It's a wonderful family beach and so peaceful."
Jennifer Froh, Fairhaven, MA

Mattapoisett Town Beach
Water Street
Mattapoisett, MA 02739
508-758-4103

Season: Memorial Day - Labor Day
Hours: 9:00 a.m. - 5:00 p.m.
Parking: Lot, resident sticker required
Fees: $4 per car per season
Sand: Coarse
Crowd: Families
Facilities: Lifeguard, restrooms, bath house, playground
Rules/Regulations: No alcohol, floats, animals

Directions: From Route 6 to North Street, left onto Water Street.

Along Mattapoisett Harbor, next to a small, white-spired church, is the town beach. The shallow waters along the wharf are perfect for children. The vista of colorful boats is a treat.

Veterans of Mattapoisett Memorial Park

Ned's Point Road
Mattapoisett, MA 02739
508-758-4103

Season: Year-round
Hours: None posted
Parking: Lot
Fees: None
Sand: Coarse
Crowd: Mixed
Facilities: Restrooms, picnic tables

Rules/Regulations: No alcohol

Directions: From Route 6 (Marion Road) to the fork. From Marion Road turn left onto Ned's Point Road.

You'll find a rocky shore at the wide open grassy park on the tip of Ned's Point. A small white lighthouse marks its location on the Mattapoisett Harbor. Swimmers head to the sandy area on the left edge, near the exit. There are sand bars at low tide. Windsurfers are welcome.

Swifts Neck and Swifts Beach
Swifts Beach Road
Wareham, MA 02571
508-291-3182

Season: Memorial Day - Labor Day
Hours: Sunrise - 9:00 p.m.
Parking: Lots and roadside
Fees: $5 per car
Sand: Soft
Crowd: Mixed
Facilities: Lifeguard, restrooms, benches, boat ramp, picnic table, playground
Rules/Regulations: No alcohol, glass containers, fires, animals, improper language, swimming in boat channels, obstructing guard stands, bathing after 9:00 p.m., ball playing without lifeguard authorization, floats beyond line buoys, unattended children under 8, loud radios

Directions: From Route 6 to Swifts Beach Road.

These two sandy beaches sit on either side of a spit of land that juts into Wareham River. In addition to the pleasant view of Buzzards Bay, notice the neighborhood homes that were rebuilt on concrete stilts after the original structures were damaged or threatened by storms.

"We come here because it's quiet, not rowdy."
Alfonso Desimone, Wilmington, MA

The ridges in blue-back oyster shells are growth lines like the rings of a tree.

Little Harbor Beach
Little Harbor Road
Wareham, MA 02571
508-291-3182

Season: Mid June - Labor Day
Hours: 10:00 a.m.- 4:00 p.m.
Parking: Lot
Fees: Nonresidents, $5 per car
Sand: Soft
Crowd: Mixed
Facilities: Restrooms, public telephone, lifeguard
Rules/Regulations: No alcohol, glass containers, fires, animals, improper language, swimming in boat channels, obstructing guard stands, bathing after 9:00 p.m., ball playing without lifeguard authorization, floats beyond line buoys, unattended children under 8, loud radios

Directions: From Route 6 to Great Neck Road. Turn right on Stockton Shortcut to Little Harbor Road. Follow to end.

What a nice surprise. This beach is well worth the long drive on narrow, twisting roads. It faces Buzzards Bay and looks as if it has remained unchanged for years. While the waters are gentle, windsurfers enjoy (and are permitted on) the right-hand side of the beach, which is near the entrance to Little Harbor.

"It's a good spot for windsurfers."
Walter Edwards, Plainville, MA

Shell Point Beach
South Avenue
Wareham, MA 02571
508-291-3182

Season: Year-round
Hours: Sunrise - 9:00 p.m.
Parking: Lot
Fees: None
Sand: Coarse
Crowd: Mixed
Facilities: None, but beach is adjacent to Onset and its facilities may be used

Rules/Regulations: No alcohol, glass containers, fires, animals, improper language, swimming in boat channels, obstructing guard stands, bathing after 9:00 p.m., ball playing without lifeguard authorization, floats beyond line buoys, unattended children under 8, loud radios

Directions: From Route 6 to Main Street, right at the fork to Central Avenue. Cross Onset Avenue, continue on Central Avenue to the entrance on South Avenue.

Sand is extremely well-groomed at this beach, which -- despite its name -- doesn't have many shells. It sits at the head of Shell Point Bay, just off Onset Bay. With a grassy hillside park nearby, the spot is quiet and relaxing.

Onset Beach
Onset Avenue
Wareham, MA 02571
508-291-3182

Season: Mid June - Labor Day
Hours: 9:00 a.m. - 9:00 p.m.
Parking: Short term parking lot; public lot nearby
Fees: $1 an hour
Sand: Soft
Crowd: Families
Facilities: Lifeguard, restrooms, swimming lessons, boat launch, nearby restaurants
Rules/Regulations: No alcohol, glass containers, fires, animals, improper language, swimming in boat channels, obstructing guard stands, bathing after 9:00 p.m., ball playing without lifeguard authorization, floats beyond line buoys, unattended children under 8, loud radios

Directions: From Route 6 to Main Street. Left onto Onset Avenue.

This village beach has calm waters and a long, narrow swath of sand. If you enjoy boating action, Onset sits right next to a busy wharf. Be sure to have a snack at the Hungry Beachcomber Restaurant. (It's right on the beach.) All proceeds benefit the Wareham Recreation department.

"Everything you need is right here."
Linda Sauta, Hudson, MA

Special Notes: *Yankee* magazine voted nearby Water Wizz Water Park, at the intersection of routes 6 and 28, as New England's best. The place has more than 1,000 feet of water slides, a lazy river, a tube ride, and miniature golf. In summer it's open between 10:00 a.m. and 6:30 p.m. Call 508-295-3255.

White Horse Beach
Taylor Avenue
Plymouth, MA 02360
508-830-4095

Season: Memorial Day - Labor Day
Hours: 9:00 a.m. - 5:00 p.m. (facilities), beach closes at 9:00 p.m.
Parking: Limited roadside
Fees: $3 per car
Sand: Soft with stones
Crowd: Mixed
Facilities: Boat launch
Rules/Regulations: No alcohol, unleashed dogs, glass, open fires (without a permit), loud radios or musical instruments

Directions: From Route 3, exit 3, to Clark Road which becomes Beaver Dam Road. Cross Route 3A onto White Horse Road and right onto Taylor Avenue.

This beach once had a reputation for wild nightlife, but times have changed and families now predominate. A sandy path, flanked by grassy dunes and homes, leads to the open ocean beach. The drop off into the water is gradual, and there's no undertow.

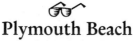

Plymouth Beach
aka Long Beach
Warren Avenue
Plymouth, MA 02360
508-830-4095

Season: Memorial Day - Labor Day
Hours: 9:00 a.m. - 4:00 p.m. (facilities), beach closes at
9:00 p.m.
Parking: Large lot
Fees: $5 per car weekdays, $8 weekends
Sand: Soft with stones
Crowd: Families
Facilities: Lifeguard, restrooms, bath house, snack bar
Rules/Regulations: No alcohol, unleashed dogs, glass, open
fires (without a permit), loud radios or musical instruments

Directions: From Route 3 S, take the Plimouth Plantation
Highway and turn left onto Route 3A (Warren Avenue).

This protected beach, with wonderfully warm water, is a
popular family spot. Four-wheel drive vehicles with stickers
can drive along the beach on a sandy, unimproved path. You
can see all the way to the Miles Standish Monument, Gurnet
Point, and, if you've got really good eyes (and conditions are
right), Cape Cod.

"It's scenic and our favorite."
    Dick and Helen Fitzhenry, Westwood, MA

Special Notes: The Plymouth Rock Trolley stops here and at
more than 40 historical sites in the area. Call 508-747-3419
or 747-2240.

Stephen's Field Beach
Winter Street
Plymouth, MA 02360
508-830-4095

Season: Mid June - Labor Day
Hours: 9:00 a.m. - 5:00 p.m. (facilities), beach closes at
9:00 p.m.
Parking: Lot
Fees: None
Sand: Coarse
Crowd: Mixed
Facilities: Restrooms, soda dispenser, picnic table, playground,
boat launch, ball field
Rules/Regulations: No alcohol, unleashed dogs, glass, open
fires (without a permit), loud radios or musical instruments

Directions: From Route 3, exit 6, onto Samoset Street. Turn right on Route 3A (Main Street) and pass Plymouth Rock. Turn left on Winter Street.

The village of Plymouth Harbor is a busy place. Visitors come to get their fill of Pilgrim history and learn about cranberries. Just to the south of Plymouth Rock is a small park with a quiet beach and shallow, gentle waters. From here you can look out to the end of Plymouth Beach.

Nelson Beach
Nelson Street
Plymouth, MA 02360
508-830-4095

Season: Mid June - Labor Day
Hours: 9:00 a.m. - 5:00 p.m. (facilities), beach closes at 9:00 p.m.
Parking: Lot
Fees: None
Sand: Coarse
Crowd: Mixed
Facilities: Lifeguard, restrooms, snack bar
Rules/Regulations: No alcohol, unleashed dogs, glass, open fires (without a permit), loud radios or musical instruments

Directions: From Route 3, exit 6, onto Samoset Street and left onto Route 3A (Main Street). Turn right onto Nelson Street.

This small beach and park in North Plymouth is a restful spot, however, there's not much sand for lounging. The water is shallow and calm. And the view, which includes Plymouth Beach, Saquish Head, and Miles Standish Monument, is restful.

Grays Beach
Grays Beach Road
Kingston, MA 02364
617-585-0533/0502/0520

Season: Memorial Day - Labor Day
Hours: 9:00 a.m. - 5:00 p.m.
Parking: Lot

Fees: $3 per car weekdays, $5 weekends
Sand: Coarse
Crowd: Families
Facilities: Lifeguard, restrooms, bath house, snack bar, playground, basketball and tennis courts
Rules/Regulations: None posted

Directions: From Route 3, exit 9, onto Route 3A (Main Street). Turn left onto Howlands Lane and right onto Grays Beach Road.

The swimming area at this small park beach is designated by a line of buoys, but at low tide shallow waters extend far beyond that protective enclosure. From here you can look out to the Miles Standish Monument.

Ellison Beach
aka **Shipyard Lane Beach**
Shipyard Lane
Duxbury, MA 02332
617-934-2866

Season: Year-round
Hours: None posted
Parking: Lot for residents only
Fees: None
Sand: Rocky
Crowd: Mixed
Facilities: Boat launch, bench, raft
Rules/Regulations: No unleashed animals, glass

Directions: From Route 3, exit 10, follow Route 3A to Depot Street. Turn left onto Washington Avenue and right onto Shipyard Lane.

The property where this beach is located was a generous gift of Eben Ellison and thus named for him. Shipyard Lane is a narrow road (you will miss it if you aren't looking) in a quiet neighborhood. The beach is similarly peaceful and has pleasant views of boats bobbing silently at their moorings. If you're not a resident, the only way you'll get on this beach is if you're vacationing in the area and can walk or bicycle.

Special Notes: Hungry for pizza? From this beach, turn left onto Washington Avenue, then left again at the Exxon Station onto Standish Street. Duxbury Pizza is on the left. Call 617-934-6568.

Duxbury Town Beach
Powder Point Avenue
Duxbury, MA 02332
617-934-2866

Season: Memorial Day - Labor Day
Hours: 8:00 a.m. - 11:00 p.m.; lot for four-wheel drive vehicles opens at 6:00 a.m.
Parking: Resident lot; nonresident roadside parking available only for four-wheel drive vehicles with oversand permits
Fees: Residents, $35 per season per car, $80 per season for four-wheel drive sticker; nonresidents, $160 per season per car.)
Sand: Soft
Crowd: Mixed
Facilities: Restrooms
Rules/Regulations: No unleashed animals, alcohol, fires, fireworks, overnight camping, glass, litter, fire; no walking in dunes, beach grass, or fenced-in areas

Directions: From Route 3, exit 11, to Route 14 which ends at Route 3A. Head straight, onto St. George Street, straight again onto Powder Point Avenue, and cross the bridge.

It's worth a drive here just to go on the long wooden plank bridge that crosses over Back River, a salt water bay. Powder Point Bridge is the longest tropical hardwood bridge in the U.S. It was rebuilt in 1987 and is a popular place to fish. This undeveloped barrier beach heads to the south for miles to Gurnet and Saquish Points. Off-road vehicles with stickers have access to an area of beach that has been set aside for their use.

Special Notes: If you're a real fan of this beach -- and who wouldn't be -- there is a legal way to get nonresident access. You can join the Duxbury Beach Bath House. For information call 617-837-3112, or try the Duxbury Harbor Master at 617-934-2866.

Duxbury State Reservation
Gurnet Street
Duxbury, MA 02332
617-934-2866

Season: Year-round
Hours: 9:00 a.m. - 8:00 p.m.
Parking: Lot
Fees: $5 per car weekdays, $8 weekends
Sand: Soft
Crowd: Families
Facilities: Lifeguard, restrooms, bath house, snack bar
Rules/Regulations: None posted

Directions: From Route 3 to Route 139, right on Canal Street. This changes into Gurnet Road. Follow to end.

This family beach is perfect for swimmers: There's a gradual drop-off with little undertow, and the bay side water offers temperatures 15 degrees higher than the open ocean. Public access is at the northern end of the barrier beach, *not* near the town beach bridge.

"Good facilities, easy parking -- a nice beach."
Susan Northridge, South Weymouth, MA

Special Notes: If you've got a hankering for homemade ice cream or frozen yogurt, head to Farfar's Danish Ice Cream Shop (617-934-5152) at 272 Saint George St.

Brant Rock Beach
Ocean Street
Marshfield, MA 02050
617-834-5540

Season: July 1 - Labor Day
Hours: 10:00 a.m. - 4:30 p.m., weekends until 6:00 p.m.
Parking: Limited roadside; lot nearby
Fees: Residents, $15 per season per car; nonresidents, $5 per car weekdays, $8 weekends
Sand: Soft
Crowd: Families

Facilities: Lifeguard; shops, snack bars, and restaurants nearby
Rules/Regulations: No alcohol, dogs, fires, glass, floats on offshore wind days

Directions: From Route 3, exit 11, to Route 14, to Route 3A. Cross Route 3A onto Tremont Street, then turn right onto Route 139 to the intersection of Ocean Street and Dyke Street.

This is an old-fashioned and unpretentious seaside village. At the edge of the beach is a small rock island which has been incorporated into a jetty and makes a fun walk. If you're going for a swim, be wary of undertows. Bird lovers should keep an eye out for Comerants.

"It's just down the street from my house. It's a nice, clean open ocean beach."
　　　Marie Smith, Marshfield, MA

Sunrise Beach
Foster Avenue
Marshfield, MA 02050
617-834-5540

Season: July 1 - mid August
Hours: 10:00 a.m. - 4:30 p.m., weekends until 6:00 p.m.
Parking: None
Fees: None
Sand: Soft
Crowd: Families
Facilities: Lifeguard on weekends only
Rules/Regulations: No alcohol, dogs, fires, glass, floats on offshore wind days

Directions: From Route 3, exit 11, to Route 14 to Route 3A. Cross Route 3A onto Tremont Street, then turn right onto Route 139 to the intersection of Ocean Street. From Ocean Street, turn left on any of the numbered streets (1st through 12th) to Foster Avenue.

There is very little access between residences to this sandy stretch. This long, narrow beach -- a mixture of sand and rocks -- is used primarily by the adjacent neighborhood.

Rexhame Town Beach
Winslow Street
Marshfield, MA 02050
617-834-5540

Season: Memorial Day - Labor Day (weekends only
until July 1)
Hours: 10:00 a.m. - 4:30 p.m., until 6:00 p.m. on weekends
Parking: Lot
Fees: Residents, $15 per season per car; nonresidents, $5 per
car weekdays, $10 weekends
Sand: Super soft with stones
Crowd: Families
Facilities: Lifeguard, restrooms, snack bar
Rules/Regulations: No alcohol, dogs, fires, glass, floats on
offshore wind days

Directions: From Route 3, exit 12, to Route 139. Turn left
onto Winslow Street and follow to the end.

Walk up a short, sandy path and over some grassy dunes to get
to this popular beach. The surf is good, but there's a mild
undertow.

*"This is a real family beach. There are lots of mothers and young
children."*
          Kristen Finn, Marshfield, MA

Special Notes: Marshfield's agricultural fair, a week-long
event held near the end of August, is one of the oldest such
fairs in Massachusetts. Call 617-834-6629.

Humarock Beach
Marshfield Avenue
Scituate, MA 02066
617-545-8738

Season: Late June - Labor Day
Hours: 10:00 a.m. - 5:00 p.m.
Parking: Lot, residents only
Fees: None
Sand: Soft with small stones

Crowd: Mixed
Facilities: Lifeguard, restrooms; stores nearby
Rules/Regulations: No alcohol, animals, cans, glass

Directions: From Route 3, exit 12, to Route 139. Turn left onto Furnace Street and left onto Ferry Street. Cross South River on Marshfield Avenue to the end.

This long barrier beach is lined with turn-of-the-century cottages. Proof of how storms change the shoreline: It was named because of its rocks, but severe storms have since washed them away, leaving a beautifully sandy beach.

Peggotty Beach
Town Way
Scituate, MA 02066
617-545-8738

Season: Late June - Labor Day
Hours: 10:00 a.m. - 5:00 p.m.
Parking: Lot, residents only
Fees: None
Sand: Soft with stones
Crowd: Mixed
Facilities: None
Rules/Regulations: No alcohol, animals, cans, glass

Directions: From Route 3, exit 13, go north on Route 53. Right on Route 123 to Route 3A. At this intersection, go straight on Country Way, and immediately right onto New Driftway, which becomes New Kent Street. Turn right onto Gilson Road, then left onto Town Way.

A boardwalk through dunes (currently under restoration) provides access to this scenic, crescent-shaped beach. Small boat fans will enjoy the sight of dinghies moored offshore.

Sand Hills Beach
Oceanside Drive
Scituate, MA 02066
617-545-8738

Season: Late June - Labor Day
Hours: 10:00 a.m. - 5:00 p.m.
Parking: Lots, residents only
Fees: None
Sand: Soft with stones
Crowd: Mixed
Facilities: None
Rules/Regulations: No alcohol, animals, glass

Directions: From intersection of routes 123 and 3A, take Country Way to First Parish Road to Beaver Dam Road, left onto Jericho Road to Turner Road to Oceanside Drive near Kenneth Road.

This rocky beach, located in a residential area, has many stones with only a bit of sand. A sea wall keeps churning water from hitting the road during storms. A storm overflow pipe protrudes onto the beach, so the water quality might not be at its best following heavy rains.

Egypt Beach
Egypt Beach Road
Scituate, MA 02066
617-545-8738

Season: Late June - Labor Day
Hours: 10:00 a.m. - 5:00 p.m.
Parking: Lot, residents only
Fees: None
Sand: Soft with stones
Crowd: Families
Facilities: None
Rules/Regulations: No alcohol, animals, cans, glass

Directions: From the intersection of routes 123 S and 3A, take Country Way to Curtis Street, to Mann Hill Road. Turn right onto Hatherly Road and left onto Egypt Beach Road.

The great stone wall that protects the pond behind North Scituate Beach extends along this shoreline. The homes along here have been constructed on stilts to protect them from storms.

"The rocks at the point keep my boys occupied looking for crabs."
Jean Munro, Marshfield, MA

North Scituate Beach
Surfside Road
Scituate, MA 02066
617-545-8738

Season: Year-round
Hours: None posted
Parking: Lot, residents only
Fees: None
Sand: Soft with small stones
Crowd: Mixed
Facilities: None
Rules/Regulations: No alcohol, animals, glass

Directions: From Route 3A, turn onto Henry Turner Bailey Road. Cross Country Way, turn right onto Gannett Road, straight onto Glades Road, and right onto Surfside Road.

A great, tall waterbreak of smooth fist-size stones is all that separates the forceful Atlantic from quiet Musquashicut Pond. The beach is long and narrow, but spacious just the same.

"In my thinking, Scituate is New England -- rugged coast and sandy beaches."
Lillian Rocket, Abington, MA

Minot Beach
Glades Road
Scituate, MA 02066
617-545-8738

Season: Year-round
Hours: None posted
Parking: None at beach
Fees: None
Sand: Soft
Crowd: Mixed
Facilities: None
Rules/Regulations: No alcohol, animals, glass

Directions: From Route 3A turn onto Henry Turner Bailey Road, go across Country Way to Gannett Road and left onto Glades Road.

This is a large sandy beach, and at low tide you can walk a short way out to an island.

"Little kids can wade in the inlet and the tide pools are fun."
Peggy Dinger, Scituate, MA

Special Notes: Although all Scituate beaches are open to the public, they have resident-only parking lots (in season). One option is to park at Scituate Harbor and ride your bike to the beaches. You can also walk to Pegotty Beach from Scituate Harbor.

Nantasket Beach Reservation
Nantasket Avenue
Hull, MA 02045
617-727-8856

Season: Year-round; facilities open late June - early September
Hours: Sunrise - sunset
Parking: Lot and roadside
Fees: $2-6 depending on day and time of year; $1 for seniors
Sand: Super soft with some stones
Crowd: Mixed
Facilities: Lifeguard, restrooms, bath house, snack bar (10:00 a.m. - 6:00 p.m.)
Rules/Regulations: No alcohol

Directions: From Route 3A South to Washington Boulevard in Hingham to Nantasket Avenue in Hull.

This 1.3-mile-long barrier beach has seen better days. In the mid-19th century it was a well-known resort. The Metropolitan District Commission (MDC) is now managing the area and doing much-needed improvements. At high tide the beach nearly disappears. But then many people shift to the small arcade area that still exists at the southern portion of the beach, and houses the historic "Carousel Under The Clock." The landmark carousel was salvaged from the now defunct, but once famous, amusement arcade, Paragon Park.

"I have fun throwing stones in the water with my brother and watching my footprints in the sand."
        Elizabeth Caliri (age 10), Quincy, MA

Special Notes: The Carousel Under the Clock was built in 1928 and sports 66 hand-carved horses and a Wurlitzer 153-piece band organ. Recently, the owners had contemplated selling the carousel and moving it to New York. However, at this writing, a local grass-roots group had just completed raising $1 million to purchase the carousel and so keep the landmark in its original home. Hours for the coming year haven't been finalized. In past years, it has operated from Memorial Day through Labor Day from 10:00 a.m. to 10:00 p.m., Sunday through Thursday, and until 11:00 p.m. on Friday and Saturday nights. Off season, after March 29 and until October 31, it's been open weekends 10:00 a.m. to 9:00 p.m.

Stony Beach
Nantasket Avenue
Hull, MA 02045
617-727-9457

Season: Late June - Labor Day
Hours: 10:00 a.m. - 6:00 p.m.
Parking: Small lot
Fees: None
Sand: Rocks and stone
Crowd: Mixed
Facilities: None
Rules/Regulations: None posted

Directions: From Route 228 onto Nantasket Avenue across from the Lifesaving Museum.

This long, narrow beach is appropriately named: there's nary a space for a blanket or chair among the stones. However, on a clear day you can see Boston Light and the islands of Boston Harbor.

"It's a good place to sit and watch the sunset."
        Bill Townsend, Hull, MA

Special Notes: Visit the Hull Lifesaving Museum with its hands-on exhibits and knowledgeable volunteers. Open Wednesday through Sunday, 12:00 p.m. to 5:00 p.m. from July 1 to Labor Day, and weekends and holidays (except January 1) the rest of the year. A donation is suggested. Call 617-925-LIFE.

Hingham Bathing Beach
Otis Street
Hingham, MA 02043
617-741-1410

Season: Last week in June - Labor Day
Hours: None posted
Parking: Lot
Fees: None
Sand: Coarse with stones
Crowd: Mixed
Facilities: Lifeguard (for 6 hours around high tide), restrooms, bath house, bicycle rack, picnic tables, boat launch
Rules/Regulations: No dogs

Directions: On Route 3A at Otis Street.

Warm, shallow water and minimal waves are the trademarks of this town beach in Hingham Harbor. The water depth at the raft is only 8 feet, and at low tide you could walk the murky bottom all the way to Button Island. But don't try it, there's way too much boat traffic.

George Lane Beach
Neck Street
Weymouth, MA 02188
617-335-2000 x409

Season: Late June - Labor Day
Hours: 9:30 a.m. - 4:30 p.m.
Parking: Lot (must have sticker)
Fees: Residents, $3 per season per car; nonresidents, $5 per season per car; no charge for senior citizens
Sand: Coarse
Crowd: Mixed

Facilities: Lifeguard, restrooms, bath house
Rules/Regulations: No alcohol, animals, balls, floats, glass

Directions: From Route 3A onto Neck Street.
This beach has an undeniable urban feel. The view includes the factories along the Fore River and several Quincy neighborhoods.

Wessagussett Beach

Wessagussett Road
Weymouth, MA 02188
617-335-2000 x409

Season: Late June - Labor Day
Hours: 9:30 a.m. - 4:30 p.m.
Parking: Lot (must have sticker)
Fees: Residents, $3 per season per car; nonresidents, $5 per season per car; no charge for senior citizens
Sand: Coarse
Crowd: Mixed
Facilities: Lifeguard, restrooms, bath house
Rules/Regulations: No alcohol, animals, balls, floats, glass

Directions: From Route 3A to North Street and left onto Wessagussett Road.

This beach has a split "personality." The view on one side is of a marina, and on the other is factories along the Fore River. An area for swimming lessons looks toward the Germantown section of Quincy.

Special Notes: You can tour the *Salem* at the U.S. Naval Shipbuilding Museum at the Fore River Shipyard in Quincy. Open daily 10:00 a.m. to 7:00 p.m. Admission: $5 for adults, $3 for children under 12 and seniors. Call 617-479-7900.

CAPE COD, MASSACHUSETTS

Nobska Light as viewed from Nobska Beach, Falmouth

Cape Cod. For many Americans, those very words are synonymous with the image of summer we hold in our mind's eye -- the one that is sheer perfection. Ocean breezes, sand dunes, and strawberry ice cream.

While parts of the Cape, with fast-food restaurants, miniature golf courses, and congested roadways, are a far cry from this image, much of it has a special mystique. In 1961, President Kennedy signed a bill ensuring that 40 miles of his beloved Cape oceanfront would remain preserved in its natural state, free from any development. Today, his vision, the Cape Cod National Seashore, offers the country's finest beaches on the Atlantic Coast.

For history buffs, the Cape's beaches hold a special allure, for it was on these beaches that the pilgrims first set foot in the New World. Several beaches, in fact, are named for their historical significance: First Encounter Beach in Eastham is the spot where pilgrims first met local Indians. Although there was an exchange of arrows and musket fire, no one was hurt.

For more information on Cape Cod history and ecology, be sure to visit one of the National Seashore visitors centers, located in Wellfleet and Provincetown. For information call, 508-349-3785

Gray Gable Beach
Gilder Road
Bourne, MA 02532
508-759-0600

Season: July 4th weekend - Labor Day
Hours: 5:00 a.m. - 9:00 p.m.
Parking: Lot, sticker required
Fees: Residents, $10 per season per car; nonresidents, $20 per week per car, $30 per two weeks, $60 per four weeks, $100 per season (Nonresident stickers available only to those staying in town.)
Sand: Soft
Crowd: Mixed
Facilities: Lifeguard
Rules/Regulations: No alcohol, animals, open fires or grills, children under 9 unless accompanied by a person over 14, floats, ball playing

Directions: From the rotary on Route 28 near the Bourne Bridge to Trowbridge Road. Straight onto Shore Road, right onto Monument Neck Road, then right onto Presidents Road. It jogs left, then left again. Turn right onto Gilder Road.

President Grover Cleveland made this neighborhood famous when he vacationed here during the summer. This bay beach is located in a deep cove at the southern entrance to the Cape Cod Canal. Because it's U-shaped, there's lots of beach frontage. A protected swimming area is roped off in the center.

"This is a tidal beach. At high tide swimming is terrific."
Monique Ward, Bourne, MA

Special Notes: Parking stickers are available from the Bourne Department of Natural Resources. Call 508-759-0623.

Mashnee Island
Mashnee Road
Bourne, MA 02532
508-759-0600

Season: July 4th weekend - Labor Day

Hours: 5:00 a.m. - 9:00 p.m.
Parking: None
Fees: None
Sand: Soft
Crowd: Mixed
Facilities: None
Rules/Regulations: No alcohol, animals, open fires or grills, children under 9 unless accompanied by a person over 14, floats, ball playing

Directions: From the rotary on Route 28 near the Bourne Bridge to Trowbridge Road. Straight onto Shore Road, right onto Monument Neck Road, then right onto Presidents Road. It jogs left, and then left again, to Mashnee Road.

Because there's no parking allowed along the narrow, man-made dike where the remote beaches on Mashnee Island are located, the best way to arrive is by boat or bicycle. (You could walk, but it would be a hike.) It's a beautiful area, with beaches facing into the calm waters of Phinneys Harbor and Onset Bay.

Monument Beach

Emmons Road
Bourne, MA 02553
508-759-0600

Season: July 4th weekend - Labor Day
Hours: 5:00 a.m. - 9:00 p.m.
Parking: Lots
Fees: Residents, $10 per season per car; nonresidents, $20 per week per car, $30 per two weeks, $60 per four weeks, $100 per season (Nonresident stickers available only to those staying in town.)
Sand: Coarse
Crowd: Families
Facilities: Lifeguard, restrooms, bath house, snack bar, raft with diving board, benches
Rules/Regulations: No alcohol, animals, open fires or grills, children under 9 unless accompanied by person over 14, floats, ball playing

Directions: From Route 28 to Clay Pond Road, straight onto Beach Street to Shore Road to Emmons Road.

Located high on Buzzards Bay and within the shelter of Phinneys Harbor, the beach has warm, gentle water. It's perfect for people who want a small, intimate space where they can park nearby. The harbor is busy with small boats and is particularly scenic at sunset.

Barlows Landing Beach

Barlows Landing Road
Bourne, MA 02559
508-759-0600

Season: July 4th weekend - Labor Day
Hours: 5:00 a.m. - 9:00 p.m.
Parking: Lot, sticker required
Fees: Residents, $10 per season per car; nonresidents, $20 per week per car, $30 per two weeks, $60 per four weeks, $100 per season (Nonresident stickers available only to those staying in town.)
Sand: Soft
Crowd: Mixed
Facilities: Lifeguard, swimming raft, boat landing, benches
Rules/Regulations: No alcohol, animals, open fires or grills, children under 9 unless accompanied by a person over 14, floats, ball playing

Directions: From Route 28 to the end of Barlows Landing Road.

This is a small neighborhood beach located within the quiet protection of Pocasset Harbor.

Hen's Cove

Circuit Avenue
Bourne, MA 02559
508-759-0600

Season: July 4th weekend - Labor Day
Hours: 5:00 a.m. - 9:00 p.m.
Parking: Lot, sticker required
Fees: Residents, $10 per season per car; nonresidents, $20 per week per car, $30 per two weeks, $60 per four weeks, $100 per

season (Nonresident stickers available only to those staying in town.)
Sand: Coarse
Crowd: Families
Facilities: Lifeguard, swimming raft
Rules/Regulations: No alcohol, animals, open fires or grills, children under 9 unless accompanied by a person over 14, floats, ball playing, snorkels/masks

Directions: From Route 28 to Landing Road, left onto Shore Road, to Island Drive, right onto Bell Buoy Road.

The medium-sized, crescent-shaped beach within Hen's Cove attracts locals who use it as a place to meet, visit, and play. The water is calm, just right for young children.

Sagamore Beach
Standish Road
Bourne, MA 02561
508-759-0600

Season: July 4th weekend - Labor Day
Hours: Sunrise - 10:00 p.m.
Parking: Lot, sticker required
Fees: Residents, $10 per season per car; nonresidents, $20 per week per car, $30 per two weeks, $60 per four weeks, $100 per season (Nonresident stickers available only to those staying in town.)
Sand: Coarse
Crowd: Families
Facilities: Lifeguard
Rules/Regulations: No alcohol, animals, open fires or grills, children under 9 unless accompanied by a person over 14

Directions: From Route 3, right onto Scusset Beach Road, left onto Williston Road, right onto Standish Road.

On Cape Cod Bay, north of Scusset Beach Reservation, is a quiet, sandy beach where you can walk for miles. On a clear night you can see the lights of Provincetown.

> The Cape Cod National Seashore includes more than 43,000 acres.

Megansett Beach

County Road
Falmouth, MA 02540
508-548-8500

Season: July 4th weekend - Labor Day (some weekends after Memorial Day)
Hours: 9:00 a.m. - 5:00 p.m.
Parking: Lot, sticker required
Fees: Residents, $10 per season per car; nonresidents, $20 per week per car, $30 per two weeks, $60 per four weeks, $100 per season (Nonresident stickers available only to those staying in town.)
Sand: Coarse
Crowd: Mixed
Facilities: Lifeguard
Rules/Regulations: No alcohol, open fires, floats

Directions: From Route 28A, across from Route151, to County Road, through the intersection with Chester Road, to the end of County Road in North Falmouth.

A long jetty separates Megansett Beach from a marina. Waters are calm, and the views of Buzzards Bay and Bourne's Scraggy Neck are pleasant.

Special Notes:. Resident stickers are purchased at the Surf Drive Beach bath house with proof of residency or a rental agreement.

Old Silver Beach

Quaker Road
Falmouth, MA 02540
508-548-8500

Season: July 4th - Labor Day (some weekends after Memorial Day)
Hours: 9:00 a.m. - 5:00 p.m.
Parking: Lot; gates lock at 8:00 p.m.
Fees: $10 per car; $4 per car for local hotel and motel guests with stickers (Most hotels and motels sell beach stickers at their front desks.)
Sand: Soft with stones

Crowd: Families
Facilities: Lifeguard, restrooms, bath house, snack bar, public telephones
Rules/Regulations: No alcohol, open fires, floats, windsurfing between 9:00 a.m. and 5:00 p.m.

Directions: From Route 28 at the exit for Route 151 (Nathan Ellis Road), turn toward North Falmouth, then left onto Wild Harbor Road, and left onto Quaker Road.

This popular and easy-to-reach Buzzards Bay beach has two sections -- one for residents and one for the general public. Generally, the water is calm; however, between the two beaches is a jetty and inlet where the currents can be a surprise at high tide. Further out, a sand bar keeps the water somewhat shallow for a while. It's a good idea to arrive around 9:00 a.m. to get a spot.

"The beautiful sand is like a velvet carpet."
Harry Donahue, Wrentham, MA

Special Notes: If you're a fan of old-fashioned diners, don't miss Betsey's Diner at 457 Main St., 508-540-4446. With authentic furnishings, homebaked pies, hand-cut donuts, and roast turkey dinner specials, the place is the genuine article.

Chapoquoit Beach
Chapoquoit Road
Falmouth, MA 02540
508-548-8500

Season: July 4th - to Labor Day (some weekends after Memorial Day)
Hours: 9:00 a.m. - 5:00 p.m.
Parking: Lot, resident sticker required
Fees: None
Sand: Soft
Crowd: Mixed
Facilities: Lifeguards, portable restrooms, mobile snack vendor
Rules/Regulations: No alcohol, open fires, floats, windsurfing except for designated area

Directions: From Route 28A (West Falmouth Highway) to Chapoquoit Road in West Falmouth

The parking lot sits above the water's edge and has a great wide open view. Below the sea wall is a shallow but long sand area. The Buzzards Bay surf is only benignly rough, so surfing is permitted anytime.

Wood Neck Beach
Wood Neck Road
Falmouth, MA 02540
508-548-8500

Season: July 4th - Labor Day (some weekends after Memorial Day)
Hours: 9:00 a.m. - 5:00 p.m.
Parking: Lot, resident sticker required
Fees: None
Sand: Soft
Crowd: Mixed
Facilities: Lifeguard, portable restrooms, mobile snack vendor
Rules/Regulations: No alcohol, open fires, floats, windsurfing between 9:00 a.m. and 5:00 p.m.

Directions: From Route 28A, where West Falmouth Road joins Palmer Avenue, take Sippewissett Road. Turn right onto Wood Neck Road and follow to end.

At high tide, this dune-backed beach on Buzzards Bay is rocky at the water's edge. Look into the water to find sandy paths between the rocks: Follow them and you'll eventually reach a soft ocean floor. At low tide, you can walk 60-80 yards out. Swimmers (including children) have fun riding the gentle currents into the nearby river.

Stoney Beach
Gosnold Road
Woods Hole, MA 02543
508-548-8500

Season: July 4th - Labor Day (some weekends after Memorial Day)

Hours: 9:00 a.m. - 5:00 p.m.; beach closes at 10:00 p.m.
Parking: Lot, resident sticker required
Fees: None
Sand: Soft
Crowd: Families
Facilities: Lifeguard, outside shower, water bubbler, bicycle rack
Rules/Regulations: No alcohol, open fires, floats, windsurfing between 9:00 a.m. and 5:00 p.m.

Directions: Follow Woods Hole Road to end. Turn onto Albatross Street. The National Marine Fisheries Aquarium is on the corner. Left onto Spencer Baird Road, right onto Bigelow, then left onto Gosnold Road (no sign).

This Quissett Harbor beach used to be a dock for the Woods Hole area. Now it's a small, sandy beach with jetties on either side where you can enjoy the Vineyard Sound water and watch the ferries to and from the Islands. The water is calm and shallow.

Special Notes: The National Marine Fisheries Aquarium on the corner of Water Street and Albatross Street in Woods Hole is open all year long and there is no entrance fee. A combination of research, public display, and public education, it's the oldest such museum in the world. Exhibits include 20 fish tanks, a hands-on touch tank for kids, and displays on conservation and management. Sometimes, you can see marine mammals being held for rehabilitation. For information, call 508-548-5123.

Nobska Beach
Nobska Road
Woods Hole, MA 02543
508-548-8500

Season: July 4th - Labor Day (some weekends after Memorial Day)
Hours: None posted
Parking: Roadside; it's also on a bicycle path
Fees: None
Sand: Soft
Crowd: Families
Facilities: Changing rooms

Rules/Regulations: No alcohol, open fires, floats, windsurfing between 9:00 a.m. and 5:00 p.m.

Directions: From Route 28 to Locust, which becomes Woods Hole Road, to Nobska Road.

From this beach is a wonderfully picturesque view north to Nobska Light. The water is gentle, thanks to protection from Little Harbor. Beachgoers seem to enjoy waving to travelers aboard the Steamship Authority's ferry to Martha's Vineyard which passes close by.

Special Notes: The grounds of Nobska Light, built in 1828 and on the National Register of Historic Places, can be visited year-round.

Surf Drive Beach
Surf Drive
Falmouth, MA 02540
508-548-8500

Season: July 4th - Labor Day (some weekends after Memorial Day)
Hours: 9:00 a.m. - 5:00 p.m.
Parking: Lots; gates lock at 8:00 p.m.
Fees: Nonresidents, $5 per car weekdays, $8 per car weekends and holidays; $4 per car for local hotel and motel guests with stickers (Most hotels and motels sell beach stickers at their front desks.)
Sand: Coarse
Crowd: Mixed
Facilities: Lifeguard, restrooms, bath house, snack bar, bicycle rack, public telephone (Stickers are available here; the office is open from 9:00 a.m. to 4:00 p.m.)
Rules/Regulations: No alcohol, open fires, floats, windsurfing between 9:00 a.m. and 5:00 p.m.

Directions: From Route 28 to Shore Street to Surf Drive.

This is a wonderful beach for children because it has a protected salt water pool. The shore curves gracefully in and out, and the beach is backed by low dunes. Surfers are welcome after 5:00 p.m. A bicycle path runs by the western end.

The Tides
Grand Avenue
Falmouth, MA 02540
508-548-8500

Season: Year-round
Hours: Sunrise - sunset
Parking: Small lot
Fees: None
Sand: Shells
Crowd: Mixed
Facilities: Benches
Rules/Regulations: No alcohol, open fires, floats

Directions: From Route 28 to Falmouth Heights Road, turn right at the intersection of Grand Avenue.

Named for the motel it sits next to, few people frequent this Vineyard Sound beach for swimming. It's too shell-covered. However, it is a fun place to watch the Island Queen ferry and other boats pass through the nearby entrance to Falmouth's inner harbor.

"I enjoy just sitting here in the sun and watching the boats going out."
Mary Thomas, Falmouth, MA

Falmouth Heights Beach
Shore Street
Falmouth, MA 02540
508-548-8500

Season: July 4th - Labor Day (some weekends after Memorial Day)
Hours: 9:00 a.m. - 5:00 p.m.
Parking: Lot, resident sticker required (cars are towed after 8:00 p.m.); also metered roadside parking
Fees: Meters are $.25/half hour with a 2-hour limit
Sand: Soft
Crowd: Families
Facilities: Lifeguard, portable restrooms; restaurants and shops nearby

Rules/Regulations: No alcohol, open fires, floats; windsurfing between 9:00 a.m. to 5:00 p.m.

Directions: From Route 28, continue straight onto Falmouth Heights Road. Turn right onto Main Street, then left onto Shore Road. Follow to end.

At Falmouth Heights, this Vineyard Sound beach is bordered by Falmouth Inner Harbor and Little Pond. In addition to a flat, sandy beach, visitors will find a grassy park with benches. This is the only beach in Falmouth for which there is no access for the handicapped.

Special Notes: The Barnstable County Fair is held at the end of July in Falmouth at fairgrounds located on Route 151. There are amusements, food, crafts, animal exhibits, and competitions. For information, call 508-362-3225.

Bristol Beach
Maravista Road
Falmouth, MA 02540
508-548-8500

Season: July 4th - Labor Day (some weekends after Memorial Day)
Hours: 9:00 a.m. - 5:00 p.m.
Parking: Lot, residents sticker required
Fees: None
Sand: Coarse
Crowd: Families
Facilities: Lifeguard, portable restrooms
Rules/Regulations: No alcohol, open fires, floats, windsurfing between 9:00 a.m. and 5:00 p.m.

Directions: From Route 28 in East Falmouth to Maravista Road by Great Pond.

A series of short jetties break up this section of sandy beach. Looking out into Vineyard Sound you'll see Martha's Vineyard.

Menauhant Beach

Menauhant Road
Falmouth, MA 02540
508-548-8500

Season: July 4th - Labor Day (some weekends after Memorial Day)
Hours: 9:00 a.m. - 5:00 p.m.
Parking: Lot; gates lock at 8:00 p.m.
Fees: Nonresidents, $5 per car weekdays, $8 per car weekends and holidays; $4 per car for local hotel and motel guests with stickers (Most hotels and motels sell beach stickers at their front desks.)
Sand: Soft
Crowd: Families
Facilities: Lifeguard, portable restrooms, bath house, mobile snack vendor
Rules/Regulations: No alcohol, open fires, floats, windsurfing between 9:00 a.m. and 5:00 p.m.

Directions: From Route 28 in East Falmouth to the end of either Davisville or Central Avenue to Menauhant Road.

This Vineyard Sound beach is really two beaches: Sand sits on either side of the inlets to Bourne Pond and Eel Pond. Boulders were put in place to help protect the dunes, and little jetties stretch into the water. Be careful of occasional rip tides at the Bourne Pond inlet. Surfers are welcome after 5:00 p.m.

"It's convenient because you park the car and you're right there."
Elinor Nelson, Newton, MA

South Cape Town Beach

Great Oak Road
Mashpee, MA 02649
508-539-1416

Season: Memorial Day - Labor Day
Hours: 9:00 a.m. - 4:00 p.m.
Parking: Lot, resident sticker required
Fees: None
Sand: Soft

Crowd: Families
Facilities: Lifeguards, portable restrooms, ice cream truck
Rules/Regulations: No alcohol, balls, open fires without permit, glass, boats

Directions: From the rotary at the intersection of routes 6 S, 151, and 28 to Great Oak Road

A Vineyard Sound beach, this sits adjacent to South Cape State Beach at the end of Great Neck. If you look carefully, you'll see mute swans (so named because they truly make no sound) flying between marshes.

"This beach has a tremendous amount of character."
Shirley Heifetz, Mashpee, MA

Special Notes: On July 4th weekend, the Wampanoag tribe holds a 3-day PowWow that includes a wonderful clambake in addition to dances, crafts, and demonstrations. For information, call 508-477-0208.

South Cape Beach State Park
Great Oak Road
Mashpee, MA 02649
508-457-0495

Season: Memorial Day - Labor Day
Hours: 9:00 a.m. - 4:00 p.m.
Parking: Lot
Fees: $2 per car
Sand: Soft
Crowd: Families
Facilities: Lifeguard, portable restrooms, hiking, shore fishing, sailboarding.
Rules/Regulations: No alcohol, animals on the beach, floats, surfing, fires without permit; windsailing is permitted 150 feet from bathers

Directions: From the intersection of routes 6 S, 151, and 28 to Great Neck Road to Great Oak Road.

A wide, sandy path leads between the dunes to this relatively unknown -- and thus uncrowded -- Vineyard Sound beach. If you've always wanted a view of the water from the lifeguard's perspective, there's a wonderful wooden deck with benches that also provides shade for children who play in the soft sand underneath. Only a small portion of this long beach is guarded. Be sure to check out the hiking trails within the park.

"You could write a chapter on this beach. I've walked its two-and-a-half miles every Christmas week for the past twenty five years."
Dick Kendall, Falmouth, MA

Oregon Beach
Rushy Marsh
Cotuit, MA 02635
508-790-6345

Season: Memorial Day - Labor Day
Hours: 9:00 a.m. - 9:00 p.m.
Parking: Lot, resident sticker required
Fees: None
Sand: Soft
Crowd: Mixed
Facilities: None
Rules/Regulations: No alcohol, animals, glass, open fires, snorkels

Directions: From Route 28 in Cotuit at the Mashpee line, to Main Street and left onto Rushy Marsh.

There is only a small access point for this beach, which ends where Meadow Point meets Vineyard Sound. The setting is natural, with marshes, grasses, and trees. Only a few distant homes are visible.

Special Notes: The weekly stickers sold to visitors are not valid at resident beach parking lots in Barnstable. However, all Barnstable beaches are open for walk-ins at no charge. Weekly visitor beach parking stickers for Barnstable's public beaches are sold between 8:00 a.m. and 5:00 p.m. at the Recreation Department at The Kennedy Skating Rink, 141 Bassett Lane, Hyannis.

Marine erosion wears the Cape away at the rate of three feet a year, more in some places.

Loop Beach
Ocean View Avenue
Cotuit, MA 02635
508-790-6345

Season: Memorial Day - Labor Day
Hours: 9:00 a.m. - 9:00 p.m.
Parking: Lot, resident sticker required
Fees: None
Sand: Soft
Crowd: Mixed
Facilities: Lifeguard, restrooms (close at 4:30 p.m.), outside shower, water bubbler, swimming lessons, mobile food vendor
Rules/Regulations: No alcohol, animals, glass, open fires, snorkels

Directions: From Route 28 in Cotuit, at the Mashpee town line, to Main Street. Just beyond the library (on right), turn left onto Ocean View Avenue (one-way street).

At the entrance to Cotuit Bay, across from Sampsons Island, is a pleasant beach that is mostly sand but has some small stones.

Ropes Beach
Old Shore Road
Cotuit, MA 02635
508-790-6345

Season: Memorial Day - Labor Day
Hours: 9:00 a.m. - 9:00 p.m. (facilities until 4:30 p.m.)
Parking: Lot, resident sticker required
Fees: None
Sand: Soft
Crowd: Mixed
Facilities: Lifeguard, restrooms, raft, bicycle rack
Rules/Regulations: No alcohol, animals, glass, open fires, snorkels

Directions: From Route 28 in Cotuit to Putnam Street to Old Shore Road.

Located deep within Cotuit Bay across from Osterville Grand Island, this is a small beach near a private golf course. Buoys mark the swimming area to protect bathers from the boats traveling along the bayside waters.

Dowses Beach

East Bay Road
Osterville, MA 02655
508-790-6345

Season: Memorial Day - Labor Day
Hours: 9:00 a.m. - 9:00 p.m.
Parking: Lot, resident sticker required
Fees: None
Sand: Soft
Crowd: Families
Facilities: Lifeguard, restrooms (close at 4:30 p.m.), bath house, outside shower, ice cream truck (stays here all summer, sponsored by Osterville Rotary), swimming lessons
Rules/Regulations: No alcohol, animals, glass, open fires, snorkels

Directions: From Main Street in Osterville Village to the end of East Bay Road.

A long entranceway runs along a salt water marsh and pond to this beach on Nantucket Sound. There water is warm, calm, and shallow a good distance out. Or, you can swim on the salt water pond side for even more protection. A jetty at the inlet entrance is popular with fishing fans.

"Great for children -- the wind waves give great rides."
Marty Stein, Oakland, RI

Craigville Beach

Craigville Beach Road
Centerville, MA 02632
508-790-6345

Season: Memorial Day - Labor Day
Hours: 9:00 a.m. - 9:00 p.m. (gates lock at 9:00 p.m.)
Parking: Lot
Fees: Nonresidents, $8 per day per car, $35 per week
Sand: Super soft

Crowd: Mixed, but lots of teens
Facilities: Lifeguard, restrooms (close at 4:30 p.m.), bath house, snack bar, outside shower
Rules/Regulations: No alcohol, animals, balls, glass, open fires, Frisbees, kites, snorkels, loud music, surfing

Directions: From Route 28 in Centerville to Old Stage Road, which becomes Main Street, to Craigville Beach Road.

The warmest water in Massachusetts is found here on Nantucket Sound at Centerville Harbor. The surf is calm and the pale beige sand is quite fine. For these reasons, people flock here. If you want to get in to the parking lot, arrive early, before 9:00 a.m. Popular with teens, it has been jokingly called "Muscle Beach" for the young athletes who play volleyball on the sand.

"It's clean and easy to get to."
Lorraine Doherty, Quincy, MA

Special Notes: If you've got a yen for ice cream, head straight to Four Seas (360 South Main St.) in nearby Centerville. It's got some of the best ice cream on the Cape -- and you can get sandwiches too.

William H. Covell Memorial Beach
Craigville Beach Road
Centerville, MA 02632
508-790-6345

Season: Memorial Day - Labor Day
Hours: 9:00 a.m. - 9:00 p.m.
Parking: Lot, resident sticker required
Fees: None
Sand: Soft
Crowd: Mixed
Facilities: Lifeguard, restrooms (close at 4:30 p.m.), bath house, volleyball nets, swimming lessons, mobile food vendor
Rules/Regulations: No alcohol, animals, glass, open fires, surfing, snorkels

Directions: From Route 28 in Centerville to Main Street to Craigville Beach Road. Pass Craigville Beach, follow to bend in road, across from Elizabeth Drive.

Residents prefer this sandy beach, which is not too far from popular Craigville. It is a good-sized, rectangular area of sand which enjoys the same water conditions as its public neighbor.

East Beach

Irving Street
Hyannis, MA 02601
508-790-6345

Season: Memorial Day - mid August
Hours: 9:00 a.m. - 9:00 p.m.
Parking: Lot, resident sticker required
Fees: None
Sand: Soft
Crowd: Mixed
Facilities: None
Rules/Regulations: No alcohol, animals, glass, open fires, snorkels

Directions: From Route 28 in Hyannis to West Main Street to Scudder Street, left onto Irving, a one-way, unmarked street.

This small beach, within Hyannis Harbor, probably hasn't changed in years. While it's unspectacular for a Cape beach -- and decidedly no-frills -- it is pleasant. There's a scenic wooden pier, which belongs to a local club, and plenty of small boats all about.

Keyes Memorial Beach

aka Orrin Keyes Beach
Ocean Avenue
Hyannis, MA 02601
508-790-6345

Season: Memorial Day - Labor Day
Hours: 9:00 a.m. - 9:00 p.m.
Fees: Nonresidents, $8 per day per car; $35 per week
Parking: Lot
Sand: Soft
Crowd: Families

Facilities: Lifeguard, restrooms (close at 4:30 p.m.), bath house, snack bar, picnic area, grills, volleyball nets
Rules/Regulations: No alcohol, animals, glass, open fires, snorkels

Directions: From the intersection of routes 6 S, 132, and 28 in Hyannis to Barnstable Road to Main Street, left onto Sea Street to Ocean Avenue.

Also known as Sea Street Beach, this Hyannis park offers a small wooded hill, a nice lookout area from which to view Hyannis Harbor, and a good-sized sandy beach. From the lookout area, the dunes drop quickly. The parking lot is on the lower level, which is near the beach. But facilities are up on the hillside, amongst the trees.

Special Notes: Looking for "fast food," but not a hamburger chain? Try Cooke's Seafood at 1220 Route132 in Hyannis. Call 508-775-0450.

Kalmus Park Beach

Hawes Avenue
Hyannis, MA 02601
508-790-6345

Season: Memorial Day - Labor Day
Hours: 9:00 a.m. - 9:00 p.m.
Parking: Lot
Fees: Nonresidents, $8 per week per car; $35 per week
Sand: Coarse with stones and shells
Crowd: Families
Facilities: Lifeguard, restrooms (close at 4:30 p.m.), bath house, snack bar, picnic tables, volleyball nets, swimming lessons
Rules/Regulations: No alcohol, animals, glass, open fires, snorkels; sailboard users must not rig in the parking lot or dunes and must stay a safe distance from swimmers

Directions: From the intersection of routes 28 and 132 in Hyannis to Barnstable Road, then straight onto Ocean Street to the end.

This barrier beach on Lewis Bay has lots of finely crushed shells and small stones mixed in with the sand. Bring a beach chair to settle in and watch the island ferries, pleasure boats, and colorful windsurfers. (Windsurfing is permitted only in designated areas.) Although the parking lot is large, it fills up early. Try arriving by 9:00 a.m.

Veterans' Park Beach
Ocean Street
Hyannis, MA 02601
508-790-6345

Season: Memorial Day - Labor Day
Hours: 9:00 a.m. - 9:00 p.m.
Parking: Lot
Fees: Nonresidents, $8 per day per car; $35 per week
Sand: Coarse
Crowd: Families
Facilities: Lifeguard, restrooms (close at 4:30 p.m.), bath house, snack bar, picnic area, swings, grills, volleyball nets
Rules/Regulations: No alcohol, animals, glass, open fires, snorkels

Directions: From routes 132 and 28 in Hyannis, to Barnstable Road to Ocean Street.

The parking lot for this beach is full for a variety of reasons: its family-friendly sheltered waters, its proximity to the ferry and tour boat docks, as well as to the JFK Memorial. There is a nice tree-shaded park behind the beach with picnic tables and grills, and you can see all the activity in busy Hyannis Harbor.

Special Notes: Kidz Connection is a new indoor playground, located at the Cape Cod Mall on Route 132. Call 508-771-8090.

Mill Way Beach
Mill Way Beach Road
West Barnstable, MA 02668
508-790-6345

Season: Memorial Day - mid August
Hours: 9:00 a.m. - 9:00 p.m.
Parking: Small lot, resident sticker required
Fees: None

Sand: Soft
Crowd: Mixed
Facilities: Restrooms (close at 4:30 p.m.), bath house, mobile food vendor
Rules/Regulations: No alcohol, animals, glass, open fires, snorkels

Directions: From Route 6A in West Barnstable to Mill Way Beach Road at the lights.

One of two Barnstable beaches on Cape Cod Bay, there's lots of sea grass in the water. Fortunately, a small area is cleared for bathers. Swimming lessons are offered.

Bay View Beach

Bay View Street
Yarmouth, MA 02673
508-398-2231

Season: Memorial Day - Labor Day
Hours: 8:00 a.m. - 10:00 p.m.
Parking: Lot
Fees: None
Sand: Stony
Crowd: Mixed
Facilities: Lifeguards, restrooms, snack bar, boat ramp, restaurant
Rules/Regulations: No alcohol, animals, floats, Frisbees/balls except in lifeguard-specified area

Directions: From Route 28 in West Yarmouth to the end of Bay View Street (the road beyond Cape Cod Hospital).

From its vantage point at the head of Lewis Bay on Nantucket Sound, sunbathers can watch ferries come and go from Martha's Vineyard and Nantucket. The beach area has many rocks and is relatively small.

Special Notes: Yarmouth beach stickers are available at the town hall. Some lodging facilities offer daily discounted beach stickers for $5. Many of the town's smaller beaches have free parking, but those lots are usually small.

Colonial Acres
Standish Way
Yarmouth, MA 02673
508-398-2231

Season: Memorial Day - Labor Day
Hours: 8:00 a.m. - 10:00 p.m.
Parking: Lot
Fees: None
Sand: Coarse
Crowd: Mixed
Facilities: Portable restrooms, mobile snack vendors, public telephone
Rules/Regulations: No alcohol, animals, Frisbees/balls except in lifeguard-specified area, floats

Directions: From Route 28 in West Yarmouth to Standish Way (this grass-divided street may be unmarked -- it sits between Berry Avenue and Wimbledon Drive) to the end, beyond the Colonial Acres Resort.

A sturdy wooden footbridge carries you over a small salt waterway to a sizable beach. Because it's away from land and dwellings, it feels remote. There is, however, a lot of boat activity. Water quality is questionable in the creek and swimming there is prohibited.

Englewood Beach
Berry Avenue
Yarmouth, MA 02673
508-398-2231

Season: Memorial Day - Labor Day
Hours: 8:00 a.m. - 10:00 p.m.
Parking: Lot
Fees: None
Sand: Soft
Crowd: Mixed
Facilities: Restrooms, mobile snack vendor, public telephone, boat launch, benches, playground
Rules/Regulations: No alcohol, animals, floats, boat trailers, Frisbees/balls except in lifeguard-specified area

Directions: From Route 28 in West Yarmouth (across from the police station) to the end of Berry Avenue.

Here's a small but scenic beach in very protected water. It's the perfect location for swimming and sailing lessons, which the Recreation Department offers during July and August. Registration for residents is held after Memorial Day weekend; nonresident registrations are taken on an ongoing basis after the third week in June. Lessons are also available at Sea Gull Beach, Parker's River, and Dennis Pond. Call 508-398-2231, ext. 284.

Sea Gull Beach
Sea Gull Road
Yarmouth, MA 02674
508-398-2231

Season: Memorial Day - Labor Day
Hours: 8:00 a.m. - 10:00 p.m.
Parking: Lot
Fees: Residents, $15 per season per car; nonresidents, $8 per day per car; $35 per week, $75 per season
Sand: Coarse
Crowd: Families
Facilities: Lifeguard, restrooms, bath house, snack bar, public telephone
Rules/Regulations: No alcohol, animals, floats, Frisbees/balls except in lifeguard-specified area

Directions: From Route 28 in West Yarmouth to South Sea Avenue to Sea Gull Road.

Facing Nantucket Sound and backed by low, sheltering dunes, this is the largest and most popular salt water beach in Yarmouth. The sand drops gently into the ocean, the water is warm, and the current is gentle. To the left is Lewis Pond and marshland, with Great Island to the right.

"The beach is wide and long and nice for walking and shell collecting."
     Marianne Batgos, Wayne, PA

Thatcher Beach

South Shore Drive
Yarmouth, MA 02673
508-398-2231

Season: Memorial Day - Labor Day
Hours: 8:00 a.m. - 10:00 p.m.
Parking: Lot
Fees: None
Sand: Soft
Crowd: Mixed
Facilities: None
Rules/Regulations: No alcohol, animals, Frisbees/balls except in lifeguard-specified area, floats

Directions: From Route 28 in South Yarmouth to Seaview Avenue. Turn right onto South Shore Drive.

At this beach, the tide comes right up to the sea wall. A concrete walk at the top of the shallow beach holds benches. This setup is similar to Sea View Beach, but Thatcher is a bit larger and has three jetties poking out from the shore.

Sea View Beach

South Shore Drive
Yarmouth, MA 02673
508-398-2231

Season: Memorial Day - Labor Day
Hours: 8:00 a.m. - 10:00 p.m.
Parking: Lot
Fees: $7 per car
Sand: Soft
Crowd: Mixed
Facilities: Portable restrooms, mobile snack vendor, bicycle rack, benches, shaded picnic tables
Rules/Regulations: No alcohol, animals, Frisbees/balls except in lifeguard-specified area, floats

Directions: From Route 28 in South Yarmouth to South Shore Drive.

A concrete walkway borders this small beach. Its benches are a perfect spot to view the action in Nantucket Sound. A few steps down and you're at the beach, which is defined by jetties.

Parker's River South Beach
South Shore Drive
Yarmouth, MA 02673
508-398-2231

Season: Memorial Day - Labor Day
Hours: 8:00 a.m. - 10:00 p.m.
Parking: Lot
Fees: Residents, $15 per season per car; nonresidents, $8 per day per car; $35 per week, $75 per season
Sand: Soft
Crowd: Mixed
Facilities: Restrooms, snack bar, public telephone, swings, benches
Rules/Regulations: No alcohol, animals, Frisbees/balls except in lifeguard-specified areas, floats

Directions: From Route 28 in South Yarmouth to South Shore Drive.

Despite its name, this beach is not precisely at Parker's River -- but it's close. At high tide, the water comes right up to the sea wall. This doesn't seem to bother bathers too much. Above the sea wall there's a grassy area with a playground, benches, and a gazebo.

South Middle Beach
South Shore Drive
Yarmouth, MA 02675
508-398-2231

Season: Memorial Day - Labor Day
Hours: 8:00 a.m. - 10:00 p.m.
Parking: Small lot, resident sticker required
Fees: None
Sand: Soft
Crowd: Mixed
Facilities: Restrooms, mobile snack vendor, public telephone

Rules/Regulations: No alcohol, animals, floats, Frisbees/balls except in lifeguard-designated area

Directions: Route 28 in South Yarmouth to South Shore Road near Judan Way.

Follow the pathway through the woods and dunes and you'll come out to a fairly unpopulated stretch of beach.

"It's clean, with nice, deep sand dunes and not too many people."
John Bell, Rochester, NY

Bass River Beach
aka Smuggler's Beach
South Shore Drive
South Yarmouth, MA 02673
508-398-2231

Season: Memorial Day - Labor Day
Hours: 8:00 a.m. - 10:00 p.m.
Parking: Lot
Fees: Residents, $15 per season per car; nonresidents, $8 per day per car; $35 per week, $75 per season
Sand: Soft
Crowd: Mixed
Facilities: Restrooms, snack bar, picnic tables, fishing, boat ramp, public telephone, bicycle rack
Rules/Regulations: No alcohol, animals, floats, Frisbees/balls except in lifeguard-specified areas

Directions: From Route 28 in South Yarmouth to Main Street to South Shore Drive.

This Nantucket Sound beach is backed by dunes and borders the Bass River, which is among the largest tidal rivers on the East Coast. The large wooden dock is a good spot if you're interested in catching some striped bass or bluefish.

Special Notes: Tour boat aficionados should check out the *Starfish*. It offers 1.5-hour tours down the Bass River. It docks in West Dennis at Waterfront Park. For information, call 508-362-5555.

Windmill Beach
Willow Street
Yarmouth, MA 02673
508-398-2231

Season: Memorial Day - Labor Day
Hours: 8:00 a.m. - 10:00 p.m.
Parking: Lot
Fees: None
Sand: Soft
Crowd: Mixed
Facilities: None
Rules/Regulations: No alcohol, animals, floats, Frisbees/balls except in lifeguard-specified areas

Directions: From Route 28 in South Yarmouth to the end of Willow Street.

The small beach at this park is just a stone's throw from the mouth of the Bass River. The windmill -- one of the oldest on Cape Cod -- for which the beach was named, is not original to this location. It was moved here in 1866 and donated to the town in 1953.

Gray's Beach
aka Bass Hole
Center Street
Yarmouth, MA 02673
508-398-2231

Season: Memorial Day - Labor Day
Hours: 8:00 a.m. - 10:00 p.m.
Parking: Lot; gates lock at 10:00 p.m.
Fees: None
Sand: Soft
Crowd: Families
Facilities: Restrooms, picnic pavilion, playground, public telephone, boat launch, bicycle rack
Rules/Regulations: No alcohol, animals

Directions: From Route 6A to the end of Center Street.

The swings in tide bring drastic changes to this inlet beach, Yarmouth's only one on Cape Cod Bay. While the water looks placid, visitors should be aware there can be dangerous crosscurrents. Be sure to explore the marshes by walking along the 860-foot wooden boardwalk, which reaches almost to Chapin Memorial Beach on the bay and ends at a nice deck. (Chapin's dunes obstruct the bay view from this beach.)

West Dennis Beach

Lighthouse Road
Dennis, MA 02638
508-760-6112

Season: 2nd Saturday in June - Labor Day
Hours: 8:00 a.m. - 5:00 p.m.
Parking: Lot
Fees: Nonresidents, $8 per day per car, $25 per week (Saturday through Friday), $125 per season
Sand: Coarse
Crowd: Families
Facilities: Lifeguards, restrooms, bath house, snack bar, playground, public telephone
Rules/Regulations: No alcohol, animals, in-line skates, skateboards, kite flying except in designated areas, fires without permit, boating or fishing

Directions: From Route 28 in West Dennis to School Street to Lighthouse Road.

This popular Nantucket Sound beach is known for its annual volleyball tournaments. Watch for windsurfers, too. Notice the half-finished breakwater? Construction began in 1837, but the project was abandoned when a sand bar formed on the shore side and engineers felt their work was a failure. This is touted as the most handicapped accessible beach in Dennis, although Corporation, Mayflower, and Scargo beaches have wheelchair ramps too.

"The shells here are different from the north side beaches."
Elaine Fisher, Dennis, MA

Special Notes: Daily parking passes may be purchased at any beach location where there is an attendant. These stickers are good for the entire day at all Dennis beaches except Cold

Storage Beach, Harbor View Beach, and Bay View Beach, which are for residents only. Weekly and seasonal passes are also available at the town hall seven days a week. For sticker information call 508-394-8300, ext. 159.

South Village Road Beach
South Village Road
Dennis, MA 02638
508-760-6112

Season: 2nd Saturday in June - Labor Day
Hours: 9:00 a.m. - 5:00 p.m.
Parking: Lots
Fees: Nonresidents, $8 per day per car, $25 per week (Saturday through Friday), $125 per season
Sand: Coarse
Crowd: Mixed
Facilities: Lifeguard, mobile snack vendor
Rules/Regulations: No alcohol, animals, in-line skates, skateboards, kite flying except in designated areas, fires without permit

Directions: From Route 28 to Swan River Road, right onto Lower County Road, and left onto South Village Road.

This Nantucket Sound beach has a spacious feel because, unlike some Cape beaches, houses are not crowded along the perimeter. That's not to say, however, there aren't a few around. Nearby is the Swan Pond River Common boat landing, which is open from 9:00 a.m. to 8:00 p.m. Neither swimming nor jet ski use is permitted in the river.

Special Notes: Dennis pulls out all the stops for its annual "Dennis Festival Days," which are held during the last week in August. There's an antique auto parade, kite flying and sand castle contests, church suppers, bingo, and more. Call 800-243-9920.

Cape Cod juts farther out into the Atlantic Ocean than any other piece of land in the United States.

Haigis Beach

Old Wharf Road
Dennis, MA 02638
508-760-6112

Season: 2nd Saturday in June - Labor Day
Hours: 9:00 a.m. - 5:00 p.m.
Parking: Lot
Fees: Nonresidents, $8 per day per car, $25 per week (Saturday through Friday), $125 per season
Sand: Coarse
Crowd: Mixed
Facilities: Lifeguard, restrooms, mobile snack vendor, public telephone, swings
Rules/Regulations: No alcohol, animals, in-line skates, skateboards, kite flying except in designated areas, fires without permit, scuba diving, fishing, wind surfing

Directions: From Route 28 to Swan River Road, left onto Lower County Road, and right onto Old Wharf Road to the beach (across from Ocean Drive) in Dennisport.

This Nantucket Sound beach disappears at high tide. But above the sea wall, there's a nice play area, complete with swings, where families can wait out the tides.

Glendon Road Beach

Glendon Road
Dennis, MA 02638
508-760-6112

Season: 2nd Saturday in June - Labor Day
Hours: 9:00 a.m. - 5:00 p.m.
Parking: Lot
Fees: Nonresidents, $8 per day per car, $25 per week (Saturday through Friday), $125 per season
Sand: Coarse
Crowd: Mixed
Facilities: Lifeguard, restrooms, snack bar, public telephone
Rules/Regulations: No alcohol, animals, in-line skates, skateboards, kite flying except in designated areas, fires without permit

Directions: From Route 28 to Swan River Road, left onto Lower County Road, right onto Glendon Road, to the intersection of Old Wharf Road.

This beach, a medium-sized one for the area, is broken up by three jetties. Off to the right, Great Island in Hyannis is visible. Otherwise, the view is open into Nantucket Sound.

Special Notes: Head over to Sundae School Ice Cream Parlor, at the corner of Lower County Road and Sea Street, where you'll find fresh fruit sundaes with real whipped cream. They also offer special calorie-counter treats. Call 508-394-9122.

Sea Street Beach
Sea Street
Dennis, MA 02638
508-760-6112

Season: Second Saturday in June - Labor Day
Hours: 9:00 a.m. - 5:00 p.m.
Parking: Lot
Fees: Nonresidents, $8 per day per car, $25 per week (Saturday through Friday), $125 per season
Sand: Coarse
Crowd: Mixed
Facilities: Lifeguard, restrooms, mobile snack vendor, public telephone
Rules/Regulations: No alcohol, animals, in-line skates, skateboards, kite flying except in designated areas, fires without permit

Directions: From Route 28 to Shed Hole Road, left onto Old Wharf Road, and right onto Sea Street to the end.

One of two Sea Street beaches in Dennis, this one is in Dennisport on Nantucket Sound. Several jetties break the beach up into tidy segments. Many years ago, shells from this beach were used to pave Sea Street, which was formerly called Shell Road.

"I like it here when the wind is blowing from the north and the rock sea wall protects you."
        Hank Workman, Sharon, MA

Raycroft Parkway Beach
Raycroft Beach Parkway
Dennis, MA 02638
508-760-6112

Season: Second Saturday in June - Labor Day
Hours: 9:00 a.m. - 5:00 p.m.
Parking: Lot
Fees: Nonresidents, $8 per day per car, $25 per week (Saturday through Friday), $125 per season
Sand: Coarse
Crowd: Mixed
Facilities: None
Rules/Regulations: No alcohol, animals, in-line skates, skateboards, kite flying except in designated areas, fires without permit

Directions: From Route 28 to Sea Street, to the Old Wharf Road and Raycroft Beach Parkway intersection. Turn left to the beach, which is across from Carr Road.

It's a quick climb down a flight of stairs to reach this very small, quiet beach.

Depot Street Beach
Depot Street
Dennis, MA 02638
508-760-6112

Season: Second Saturday in June - Labor Day
Hours: 9:00 a.m. - 5:00 p.m.
Parking: None
Fees: None
Sand: Coarse
Crowd: Mixed
Facilities: None
Rules/Regulations: No alcohol, animals, in-line skates, skateboards, kite flying except in designated areas, fires without permit

Directions: From Route 28 to Depot Street where it intersects with Chase Avenue.

This is primarily an access to Nantucket Sound. There is little more than a narrow sand pathway to a postage-stamp-size beach.

Sea Street Beach
Old Wharf Road
Dennis, MA 02638
508-760-6112

Season: 2nd Saturday in June - Labor Day
Hours: 9:00 a.m. - 5:00 p.m.
Parking: Lot
Fees: Nonresidents, $8 per day per car, $25 per week (Saturday through Friday), $125 per season
Sand: Soft
Crowd: Mixed
Facilities: Lifeguard, restrooms, mobile snack vendor
Rules/Regulations: No alcohol, animals, in-line skates, skateboards, kite flying except in designated area, fires without permit

Directions: From Route 6A in East Dennis to Sea Street to Old Wharf Road.

This Sea Street Beach, located on Cape Cod Bay in East Dennis, sits between Cold Storage Beach and Paines Creek Beach. It has a gentle surf, soft sand, and a boardwalk.

"It's nice for my grandchildren -- safe because of the distance you can walk out."
Josephine Breau, Waltham, MA

Inman Road Beach
Depot Street
Dennis, MA 02638
508-760-6112

Season: Second Saturday in June - Labor Day
Hours: 9:00 a.m. - 5:00 p.m.
Parking: Lot
Fees: Nonresidents, $8 per day per car, $25 per week (Saturday through Friday), $125 per season

Sand: Soft
Crowd: Mixed
Facilities: Lifeguard, restrooms, mobile snack vendor, bicycle rack, restaurant, public telephone
Rules/Regulations: No alcohol, animals, in-line skates, skateboards, kite flying except in designated areas, fires without permit

Directions: From Route 28 to Sea Street, left onto Lower County Road, right onto Depot Street.

Walk down a short path through dunes to this small sandy beach on Nantucket Sound. A good spot for shell seekers.

Cold Storage Beach

Cold Storage Road
Dennis, MA 02638
508-760-6112

Season: Second Saturday in June - Labor Day
Hours: 9:00 a.m. - 5:00 p.m.
Parking: Lot, resident sticker required
Fees: None
Sand: Soft
Crowd: Mixed
Facilities: Lifeguard, restrooms, fishing, boat launch, mobile snack vendor
Rules/Regulations: No alcohol, animals, in-line skates, skateboards, kite flying except in designated areas, fires without permit

Directions: From Route 6A to School Street, right onto Pleasant Street, left onto Cold Storage Road.

Although the dunes are nice at this Cape Cod Bay beach, and it has shallow flats for walking, its most striking feature is the beautifully constructed jetty on the left, near the Sesuit Harbor entrance.

"We like the long jetty for walking and watching the boats come in."
Michelle Lyford, Goffstown, NH

Harborview Beach

Sesuit Neck Road
Dennis, MA 02638
508-760-6112

Season: Second Saturday in June - Labor Day
Hours: 9:00 a.m. - 5:00 p.m.
Parking: Lot, resident sticker required
Fees: None
Sand: Soft
Crowd: Mixed
Facilities: Lifeguard, mobile snack vendor
Rules/Regulations: No alcohol, animals, in-line skates, skateboards, kite flying in designated areas, fires without permit

Directions: From Route 6A to Bridge Street, right on Sesuit Neck Road.

This small beach has a beautiful stone jetty, almost a twin, albeit smaller, to its neighbor at Cold Storage. Both jetties line the entrance to Sesuit Harbor.

Howe Street Beach

Howe Street
Dennis, MA 02638
508-760-6112

Season: 2nd Saturday in June - Labor Day
Hours: 9:00 a.m. - 5:00 p.m.
Parking: Lot
Fees: Nonresidents, $8 per day per car, $25 per week (Saturday through Friday), $125 per season
Sand: Soft
Crowd: Families
Facilities: Lifeguard, mobile snack vendor
Rules/Regulations: No alcohol, animals, in-line skates, skateboards, kite flying except in designated areas, fires without permit

Directions: From Route 6A to Seaside Avenue and right on Howe Street.

This beach is an extension of the larger Corporation Road Beach. It has the same smooth sand but also patches of rock.

"Mostly 'locals' go here. My son loves it and has discovered many creatures with his net and bucket."
Sue Latimer, West Yarmouth, MA

Corporation Road Beach
Corporation Beach Road
Dennis, MA 02638
508-760-6112

Season: Second Saturday in June - Labor Day
Hours: 8:00 a.m. - 5:00 p.m.
Parking: Lot
Fees: Nonresidents, $8 per day per car, $25 per week (Saturday through Friday), $125 per season
Sand: Super soft
Crowd: Families
Facilities: Lifeguard, restrooms, mobile snack vendor, boat launch, picnic area, public telephone, old swing set
Rules/Regulations: No alcohol, animals, in-line skates, skateboards, kite flying except in designated areas, fires without permit

Directions: From Route 6A to the end of Corporation Beach Road.

This capacious beach on Cape Cod Bay has smooth sand and calm surf. It's fun to explore the rocks along the breakwater, or walk to Sesuit Harbor when the tide is out. The beach's name comes from the business arrangements that were made by townsfolk who held shares in the merchant fleets that were built here.

"At high tide people can stand on the breakwater to fish."
Bill Lipsky, Nashua, NH

Bay View Beach
Bay View Street
Dennis, MA 02638
508-760-6112

Season: Second Saturday in June - Labor Day
Hours: 8:00 a.m. - 5:00 p.m.
Parking: Lot, resident sticker required
Fees: None
Sand: Soft
Crowd: Mixed
Facilities: Lifeguard
Rules/Regulations: No alcohol, animals, in-line skates, skateboards, kite flying except in designated areas, fires without permit

Directions: From Route 6A to New Boston Road, right onto Beach Street, then right onto Bay View Avenue.

This stretch of beach sits right next to Mayflower. A short boardwalk provides easy access to the beach from the parking lot.

Mayflower Public Beach

Dunes Road
Dennis, MA 02638
508-760-6112

Season: 2nd Saturday in June - Labor Day
Hours: 8:30 a.m. - 5:00 p.m.
Parking: Lot
Fees: Nonresidents, $8 per day per car, $25 per week (Saturday through Friday), $125 per season
Sand: Soft
Crowd: Mixed
Facilities: Lifeguard, restrooms, snack bar, picnic table, public telephone
Rules/Regulations: No alcohol, animals, in-line skates, skateboards, kite flying except in designated areas, fires without permit

Directions: From Route 6A to New Boston Road to Beach Street, right onto Horsefoot Point and right onto Dunes Road.

This large Cape Cod Bay beach is very popular. At low tide, you can walk far out to meet the ocean, or walk over to Cold Storage Beach. On a clear day, Wellfleet's Great Island is visible across the bay.

"The water is warm and gentle and at low tide you can walk way out."

Margaret Brown, Hollis, NH

Chapin Memorial Beach

Taunton Avenue
Dennis, MA 02638
508-760-6112

Season: Second Saturday in June - Labor Day
Hours: 9:00 a.m. - 5:00 p.m.
Parking: Lot
Fees: Nonresidents, $8 per day per car, $25 per week (Saturday through Friday), $125 per season
Sand: Soft
Crowd: Mixed
Facilities: Restrooms
Rules/Regulations: No alcohol, animals, in-line skates, skateboards, kite flying except in designated areas, fires without permit

Directions: From Route 6A to New Boston Road, right onto Beach Street, then left onto Taunton Avenue.

It's a long drive out to this beach. (If you've got a four-wheel drive vehicle you can go right onto the beach.) Low tide gets extraordinarily low: Plan for a long, long walk if you want to take a swim. Waters are typically calm. Part of Chapin shifted to Sandy Neck Beach during the Blizzard of '78. A tire reef and Christmas tree barriers, along with other conservation efforts, could not hold it in place. Sandy Neck can be viewed off to the left.

Special Notes: If you want a bird's-eye view of the beach, drive or hike to Scargo Tower, a 28-foot tall observatory that was built of stone in 1902. From Route 6A near the Cape Playhouse, take Scargo Hill Road.

Legend has it that more than 3,000 ships were lost in the dangerous shoals bordering Cape Cod, prior to the opening of the Cape Cod Canal in 1914.

Pleasant Road Beach
Pleasant Road
Harwich, MA 02645
508-430-7553

Season: June 1 - Labor Day
Hours: 6:00 a.m. - midnight
Parking: Lot, sticker required
Fees: Residents, $5 per season per car; nonresidents, $25 per week per car, $40 per two weeks, $50 per season (Nonresidents must prove they are staying in town to obtain a sticker.)
Sand: Soft
Crowd: Mixed
Facilities: Lifeguard, portable restrooms, bicycle rack, snack bar
Rules/Regulations: No alcohol, animals, glass, fires without permit

Directions: From Route 28 in West Harwich to Pleasant Road at Shore Road.

This good-sized beach is rectangular and sandy. A boardwalk cuts through the center and splits around to either side of the lifeguard chair. The view is of open Nantucket Sound.

Special Notes: Harwich beach stickers are sold 7 days a week between June 1 and Labor Day at the highway department offices on Queen Anne Street, from 9:00 a.m. to 12:00 p.m. and from 12:30 p.m. to 3:30 p.m. Red River Beach is the only Harwich beach for which a one-day sticker is available. For nonresidents, parking at all other beaches requires at least a one-week permit.

Grey Neck Road Beach
Grey Neck Road
Harwich, MA 02645
508-430-7553

Season: June 1 - Labor Day
Hours: 6:00 a.m. - midnight
Parking: Lot, sticker required

Fees: Residents, $5 per season per car; nonresidents, $25 per week per car, $40 per two weeks, $50 per season (Nonresidents must prove they are staying in town to obtain a sticker.)
Sand: Soft
Crowd: Mixed
Facilities: None,but mobile snack vendors visit
Rules/Regulations: No alcohol, animals, fires without permit, glass

Directions: From Route 28 in West Harwich to Grey Neck Road.

A flight of 25 wooden stairs conveys you to a small sliver of sand that sits between two jetties. The Nantucket Sound waters are gentle.

"The water is warm and the sand is nice, not all icky."
Rebecca Greenwald, Larchmont, NY

Earle Road Beach
Earle Road
Harwich, MA 02645
508-430-7553

Season: June 1 - Labor Day
Hours: 6:00 a.m. - midnight
Parking: Lot, sticker required
Fees: Residents, $5 per season per car; nonresidents, $25 per week per car, $40 per two weeks, $50 per season (Nonresidents must prove they are staying in town to obtain a sticker.)
Sand: Soft
Crowd: Mixed
Facilities: Lifeguard, portable restrooms, mobile snack vendors
Rules/Regulations: No alcohol, animals, fires without permit, glass

Directions: From Route 28 in West Harwich to Earle Road.

A short boardwalk runs down a gentle slope to this beach. The preferred swimming area is within the confines of the two jetties.

Atlantic Avenue Beach

Atlantic Avenue
Harwich, MA 02645
508-430-7553

Season: June 1 - Labor Day
Hours: 6:00 a.m. - midnight
Parking: Lot, sticker required
Fees: Residents, $5 per season per car; nonresidents, $25 per week per car, $40 per two weeks, $50 per season (Nonresidents must prove they are staying in town to obtain a sticker.)
Sand: Soft
Crowd: Mixed
Facilities: None
Rules/Regulations: No alcohol, animals, glass, fires without permit

Directions: From Route 28 to Lower County Road to Pine Street. Turn right at the end onto Atlantic Avenue.

This is a small beach on Nantucket Sound. A tiny wooden deck with benches sits at the top of a stone retaining wall. Twenty steps lead from here to the beach.

Sea Street Beach

Sea Street
Harwich, MA 02645
508-430-7553

Season: June 1 - Labor Day
Hours: 6:00 a.m. - midnight
Parking: Handicapped parking only
Fees: None
Sand: Soft
Crowd: Mixed
Facilities: None
Rules/Regulations: No alcohol, animals, glass, fires without permit

Directions: From Route 28 in Harwich Port to Sea Street.

People who come here usually park in town near the Harwich Chamber of Commerce and walk the short distance to the beach. The beach is small, with only a small area of sand that is flanked by beach houses.

Bank Street Beach
Bank Street
Harwich, MA 02645
508-430-7553

Season: June 1 - Labor Day
Hours: 6:00 a.m. - midnight
Parking: Lot, sticker required
Fees: Residents, $5 per season per car; nonresidents, $25 per week per car, $40 per two weeks, $50 per season (Nonresidents must prove they are staying in town to obtain a sticker.)
Sand: Soft
Crowd: Mixed
Facilities: Lifeguard, restrooms, bicycle rack, snack vendor
Rules/Regulations: No alcohol, animals, glass, fires without permit

Directions: From Route 28, Harwich Port, to Bank Street.

On Nantucket Sound, this is a small but pretty beach. A diagonal boardwalk takes you through high grass to the sand.

"It's a good beach for swimming."
Jean Egbert, Harwich Port, MA

Red River Beach
Deep Hole Road
Harwich, MA 02645
508-430-7553

Season: June 1 - Labor Day
Hours: 6:00 a.m. - midnight
Parking: Lot
Fees: Residents, $5 per season per car; nonresidents, $25 per week per car, $40 per two weeks, $50 per season (Nonresidents must prove they are staying in town to obtain a sticker.)
Sand: Soft

Crowd: Families
Facilities: Lifeguard, restrooms, bath house, snack bar, bicycle rack
Rules/Regulations: No alcohol, animals, fires without permit, glass

Directions: From Route 28 in South Harwich to Julian Road, Deep Hole Road, or Uncle Venies Road.

On Nantucket Sound, this calm, sandy barrier beach is the largest of the ocean beaches in this community. It runs in a long, narrow strip and has jetties poking out along the way. Small dunes sit at either end, and low wooden retaining walls are in between. While there might be too much seaweed for some people's tastes, the place is nonetheless crowded. Small sailboats may be launched from the east end.

Special Notes: Watch for the Harwich Junior Theatre's schedule. It offers four summer productions that are geared to children over age 5. It also offers drama classes for children. Call 508-432-2002.

Pleasant Bay Beach
aka **Jackknife Beach**
Pleasant Bay Road
Harwich, MA 02645
508-430-7553

Season: June 1 - Labor Day
Hours: 6:00 a.m. - midnight
Parking: Roadside, sticker required
Fees: Residents, $5 per season per car; nonresidents, $25 per week per car, $40 per two weeks, $50 per season (Nonresidents must prove they are staying in town to obtain a sticker.)
Sand: Soft
Crowd: Mixed
Facilities: None
Rules/Regulations: No alcohol, animals, fires without permit, glass, ball playing or kite flying

Directions: Along Route 28 just north of the Chatham-Harwich line near Pleasant Bay Road. Or from Route 137 near Route 6 to Pleasant Bay Road.

This small, gentle beach is on pretty Pleasant Bay, and also enjoys views of the Cape Cod National Seashore. It sits right on the Harwich-North Chatham line and both Harwich and Chatham claim this beach in their listings. A popular spot with windsurfers, it also harbors many boats.

Forest Beach
Forest Beach Road
Chatham, MA 02633
508-945-5100

Season: End of June - Labor Day Sunday
Hours: 6:00 a.m. - 5:00 p.m.
Parking: Lot, sticker required
Fees: Residents, $15 per season per car; nonresidents, $7 per day per car, $35 per week, $60 per season
Sand: Soft
Crowd: Mixed
Facilities: None
Rules/Regulations: No alcohol, animals, glass, fires without permit

Directions: From Route 28 in South Chatham to Forest Beach Road.

For years, this was a busy town landing. Today, people enjoy a small, crescent-shaped, sandy beach. The varied flights of windsurfers, the bobbing of small boats moored off shore, and the low, grassy dunes create a pleasant atmosphere.

Special Notes: Extended beach parking passes can be obtained at all Chatham beaches.

Cockle Cove Beach
Cockle Cove Road
Chatham, MA 02633
508-945-5100

Season: End of June - Labor Day Sunday
Hours: 6:00 a.m. - 10:00 p.m.
Parking: Lot, sticker required

Fees: Residents, $15 per season per car; nonresidents, $7 per day per car, $35 per week, $60 per season
Sand: Soft
Crowd: Mixed
Facilities: Lifeguard, restrooms, bicycle rack
Rules/Regulations: No alcohol, animals, glass, fires without a permit, floats within the lifeguard area

Directions: From Route 28 in South Chatham to Cockle Cove Road.

On Nantucket Sound, this small barrier beach has large sand bars that form at low tide. Similar to the beaches on the bay, it's hard to take a dip at low tide because the water is so shallow for so far out.

"It's not all that crowded here, which is nice."
Justin Fielding, Milton, MA

Ridgevale Beach
Ridgevale Road
Chatham, MA 02633
508-945-5100

Season: End of June - Labor Day Sunday
Hours: 6:00 a.m. - 10:00 p.m.
Parking: Lot, sticker required
Fees: Residents, $15 per season per car; nonresidents, $7 per day per car, $35 per week, $60 per season
Sand: Soft
Crowd: Mixed
Facilities: Lifeguard, restrooms, bath house, snack bar, boat rentals
Rules/Regulations: No alcohol, animals, glass, fires without a permit, floats within lifeguard area

Directions: Off Route 28 on Ridgevale Road in South Chatham.

This long, sandy beach on Nantucket Sound has calm water. Canoes, windsurfers, sunfish and day sailors are available to rent. For information on sailing lessons for children age 6 and up, call 508-432-4339.

Special Notes: If you're at the beach with kids and they tire of the sun and sand, head over to Chatham's well-equipped playground across from the Railroad Museum and next to Veteran's Field. It includes a multilevel, wooden jungle gym, an area for physically challenged kids, and a fenced-in area for tots.

Hardings Beach

Hardings Beach Road
Chatham, MA 02633
508-945-5100

Season: End of June - Labor Day Sunday
Hours: 6:00 a.m. - 10:00 p.m.
Parking: Lot, sticker required
Fees: Residents, $15 per season per car; nonresidents, $7 per day per car, $35 per week, $60 per season
Sand: Soft
Crowd: Mixed
Facilities: Lifeguard, restrooms, snack bar
Rules/Regulations: No alcohol, animals, glass, fires without a permit, floats within lifeguard area

Directions: From Route 28 in West Chatham to Barn Hill Road to Hardings Beach Road.

This 1.25-mile long undeveloped barrier beach along Nantucket Sound -- one of Chatham's most popular -- has a salt marsh, with low, grassy dunes, and a charming view of Stage Harbor Light and Monomoy Island. The Chatham Conservation Foundation maintains a walking trail and has a booklet describing the area's natural history.

Special Notes: *A Beachcomber's Botony* was published by the Chatham Conservation Foundation, which is a private organization and separate from the Town Conservation Commission. Write or visit them at 104 Crowell Rd., Chatham, MA 02633. During the summer its hours are 11:00 a.m. to 4:00 p.m. Copies are also available at bookstores and gift shops in the area.

Penny candy lovers shouldn't miss the Chatham Country Store at 403 Main St. Call 508-945-4667.

Oyster Pond Beach

Stage Harbour Road
Chatham, MA 02633
508-945-5100

Season: End of June - Labor Day Sunday
Hours: 6:00 a.m. - 10:00 p.m.
Parking: Lot
Fees: None
Sand: Soft
Crowd: Families
Facilities: Lifeguard, restrooms, bath house, swimming
lessons, picnic tables, benches
Rules/Regulations: No alcohol, animals, glass, fires without a
permit

Directions: From Route 28 (Main Street) to Stage Harbour
Road.

Known locally as the "Children's Beach" because of its calm
water, it's the second most popular beach in Chatham. No
ocean is visible from here, as it is located at the inner-most
region of the Oyster River. (It's got salt water.). There's an
anchored raft in the water and a small grass park nearby.

Special Notes: Town band concerts are held every Friday
evening between June 30 and September 1. They start at 8:00
p.m. at Kate Gould Park on Main Street (Route 28), not far
from the Town Office. They're immensely popular.

Monomoy Island Beaches

Chatham, MA 02633
508-945-5100

Season: End of June - Labor Day Sunday
Hours: None posted
Parking: None, boat access only
Fees: None
Sand: Soft
Crowd: Mixed
Facilities: None
Rules/Regulations: No pets, vehicles, camping, fires

Directions: To the Water Taxi, a service that ferries bathers to
South Beach, North Beach, and Monomoy Islands: from
Route 28 to Shore Road, to Chatham Fish Pier. Call 508-430-
2346.

Monomoy is made up of two islands, North Island and South
Island. North Island is smaller, with narrow sand dunes and a
large salt marsh. At low tide, there are flats on the Nantucket
Sound side that extend over a mile. South Island is much larger
and has extensive sand dunes, especially at the southern end.
There are freshwater ponds, woods, and a historic
decommissioned and restored lighthouse on the island.
Designated as a National Wilderness Area, inhabitants include
the endangered grey seal, as well as the white-tailed deer.

*"Monomoy is as pristine, primitive, and unspoiled as you would
find anywhere in New England."*
      Richard Hall, Staff Naturalist, Museum of Natural
      History, Brewster, MA

Special Notes: Monomoy is in the midst of an eco-
controversy. The U.S. Fish and Wildlife Service has plans to
drop toxic bread crumbs on this gull-dominated island. The
goal is to kill off the seagulls to make room for endangered
shore birds, such as piping plovers and terns. In the past, the
agency has tried to drive them off with dogs, guns, and other
loud noises, but to no avail. The Massachusetts Audubon
Society and many citizens oppose the mass poisoning. They
claim it's politically motivated -- an effort to prevent the birds
from nesting on public beaches and thus forcing restricted
four-wheel drive access.

South Beach Island
Chatham, MA 02633
508-945-5100

Season: End of June - Labor Day Sunday
Hours: 6:00 a.m. - 10:00 p.m.
Parking: None, boat access only
Fees: None
Sand: Soft
Crowd: Mixed
Facilities: None

Rules/Regulations: No alcohol, animals, glass, fires without a permit

Directions: To the Water Taxi, a service that ferries bathers to South Beach, North Beach, and Monomoy Islands: from Route 28 to Shore Road, to Chatham Fish Pier. Call 508-430-2346.

This 3-mile long sand "island" was formed when a winter storm broke through Nauset Beach in 1987, dividing it in half. The southern divide is now appropriately called South Beach. A new sand bar has formed which provides foot access. But many bathers take a water taxi.

Chatham Light Beach
Shore Road
Chatham, MA 02633
508-945-5100

Season: End of June - Labor Day Sunday
Hours: 6:00 a.m. - 10:00 p.m.
Parking: None (Thirty-minute-only parking is available across from the lighthouse.)
Fees: None
Sand: Soft
Crowd: Mixed
Facilities: None
Rules/Regulations: No alcohol, animals, glass, fires without a permit

Directions: From Route 28 to Shore Road.

The lighthouse offers spectacular views down to this beach which, until 1987, was in Pleasant Bay. The storm that created North and South Beaches opened this beach to the ocean currents. Today storms threaten its fragile shoreline, including this lighthouse, which was originally one of a pair of lighthouses situated here. The currents are strong and the surf -- both for swimming and wading -- is hazardous. The beach is accessible from a narrow pathway just south of the lighthouse on Morris Island Road.

Special Notes: Eldredge Taxi will transport you from a parking lot on Main Street to and from the beach. The $7 fee includes parking and transportation. Call 508-945-0068.

North Beach
Chatham, MA 02633
508-945-5100

Season: End of June - Labor Day Sunday
Hours: 6:00 a.m. - 10:00 p.m.
Parking: None, but you can park in town or at the pier and take a taxi
Fees: None
Sand: Soft
Crowd: Mixed
Facilities: None
Rules/Regulations: No alcohol, animals, glass, fires without a permit

Directions: From Route 6A or Route 28 to Main Street, to Beach Road in East Orleans. Or, take The Water Taxi: from Route 28 to Shore Road, to Chatham Fish Pier. Call 508-430-2346.

A strong January storm in 1987 changed the offshore landscape. It broke through the sand of this barrier beach on the Cape Cod National Seashore, thus creating two beaches now known as North and South. North Beach is beautiful, quiet, and remote. Although it can be reached through Nauset Beach in Orleans, it's much easier and less expensive to travel via water taxi from Chatham.

Nauset Beach
Beach Road
Orleans, MA 02653
508-240-3780

Season: Memorial Day - Labor Day
Hours: 6:00 a.m. - 10:00 p.m.
Parking: Lot, limited spaces for RVs
Fees: $8 per car; $5 per car pre-season (Memorial Day to 3rd weekend in June)

Sand: Coarse
Crowd: Mixed
Facilities: Lifeguard, restrooms, snack bar
Rules/Regulations: No alcohol, animals, glass, floats, snorkels, open fires

Directions: From Route 6A or Route 28 in East Orleans to Main Street, to Beach Road.

A beautiful Atlantic Ocean beach, it's co-managed by Orleans and Chatham. A favorite spot with surfers, even beginners, specific areas are set aside for them, as well as for sailboarders, and scuba and skin divers. Although it gets plenty of families, the beach draws scores of young singles. It's home to one of the largest least tern (so called because they're the smallest species of tern -- no more than 10 inches long) colonies in Massachusetts. Please remember not to disturb nesting birds.

"Great for surfing or riding the waves."
Betty Hurley, Milton, MA

Special Notes: Band concerts are held at the Nauset Beach gazebo on Monday nights from 7:00 to 9:00. Entertainment ranges from country to jazz.

Rock Harbor Beach
Rock Harbor Road
Orleans, MA 02642
508-240-3700

Season: Year-round
Hours: 6:00 a.m. - 10:00 p.m.
Parking: Small lot
Fees: None
Sand: Coarse
Crowd: Mixed
Facilities: Portable restrooms, benches
Rules/Regulations: No alcohol, animals

Directions: From Route 6A at the rotary, take the Rock Harbor Road exit and follow to Rock Harbor, Eastham.

Most people come to Rock Harbor to catch a fishing boat for Cape Cod Bay or to simply watch the harbor activity. There is, however, a very small sandy beach at the mouth of the harbor, between a jetty on the harbor side and a marsh on the other. Wondering about the line of dead trees in the water? It marks the channel for the boats.

"A peaceful place to enjoy the view of the harbor or a sunset."
Heather Ormsby, New Boston, NH

Special Notes: To charter a boat, call the Rock Harbor Charter Boat Service at 508-255-9757.

Skaket Beach
Skaket Beach Road
Orleans, MA 02642
508-255-0572

Season: 3rd weekend June - Labor Day
Hours: 8:00 a.m. - 10:00 p.m.
Parking: Lot
Fees: $8 per car
Sand: Coarse
Crowd: Families
Facilities: Lifeguard, restrooms, snack bar, benches, public telephone, bicycle rack
Rules/Regulations: No alcohol, animals

Directions: From Route 6A, right onto West Road (at lights). Turn left on Skaket Beach Road (also called Namskaket).

Because of its location on Cape Cod Bay, this beach experiences a 9-foot tidal change. Although the beach is only a half-mile wide, at low tide you feel as though you could walk through the calm waters all the way to Sandy Neck in Barnstable.

Coast Guard Beach
Doane Road
Eastham, MA 02642
508-349-3785

Season: Last Saturday in June - Labor Day
Hours: 6:00 a.m. - midnight

Parking: Small lot; also free parking and a beach shuttle at Little Creek parking lot nearby
Fees: $5 per car at beach lot; $3 for walk-ins
Sand: Soft
Crowd: Mixed
Facilities: Lifeguard, restrooms, bath house
Rules/Regulations: No alcohol, animals, beach parties after 7:00 p.m. without a permit, surfing in main beach area, open fires, glass, floats

Directions: From Route 6 to the end of Doane Road. Look for signs to Little Creek parking lot.

The Cape Cod National Seashore and the Outer Cape begin here. Surfers love it. Even on calm days the waves roll in off the Atlantic. The wide, mile-long expanse of sand provides a real "big beach" feeling. The dunes are majestic, and the water sparkles. Henry Beston wrote *The Outermost House* here, and it gives readers a real feeling for the earlier days on "The Great Beach."

Special Notes: Fees paid at one National Seashore beach are good for all other National Seashore beaches on the day of purchase. If you're interested in viewing the seashore from a different perspective, take a tour of the shoreline, marshes, and nearby coves by boat. Call Seashore Park Boat Tours at 508-385-2063.

Nauset Light Beach
Cable Road
Eastham, MA 02642
508-349-3785

Season: Last Saturday in June - Labor Day
Hours: 6:00 a.m. - midnight
Parking: Small lot; free shuttle available from nearby Little Creek parking lot
Fees: $5 per car, $3 for walk-ins
Sand: Super soft
Crowd: Mixed
Facilities: Lifeguards, restrooms, bath house
Rules/Regulations: No alcohol, animals, surfing in main beach area, glass, open fires, floats, snorkels

Directions: From Route 6 to Cable Road. Or, park at Little Creek parking lot and ride the free shuttle.

Climb down steep wooden stairs to reach this beautiful and popular mile-long Atlantic Ocean beach. Located within the Cape Cod National Seashore, it has some of the best surfing around. Shell seekers won't be disappointed either.

"You can walk forever along the shore."
Tom Sullivan, Greenfield, NH

Special Notes: For more information on the Cape Cod National Seashore, which stretches from Chatham all the way to Provincetown, visit one of two visitor centers. Both are open from 9:00 a.m. to 5:00 p.m. In this area, the Salt Pond Visitor Center is located on Route 6 in Eastham. Call 508-255-3421.

Sunken Meadow Beach
Sunken Meadow Road
Eastham, MA 02642
508-240-5900

Season: Last Saturday in June - Labor Day
Hours: 6:00 a.m. - midnight
Parking: Lot, sticker required
Fees: Free stickers available for residents and taxpayers; nonresidents, $5 per day per car, $20 per week, $30 per two weeks, $50 per season
Sand: Soft
Crowd: Families
Facilities: Portable restrooms
Rules/Regulations: No alcohol, animals, fires; ball/Frisbee playing is at the discretion of the attendant

Directions: From Route 6 to Massasoit Road to Sunken Meadow Road.

This Cape Cod Bay beach has fine sand, little surf, and a view that faces toward Wellfleet.

Special Notes: Passes are purchased at the Natural Resources office on Old Orchard Road. Hours are Monday through Saturday, 9:00 a.m. to 4:00 p.m. Vacationers arriving on

Sunday may bring their 1-day ticket to the Natural Resources office for credit toward their pass purchase. Call 508-240-5972.

Cooks Brook Beach
Steele Road
Eastham, MA 02642
508-240-5900

Season: Last Saturday in June - Labor Day
Hours: 6:00 a.m. - midnight
Parking: Lot
Fees: Free stickers available for residents and taxpayers; nonresidents, $5 per day per car, $20 per week, $30 per two weeks, $50 per season
Sand: Soft
Crowd: Mixed
Facilities: Portable restrooms
Rules/Regulations: No alcohol, animals, fires

Directions: From Route 6 to Massasoit Road to Steele Road.

If you've gotten a late start on the day, this beach is a good bet: it's got one of the larger parking lots of Eastham's bay beaches. Be sure to keep your eye on the water. At high tide all that remains of the beach is a narrow thread of sand.

Campground Beach
Campground Road
Eastham, MA 02642
508-240-5900

Season: Last Saturday in June - Labor Day
Hours: 6:00 a.m. - midnight
Parking: Lot
Fees: Free stickers available for residents and taxpayers; nonresidents, $5 per day per car, $20 per week, $30 per two weeks, $50 per season
Sand: Soft
Crowd: Families
Facilities: Restrooms
Rules/Regulations: No alcohol, animals, fires

Directions: From Route 6 to Massasoit Road to Campground Road at the intersection of Herringbrook Road.

At low tide you can walk way out at this Cape Cod Bay beach. When the tide is high, though, the beach disappears. Rocks have been piled up against the sandy embankments to help protect them from erosion.

"It's quiet and a lot of families come here."
Kathy O'Leary, Rensselaer, NY

Thumpertown Beach
Thumpertown Road
Eastham, MA 02642
508-240-5900

Season: Last Saturday in June - Labor Day
Hours: 6:00 a.m. - midnight
Parking: None
Fees: None
Sand: Soft
Crowd: Mixed
Facilities: None
Rules/Regulations: No alcohol, animals, fires

Directions: From Route 6 to Kingsbury Beach Road, right onto Herring Brook Road, left onto Thumpertown Road.

A wooden staircase leads visitors to a narrow band of beach on Cape Cod Bay. High embankment walls can either add to your sense of being away from it all or, at high tide, leave you without a beach to sit on.

Kingsbury Beach
Kingsbury Beach Road
Eastham, MA 02642
508-240-5900

Season: Last Saturday in June - Labor Day
Hours: 6:00 a.m. - midnight
Parking: None
Fees: None

Sand: Soft
Crowd: Mixed
Facilities: None
Rules/Regulations: No alcohol, animals, fires

Directions: From Route 6 to the end of Kingsbury Beach Road.

This is a quiet beach, more an access point really. There's no parking anywhere. Arrive by bicycle or make arrangements for drop off and pick up. From here and other nearby locations, you can see the hull of the *Gen. James Longstreet*, a World War II warship that was once used for target practice by the U.S. Air Force. (It looks like a big black rock.)

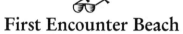

First Encounter Beach
Samoset Road
Eastham, MA 02642
508-240-5900

Season: Last Saturday in June - Labor Day
Hours: 6:00 a.m. - midnight
Parking: Lot, sticker required
Fees: Free stickers available for residents and taxpayers; nonresidents, $5 per day per car, $20 per week, $30 per two weeks, $50 per season
Sand: Super soft
Crowd: Families
Facilities: Restrooms, public telephone
Rules/Regulations: No alcohol, animals, fires

Directions: From Route 6, at the lights turn onto Samoset Road and follow to the end.

Enjoy the smooth sand and interesting stones along this wide strand of mild-mannered beach facing Cape Cod Bay. This is the spot where the Pilgrims and Wampanoag Indians are said to have had their first encounter (hence the name), exchanging arrow and musket fire. Today it's virtually unspoiled, and backed by a vast marshland. The road continues beyond the first parking area to a series of smaller ones from which narrow dune paths provide access to the beach.

Boat Meadow Beach

Bayview Road
Eastham, MA 02642
508-240-5900

Season: Last Saturday in June - Labor Day
Hours: 6:00 a.m. - midnight
Parking: None
Fees: None
Sand: Coarse
Crowd: Mixed
Facilities: None
Rules/Regulations: No alcohol, animals, fires

Directions: From Route 6 at the rotary, take the Rock Harbor Road exit. Turn right onto Bridge Street to the bend, where you continue straight on Bayview Road to the beach.

The meadow at the edge of Cape Cod Bay is a great expanse of marshland. There's a small bit of sand along the inlet, and there's a lot of grass in the water at high tide.

Marconi Beach

Marconi Beach Road
Wellfleet, MA 02667
508-349-3785

Season: Last Saturday in June - Labor Day
Hours: 7:00 a.m. - midnight
Parking: Lot
Fees: $5 per car
Sand: Soft
Crowd: Mixed
Facilities: Lifeguard, restrooms, bath house
Rules/Regulations: No alcohol, animals, fires without permit, floats, glass, snorkels, surfing in main beach area

Directions: From Route 6 to Marconi Beach Road.

Because high dunes block late afternoon sun at this Atlantic Ocean beach, you'll want to get here early. Located within the

Cape Cod National Seashore, it's named for Guglielmo Marconi, who, in 1901, transmitted the first trans-Atlantic wireless message from here. Head to the lookout platform at Marconi Station for a 360-degree view of the Atlantic and Cape Cod Bay. Surfing is allowed away from the guarded area. The National Seashore Headquarters, near the Marconi Station, is open from 8:00 a.m. to 4:30 p.m. Monday through Friday. Call 508-349-3785.

"Every day the beach looks different."
    Jessica Richard, Lunenberg, MA

Special Notes: Beach stickers are available at the "Beach Sticker Booth" on the town pier and marina in Wellfleet Harbor. (White Crest and Cahoon Hollow are the only beaches that offer a daily rate.) The booth is open between 8:30 a.m. and 4:00 p.m., except Friday and Saturday, when it remains open until 8:00 p.m. Call 508-349-9818.

LeCount Hollow Beach
LeCount Hollow Road
Wellfleet, MA 02667
508-349-2510

Season: End of June - Labor Day
Hours: 7:00 a.m. - midnight
Parking: Lot
Fees: Residents, $5 per season per car; nonresidents, $25 per week per car, $75 per season (Nonresident stickers are available only to those staying in the town of Wellfleet.)
Sand: Coarse
Crowd: Young
Facilities: Lifeguard, restrooms
Rules/Regulations: No alcohol, animals, fires without permit, glass, surfing in main beach area

Directions: From Route 6 to LeCount Hollow Road.

Very similar to other beaches along this stretch of Cape Cod National Seashore, it was named for people who used to own property here. It's now managed by the town. Of the nearby beaches, this one has the shortest trek to the beach. Sun worshippers may want to check the tide schedule -- the sand disappears at high tide.

White Crest Beach

Ocean Drive
Wellfleet, MA 02667
508-349-2510

Season: End of June - Labor Day
Hours: 7:00 a.m. - midnight
Parking: Lot, sticker required
Fees: Residents, $5 per season per car; nonresidents, $25 per week per car, $75 per season (Nonresident stickers are available only to those staying in the town of Wellfleet.)
Sand: Coarse
Crowd: Young
Facilities: Lifeguard, restrooms
Rules/Regulations: No alcohol, animals, fires without permit, glass, floats, snorkels, surfing in main beach area

Directions: From Route 6 to Ocean View Drive (between LeCount Hollow and Cahoon Hollow Roads).

A favorite spot with surfers and hang gliders, this is, in fact, the only beach managed by the town that allows them. Surfcasters too, clamor here. Some will appreciate the fact that the climb down over the dunes isn't as steep as at Cahoon Hollow Beach.

Special Notes: If your day at the beach isn't complete without an order of fried clams, head to the Clam Shack. Right on Route 6A in South Wellfleet, the place makes up for in taste what it lacks in atmosphere. Sit at one of the outdoor picnic benches and enjoy.

Cahoon Hollow Beach

Cahoon Hollow Road
Wellfleet, MA 02667
508-349-2510

Season: Last Saturday in June - Labor Day
Hours: 7:00 a.m. - midnight
Parking: Lot, sticker required
Fees: $10 per car or sticker; residents, $5 per season per car; nonresidents, $25 per week per car, $75 per season

(Nonresident stickers are available only to those staying in the town of Wellfleet.)
Sand: Coarse
Crowd: Mixed, but lots of teens and 20-somethings
Facilities: Lifeguard, restrooms, snack bar, restaurant
Rules/Regulations: No alcohol, animals, fires without permit, glass, surfing in main beach area.

Directions: From Route 6 to either Ocean View Drive or Cahoon Hollow Road.

A beautiful Atlantic Ocean beach, this is a favorite surfer hangout despite the notorious rip tide. It is backed by tall dunes, which you have to climb down to reach the beach. The Beachcomber, a hugely popular hangout bar and restaurant, housed in a former Coast Guard station, is perched above the beach. It's a favorite spot to savor the sunset.

Newcomb Hollow Beach
Ocean View Drive
Wellfleet, MA 02667
508-349-2510

Season: Last Saturday in June - Labor Day
Hours: 7:00 a.m. - midnight
Parking: Lot, sticker required
Fees: $10 per car or sticker: residents, $5 per season per car; nonresidents, $25 per week per car, $75 per season
(Nonresident stickers are available only to those staying in the town of Wellfleet.)
Sand: Soft
Crowd: Families
Facilities: Lifeguard, restrooms, snack bar
Rules/Regulations: No alcohol, animals, fires without permit, surfing in main beach area

Directions: From Route 6 to Gross Hill Road and left onto Ocean View Drive.

Scenic, beautiful, postcard perfect. That's how most people describe this Atlantic Ocean beach on the Wellfleet-Truro line. It is backed by enormously tall dunes which are kept in scale by great waves. Although within the Cape Cod National Seashore, it is under the management of the town of Wellfleet.

Special Notes: Visit the Wellfleet Bay Wildlife Sanctuary, Route 6 in Wellfleet. They offer children's programs, sunset hikes, cruises, wildlife tours, and more. For information, call 508-349-2615.

Duck Harbor Beach
aka **Black Duck Beach**
Chequessett Neck Road
Wellfleet, MA 02667
508-349-2510

Season: Last Saturday in June - Labor Day
Hours: 7:00 a.m. - midnight
Parking: Lot, sticker required
Fees: $10 per car or sticker: residents, $5 per season per car; nonresidents, $25 per week per car, $75 per season
(Nonresident stickers are available only to those staying in the town of Wellfleet.)
Sand: Coarse
Crowd: Mixed
Facilities: None
Rules/Regulations: No alcohol, animals, fires without permit, surfing in main beach area

Directions: From Route 6 to the end of Chequessett Neck Road.

Snow fencing marks a zigzag walk that leads through the dunes to this quiet beach on Cape Cod Bay. It's the place to go for Bay-side surf casting, and no license is required.

Great Hill Beach
Great Island (Wellfleet), MA 02667
508-349-2510

Season: Last Saturday in June - Labor Day
Hours: 7:00 a.m. - midnight
Parking: Lot
Fees: None
Sand: Soft
Crowd: Mixed

Facilities: Portable restrooms and picnic tables at the parking area

Rules/Regulations: No alcohol, animals, fires without permit, floats, glass, snorkels

Directions: From Route 6 to Chequessett Neck Road. Turn left just beyond Herring Creek at the hilltop into the parking area.

This long, remote barrier beach separates Wellfleet Harbor from Cape Cod Bay and is part of the Cape Cod National Seashore. It has no services, although there is parking on Sunset Hill: a four-mile (one way) trail leads down to it. Great Island's huge sand dunes are visible from Bay beaches far away. The area was once an island, but sand bars began connecting it to the mainland in the mid 1800s. Still, the name remains. If you're not in decent shape it's best to stick to the more accessible beaches: Not only is the trail long, but it's also mostly made up of soft sand. Jeremy Point, the island's tip, is under water at high tide.

Powers Landing
Chequessett Neck Road
Wellfleet, MA 02667
508-349-2510

Season: Last Saturday in June - Labor Day
Hours: 7:00 a.m. - midnight
Parking: Lot, sticker required
Fees: $10 per car or sticker: residents, $5 per season per car; nonresidents, $25 per week per car, $75 per season (Nonresident stickers are available only to those staying in the town of Wellfleet.)
Sand: Coarse with shells
Crowd: Mixed
Facilities: Portable restrooms
Rules/Regulations: No alcohol, animals, fires without permit, floats, glass, snorkels

Directions: From Route 6 to Chequessett Neck Road.

The access to the beach is wide enough for boat launching, and many small sailboats are moored here. However, it's not a beach for swimming or building sand castles.

Mayo Beach

Kendrick Avenue
Wellfleet, MA 02667
508-349-2510

Season: Last Saturday in June - Labor Day
Hours: 7:00 a.m. - midnight
Parking: Lot, sticker required
Fees: $10 per car or sticker: residents, $5 per season per car;
nonresidents, $25 per week per car, $75 per season
(Nonresident stickers are available only to those staying in the
town of Wellfleet.)
Sand: Coarse, with shells
Crowd: Mixed
Facilities: Nearby playground, tennis/basketball courts,
restrooms, snack bar, picnic table
Rules/Regulations: No alcohol, animals, fires without permit,
floats, glass, snorkels

Directions: From Route 6 to Commercial Street (across from
Long Pond Road). At the end of the road, turn right onto
Kendrick Avenue.

It's best to wear shoes to this beach because it's littered with
broken shells. Windsurfers are welcome to the right of the
main beach. And despite the occasional strong gust, the waters
are generally calm. Views include Wellfleet Harbor, Shirtail
Point, and Indian Neck Beach.

"This is safe for children and there are nice facilities."
Catherine Evangelista, Natick, MA

Special Notes: Check out the steeple clock on the First
Congregation Church in Wellfleet. It's the only town clock in
the world that strikes on "ship's time." What's ship's time you
ask? One, five, and nine o'clock are two bells. Two, six, and
ten o'clock are four bells. Four, eight, and twelve o'clock are
eight bells. The half hours are struck by adding one stroke to
the corresponding even hours.

How do you tell a quahog from a surf clam? A quahog's
shell is grayish-colored outside, and white, edged by purple,
inside. A surf clam's shell is white or cream-colored.

Indian Neck Beach

Indian Neck Road
Wellfleet, MA 02667
508-349-2510

Season: Last Saturday in June - Labor Day
Hours: 7:00 a.m. - midnight
Parking: Lot, sticker required
Fees: $10 per car or sticker: residents, $5 per season per car;
nonresidents, $25 per week per car, $75 per season
(Nonresident stickers are available only to thoose staying in
the town of Wellfleet.)
Sand: Coarse, with shells
Crowd: Families
Facilities: None
Rules/Regulations: No alcohol, animals, fires without permit,
floats, glass, snorkels

Directions: From Route 6 to Indian Neck Road.

Although this beach is just a spit of sand at the harbor
entrance, it affords a great perch for watching the action in
scenic Wellfleet Harbor. Unlike some harbors, this has a quiet
ambiance, aided, in no small part, by the nearby marshlands.
Windsurfers may launch from here and from Burton Baker
Beach. A list of surfing regulations are available at the beach
sticker booth on the town pier.

"We have been coming here for years, and the kids love it."
Ernest Froech, Albany, NY

Special Notes: Square dances are held on the town pier in July
and August, Wednesday nights from 7:30 to 10:00.

Burton Baker Beach

Indian Neck Road
Wellfleet, MA 02667
508-349-2510

Season: Last Saturday in June - Labor Day
Hours: 7:00 a.m. - midnight
Parking: Limited lot, sticker required

Fees: $10 per car or sticker: residents, $5 per season per car;
nonresidents, $25 per week per car, $75 per season
(Nonresident stickers are available only to those staying in the
town of Wellfleet.)
Sand: Coarse
Crowd: Mixed
Facilities: None
Rules/Regulations: No alcohol, animals, fires without permit,
floats, glass, snorkels

Directions: From Route 6 to Pilgrim Spring Road to Indian
Neck Road on the bend in the road by Nauset Road.

You'll miss this small access point if you're not looking for it.
On the outskirts of Wellfleet Harbor, this beach affords views
of Great Island's sandy dunes. Windsurfers may launch from
the left of the jetty, and the swimming area is marked with
buoys. This beach and Indian Neck Beach are the only ones in
Wellfleet that allow windsurfing, and then, only during certain
periods of each tide.

Ballston Beach
South Pamet Road
Truro, MA 02666
508-349-3635

Season: Last Saturday in June - Labor Day
Hours: 6:00 a.m. - midnight
Parking: Lot, sticker required
Fees: Residents, $10 per season per car; nonresidents; $20 per
week per car, $30 per two weeks, $60 per four weeks, $100 per
season (Nonresident stickers available only to those staying in
town.)
Sand: Super soft
Crowd: Families
Facilities: Restrooms
Rules/Regulations: No alcohol, glass, fires without a permit,
driving over sand, climbing on dunes, surfing in swimming
area, animals between 9:00 a.m. and 6:00 p.m

Directions: From Route 6 to South Pamet Road.

This beach experienced major topographic changes in 1993. A
dune break occurred, allowing the ocean to meet the Pamet

River. Be cautious and watch for the deep drop from the beach into the Atlantic. There's great surfing here and it's a favored fishing spot. (There's lots of bluefish and striped bass.) Although this beach is within the Cape Cod National Seashore, the town manages it.

Special Notes: You can purchase resident and nonresident beach parking stickers at the Beach Program Office in Truro center, behind the post office on Route 6A. Nonresidents must show rental/motel documentation. No fee for walkers or bicyclists. The office is open every day except Wednesday from the end of June to Labor Day between 8:00 a.m. and 3:45 p.m. Head of the Meadows and Corn Hill Beaches do not require stickers. Call 508-349-3635.

Longnook Beach
Longnook Road
Truro, MA 02666
508-349-3635

Season: Last Saturday in June - Labor Day
Hours: 6:00 a.m. - midnight
Parking: Lot, sticker required
Fees: Residents, $10 per season per car; nonresidents; $20 per week per car, $30 per two weeks, $60 per four weeks, $100 per season (Nonresident stickers available only to those staying in town.)
Sand: Super soft
Crowd: Mixed
Facilities: Restrooms
Rules/Regulations: No alcohol, glass, fires without a permit, floats, driving over sand, climbing on dunes, snorkels, surfing in swimming area, animals between 9:00 a.m. and 6:00 p.m.

Directions: From Route 6 to Longnook Road.

Surfers are welcome -- and indeed flock -- to this Cape Cod National Seashore beach. Two graded paths descend the dunes, which are up to 150 feet high.

"This beach has a starkly beautiful primitive feeling, as if you are at the edge of the world."
    Linda Rose O'Connor, Hyde Park, MA

Highland Beach
Coast Guard Road
Truro, MA 02666
508-349-3635

Season: Last Saturday in June - Labor Day
Hours: 6:00 a.m. - midnight
Parking: Lot, sticker required
Fees: Residents, $10 per season per car; nonresidents; $20 per
week per car, $30 per two weeks, $60 per four weeks, $100 per
season (Nonresident stickers available only to those staying in
town.)
Sand: Super soft
Crowd: Mixed
Facilities: Portable restrooms
Rules/Regulations: No alcohol, glass containers, fires without
a permit, driving over sand, climbing on dunes, surfers in
swimming area, animals between 9:00 a.m. and 6:00 p.m.

Directions: From Route 6, to Highland Road or South
Highland Road, to Coast Guard Road.

Some mistakenly call this sandy stretch Head of the Meadows
Beach. But it's actually a bit to the north. Nearby Highland
Light is the oldest lighthouse on Cape Cod. When the current
building was established in 1857, it sat on a 10-acre lot. Erosion
has left only 4 of those original acres.

Special Notes: The Highland House Museum houses the
collection of the Truro Historical Society and other early
shipping artifacts.

Head of the Meadow Beaches
Head of the Meadow Road
Truro, MA 02666
508-349-3785

Season: Last Saturday in June - Labor Day
Hours: 6:00 a.m. - midnight
Parking: Lots
Fees: $5 per car; $3 for walk-ins
Sand: Super soft
Crowd: Mixed

Facilities: Lifeguard (National Seashore section only), restrooms, bath house

Rules/Regulations: No alcohol, animals, between 9:00 a.m. and 6:00 p.m.: glass containers, fires without a permit, floats, driving over sand, climbing on dunes, snorkels, surfing in main beach area

Directions: From Route 6 to Head of the Meadow Road.

These two sandy beaches -- one managed by the National Seashore, the other by the town -- have gently rolling dunes that are great for families. Surfing here is fun and the undertow area is well-marked. One note: the abundant red seaweed in August can be bothersome.

Pilgrim Beach
Route 6A
Truro, MA 02666
508-349-3635

Season: Last Saturday in June - Labor Day
Hours: 6:00 a.m. - midnight
Parking: Lot, sticker required
Fees: Residents, $10 per season per car; nonresidents; $20 per week per car, $30 per two weeks, $60 per four weeks, $100 per season (Nonresident stickers available only to those staying in town.)
Sand: Soft
Crowd: Mixed
Facilities: None
Rules/Regulations: No alcohol, glass, fires without a permit, driving over sand, climbing on dunes, surfing in swimming or main beach area, animals between 9:00 a.m. and 6:00 p.m.

Directions: On the southern portion of Route 6A, near Knowles Heights Road, in North Truro.

Vacation cottages are densely clustered along this narrow strip, the last open Cape Cod Bay beach before Provincetown turns toward the Atlantic. The only access is on a path, across from the parking lot, which is wide enough for a four-wheel drive vehicle. Views include Provincetown Lighthouse and Great Island.

Great Hollow Beach

Great Hollow Road
Truro, MA 02666
508-349-3635

Season: Last Saturday in June - Labor Day
Hours: 6:00 a.m. - midnight
Parking: Lot, sticker required
Fees: Residents, $10 per season per car; nonresidents; $20 per week per car, $30 per two weeks, $60 per four weeks, $100 per season (Nonresident stickers available only to those staying in town.)
Sand: Soft
Crowd: Mixed
Facilities: Portable restrooms
Rules/Regulations: No alcohol, glass, fires without a permit, floats, glass, driving over sand, climbing on dunes, snorkels, surfing in main beach area, animals between 9:00 a.m. and 6:00 p.m.

Directions: From Route 6 to Great Hollow Road.

Early birds will be able to park near this Cape Cod Bay beach. If you arrive late, you'll be relegated to the top of the hill. Wooden stairs deliver you down to the beach, which is backed by dunes. Private residences are located on either side.

Corn Hill Beach

Corn Hill Road
Truro, MA 02666
508-349-3635

Season: Last Saturday in June - Labor Day
Hours: 6:00 a.m. - midnight
Parking: Lot, no sticker required
Fees: $5 per car; $3 for walk-ins
Sand: Coarse
Crowd: Families
Facilities: Restrooms
Rules/Regulations: No alcohol, glass, fires without a permit, climbing on dunes, surfing or swimming in main beach areas, animals between 9:00 a.m. and 6:00 p.m., driving over sand before 5:00 p.m.

Directions: From Route 6 to Castle Road to Corn Hill Road.

This sandy beach is named because the Pilgrims found a life-saving cache of corn here. Because it's a bit of a walk from the parking area, it doesn't attract a crowd. After 5:00 p.m., walkers should be aware that four-wheel drive vehicles have access to the beach.

"There are the most beautiful scallop shells -- orange, pink, white, and striped ones."
    Liz Heeley-Ray, West Yarmouth, MA

Fisher Beach
Fisher Road
Truro, MA 02666
508-349-3635

Season: Last Saturday in June - Labor Day
Hours: 6:00 a.m. - midnight
Parking: Roadside, sticker required
Fees: Residents, $10 per season per car; nonresidents; $20 per week per car, $30 per two weeks, $60 per four weeks, $100 per season (Nonresident stickers available only to those staying in town.)
Sand: Soft
Crowd: Mixed
Facilities: None
Rules/Regulations: No alcohol, glass, fires without a permit, climbing on dunes, surfing or swimming in main beach areas, animals between 9:00 a.m. and 6:00 p.m., driving over sand before 5:00 p.m.

Directions: Route 6 to Old County Road to Fisher Road.

Although this is another Cape Cod Bay vacation neighborhood, it feels more remote because the homes are set back and not directly on the water.

Ryder Beach
Ryder Beach Road
Truro, MA 02666
508-349-3635

Season: Last Saturday in June - Labor Day
Hours: 6:00 a.m. - midnight
Parking: Roadside, sticker required
Fees: Residents, $10 per season per car; nonresidents; $20 per week per car, $30 per two weeks, $60 per four weeks, $100 per season (Nonresident stickers available only to those staying in town.)
Sand: Soft
Crowd: Mixed
Facilities: None
Rules/Regulations: No alcohol, glass, fires without a permit, climbing on dunes, surfing or swimming in main beach areas, animals between 9:00 a.m. and 6:00 p.m., driving over sand before 5:00 p.m.

Directions: From Route 6 to Prince Valley Road, right on Old County Road, left onto Ryder Beach Road to the end.

It's a rather long drive to reach this Cape Cod Bay beach. At the end of the paved road are some parking spaces. From here hike up and over the steep dune hill to the quiet beach. There are some homes along the access trail, but just to the south is undeveloped marshland.

Race Point Beach
Race Point Road
Provincetown, MA 02657
508-349-3785

Season: Last Saturday in June - Labor Day
Hours: 6:00 a.m. - midnight
Parking: Lot
Fees: $5 per car; $3 for walk-ins
Sand: Super soft
Crowd: Families
Facilities: Lifeguards, restrooms, bath house, bicycle rack, public telephone
Rules/Regulations: No alcohol, animals, balls, glass, open fires, floats, snorkels, surfing in main beach area

Directions: From Route 6 to the end of Race Point Road.

It may be the great expanse of rolling dunes, or perhaps it's knowing you're at the far end of the Cape, but words cannot describe the quiet, breathtaking feeling of being here. This sweeping National Seashore beach is about 8 miles long. If you're lucky, you may have a whale sighting: Stellwagen Bank, a prime feeding area for migrating whales, is just 9 miles from here. This is also a top stop for watching sea birds. Water depths drop sharply not too far out from the beach and there is fine surfing. Sunsets can be spectacular. Province Lands Visitor Center (508-487-1256), the second of two National Seashore information points, is here. It offers guided tours, exhibits, and publications. Nearby is the Old Harbor Life-Saving Station and a branch of the Province Lands Trail, an extensive paved bicycle path through area woods and dunes.

Special Notes: Buggy tours of the dunes are available from Art's Dune Tours. Call 508-487-1950 or 508-487-1050. Guided horseback rides (for those 12 and older) may be arranged through Nelson's Riding Stable, 43 Race Point Road. Call 508-487-1112.

Herring Cove Beach
Province Land Road
Provincetown, MA 02657
508-349-3785

Season: Last Saturday in June - Labor Day
Hours: 6:00 a.m. - midnight
Parking: Lot
Fees: $5 per car; $3 for walk-ins
Sand: Soft
Crowd: Mixed
Facilities: Lifeguard, restrooms (both flush and portable), bath house, snack bar, public telephone
Rules/Regulations: No alcohol, animals, balls, fires, floats, glass, snorkels, surfing in main beach area

Directions: At the end of Route 6 on Province Land Road. This half-mile long beach on Cape Cod Bay is also part of the National Seashore. While the sand is soft, there are also plenty of rocks. The waters are fairly calm. On a clear day you can see Plymouth. While the parking lot is large, this beach is extremely popular so the lot fills up early. If you're energetic, you can bike here via the Province Lands bike trail.

"We love this beach. There are beautiful beach stones and one can walk a bit and find some privacy."
      Leslie Roitman, Milton, MA

Special Notes: Another way to tour part of the Cape Cod National Seashore is by boat. Flyer's Boat Rentals will take you out to Long Point, which is at the very end of the curve of the Cape's arm. While quiet and remote, there are two lighthouses here and two Civil War gun emplacements. Children ride free. The boat leaves Provincetown's MacMillan Wharf every half hour. Call 800-750-0898 or 508-487-0898.

Crosby Landing Beach
Crosby Lane
Brewster, MA 02631
508-896-3701

Season: Memorial Day - Labor Day
Hours: 6:00 a.m. - 10:00 p.m.
Parking: Lot, sticker required
Fees: Nonresidents, $8 per day per car, $25 per week, $45 per two weeks, $75 per season
Sand: Soft
Crowd: Mixed
Facilities: Portable restrooms
Rules/Regulations: No alcohol, animals, fires

Directions: From Route 6A to Crosby Lane.

The low dunes here help give this Cape Cod Bay beach an expansive feeling, although it really isn't any larger than other local beaches. Rocks and stones are at the shore line, and the water is warm and calm. At low tide you can walk far out into the tidal flats.

Special Notes: Brewster beach stickers can be purchased at the Brewster Town Hall Annex Building from 9:00 a.m. to 3:00 p.m. daily. Call 508-896-4511.

Linnell's Landing Beach

Linnell Road
Brewster, MA 02631
508-896-3701

Season: Memorial Day - Labor Day
Hours: 6:00 a.m. - 10:00 p.m.
Parking: Lot, sticker required
Fees: Nonresidents, $8 per day per car, $25 per week, $45 per two weeks, $75 per season
Sand: Soft
Crowd: Families
Facilities: Portable restrooms, bicycle rack
Rules/Regulations: No alcohol, animals, fires

Directions: From Route 6A to Linnell Road, East Brewster.

Like all bayside beaches, the water here is warm and calm. Amidst such a peaceful setting, it's hard to believe that 200 years ago this bay area was teaming with salt-making businesses.

"The kids look for hermit crabs -- that gives them something else to do around the water."
Alice Soderman, Brewster, MA

Ellis Landing Beach

Ellis Landing Road
Brewster, MA 02631
508-896-3701

Season: Memorial Day - Labor Day
Hours: 6:00 a.m. - 10:00 p.m.
Parking: Small lot, sticker required
Fees: Nonresidents, $8 per day per car, $25 per week, $45 per two weeks, $75 per season
Sand: Soft
Crowd: Mixed
Facilities: Portable restrooms
Rules/Regulations: No alcohol, animals, fires

Directions: From Route 6A to Ellis Landing Road.

Water here is calm and warm. Looking out across Cape Cod Bay you can see the cliffs of Great Island in Wellfleet. Just beside the parking lot, to the right, is a small parcel of conservation land which was deeded over by a generous landowner.

Point of Rocks Beach
Point of Rocks Road
Brewster, MA 02631
508-896-3701

Season: Memorial Day - Labor Day
Hours: 6:00 a.m. - 10:00 p.m.
Parking: Lot, sticker required
Fees: Nonresidents, $8 per day per car, $25 per week, $45 per two weeks, $75 per season
Sand: Soft
Crowd: Mixed
Facilities: None
Rules/Regulations: No alcohol, animals, fires

Directions: From Route 6A to Point of Rocks Road.

There are no facilities and very little parking at this Cape Cod Bay beach. While these things alone are reason enough to keep visitors away, another drawback is the amount of sea-grass in the water. Other Brewster beaches are a better bet.

Breakwater Beach
Breakwater Road
Brewster, MA 02631
508-896-3701

Season: Memorial - Labor Day
Hours: 6:00 a.m. - 10:00 p.m.
Parking: Lot, sticker required
Fees: Nonresidents, $8 per day per car, $25 per week, $45 per two weeks, $75 per season
Sand: Soft
Crowd: Mixed
Facilities: Portable restrooms, bicycle rack
Rules/Regulations: No alcohol, animals, fires

Directions: From Route 6A to Breakwater Road.

If you get a late start, this beach is a good bet because it has the biggest parking lot of all Brewster beaches. But don't think of it as a last resort; it's as nice as any local beach. Strollers will enjoy walking the Brewster Flats at low tide.

Special Notes: Brewster is home to the Brewster Whitecaps, with over 110 years of play in the Cape Cod Baseball League. Their home field is just down the road on Route 124 at the Cape Cod Regional Technical High School. (Carlton Fisk was discovered while playing for this community league!) For information, call 508-896-3913.

Saint's Landing Beach
Robbins Hill Road
Brewster, MA 02631
508-896-3701

Season: Memorial Day - Labor Day
Hours: 6:00 a.m. - 10:00 p.m.
Parking: Lot, sticker required
Fees: Nonresidents, $8 per day per car, $25 per week, $45 per two weeks, $75 per season
Sand: Soft
Crowd: Mixed
Facilities: Portable restrooms
Rules/Regulations: No alcohol, animals, fires

Directions: From Route 6A in West Brewster to Lower Road, right at the bend to Robbins Hill Road.

Next to Robbins Hill Beach on Cape Cod Bay, this small sandy beach, with boats moored nearby, has a pleasant view. It's divided by jetties and has just a little grass in the water.

Robbins Hill Beach
Robbins Hill Road
Brewster, MA 02631
508-896-3701

Season: Memorial Day - Labor Day

Hours: 6:00 a.m. - 10:00 p.m.
Parking: Lot, sticker required
Fees: Nonresidents, $8 per day per car, $25 per week, $45 per two weeks, $75 per season
Sand: Soft
Crowd: Mixed
Facilities: Portable restrooms, bicycle rack
Rules/Regulations: No alcohol, animals, fires

Directions: From Route 6A to Lower Road to Robbins Hill Road.

Even though this beach is close to the others on Cape Cod Bay, it has a secluded feeling. There are some stones at the water's edge and sea grass too.

Special Notes: On Sunday evenings during July and August, bring your blanket or beach chair and head for Drummer Boy Park on Route 6A in West Brewster. The Brewster Town Band performs weekly concerts that begin at 6:00 p.m.

Paines Creek Beach
Paines Creek Road
Brewster, MA 02631
508-896-3701

Season: Memorial Day - Labor Day
Hours: 6:00 a.m. - 10:00 p.m.
Parking: Lot, sticker required
Fees: Nonresidents, $8 per day per car, $25 per week, $45 per two weeks, $75 per season
Sand: Soft
Crowd: Mixed
Facilities: Portable restrooms, bicycle rack
Rules/Regulations: No alcohol, animals, fires

Directions: From Route 6A in West Brewster to Paines Creek Road.

Paines Creek borders this Cape Cod Bay beach. Children especially enjoy this morsel of sand, which has very warm water and little coves and inlets. Although there is quite a bit of sea grass mixed in, no one seems to mind.

"We head for the huge sand bar at low tide -- you can walk out about a mile."

Judy Robbins, Sterling, MA

Special Notes: The Cape Cod Museum of Natural History on Route 6A in West Brewster has a collection of interesting ecological and animal exhibits that examine the Cape's plant and animal life. There's a saltwater aquarium, classes and nature programs, and a trail that heads out to Wing Island. The museum is open year-round and there's no charge. Call 508-896-3867.

East Sandwich Beach

North Shore Boulevard
Sandwich, MA 02563
508-888-4910

Season: Memorial Day - Labor Day
Hours: 8:00 a.m. - 10:00 p.m.
Parking: Lot, sticker required
Fees: Residents, $15 per season per car; nonresidents, $20 per season per car
Sand: Soft
Crowd: Mixed
Facilities: None
Rules/Regulations: No alcohol, animals

Directions: From Route 6A to Ploughed Neck Road, left onto North Shore Boulevard.

Tiny, neat, and well-maintained cottages make up the neighborhood along these dunes. People who stay here like the simplistic, retro-look of the area. They don't care about frills, and are here for just the basics -- the sand, sun, and ocean.

Special Notes: Sandwich is one of the best spots on the Cape for blueberry picking. Call the Chamber of Commerce (508-759-6000) for a list of pick-your-own farms.

Within the past 3 million years, the location of the Atlantic shoreline has varied at least 100 miles in both directions.

Sandy Neck Beach

Sandy Neck Road
Sandwich, MA 02630
508-362-8300

Season: Memorial Day - Labor Day
Hours: 9:00 a.m. - 9:00 p.m.
Parking: Lot
Fees: Nonresidents, $8 per day per car, $35 per week per car
Sand: Soft with some pebbles
Crowd: Families
Facilities: Lifeguards, restrooms (close at 4:30 p.m.), bath house, snack bar, picnic tables, public telephone, swimming lessons
Rules/Regulations: No alcohol, animals, open fires, glass, snorkels

Directions: From Route 6A to Sandy Neck Road in East Sandwich at the West Barnstable line.

With its unspoiled expanse of dunes, this beach is among the more breathtaking on the Cape. It's one of the largest barrier beaches in New England and spans 8 miles of mostly pebbly shore along Cape Cod Bay. Most of the beach is part of the 1,322-acre Sandy Neck Conservation Area. The parking lot is at the western side of the beach. So if you want solitude, head toward the eastern side, which fewer people reach. The sandy roads along Sandy Neck require off-road permits, which are available at the gatehouse.

"This is a beautiful area with delightful crosswinds, although the water is quite cold."
Betty Hurley, Milton, MA

Town Beach

aka Town Neck Beach
Tupper Road
Sandwich, MA 02563
508-888-4910

Season: Memorial Day - Labor Day
Hours: 8:00 a.m. to 10:00 p.m.
Parking: Lot, sticker required

Fees: Residents, $15 per season per car; nonresidents, $20 per season per car
Sand: Soft
Crowd: Families
Facilities: Lifeguard, restrooms, bath house, snack bar
Rules/Regulations: No alcohol, animals

Directions: From Route 6A to Town Neck Road to the end of Tupper Road.

This beach, bound by the Cape Cod Canal and Dock Creek, was heavily damaged by Hurricane Bob in 1991. Since then, the town has constructed a wonderful boardwalk leading from the parking lot over the dunes and across an extensive tidal marsh to the beach. Walkers along here tend to stroll, with their heads bowed down. Why, when there is so much beauty around? Most of the boards are carved with names and messages from people who "bought" them during a fundraising construction drive.

Special Notes: Green Briar Nature Center and Jam Kitchen have nature trails and exhibits, story times, canoe trips, and workshops, including one on jam making so you can learn to make jam that doesn't dribble off the spreading knife. They are located at 6 Discovery Hill Road off Route 6 in East Sandwich, open weekdays and Saturday from 10:00 a.m. to 4:00 p.m. and Sundays from 1:00 p.m. to 4:00 p.m. Call 508-888-6870 for workshop registration.

Scusset Beach State Reservation
Scusset Beach Road
Sandwich, MA 02563
508-888-0859

Season: Memorial Day - Labor Day
Hours: 10:00 a.m. - 8:00 p.m.
Parking: Lot (gate locks at closing)
Fees: $2 per car, $15 per car for seasonal pass
Sand: Soft
Crowd: Families
Facilities: Lifeguard, restrooms, bath house, snack bar, bicycle rack, picnic tables, public telephones, fishing, campground
Rules/Regulations: No alcohol, pets on beach, floats, surfing, fires without permit

Directions: From Route 3, exit at the Sagamore Bridge. Turn onto Meetinghouse Lane at the rotary, then bear right at the first intersection to Scusset Beach Road.

This busy beach is separated from the Cape Cod Canal by a large stone jetty. Along the length of beach at this 380-acre park are low-sweeping, grassy dunes. A wooden boardwalk with a small gazebo and a sandy path lead from the parking lot to the beach. It's fun to walk out on the jetty to watch the people fishing and see the boats passing through the canal. Look to the north at the beautiful white cliffs of Manomet.

"The water is clean, and I can fish nearby while my wife swims."
Ron McIvor, Sandwich, MA

Special Notes: A paved biking and hiking trail extends 7 miles on either side of the canal. It is the longest uninterrupted trail in Massachusetts.

MARTHA'S VINEYARD, MASSACHUSETTS

Lighthouse Beach, Edgartown

Long Island may have the Hamptons. But Cape Cod has Martha's Vineyard. Summer playground of the privileged, it's second home to Hollywood celebrities, business moguls, and the idle rich. But despite its elitist image, the Vineyard is a place where even the common person can feel comfortable. Baggy cotton clothes and flip-flops are practically the island uniform. And flash, in any form on this undeniably Yankee island, is considered bad taste. (Witness the cold shoulder that car magnate Ernie Boch received when he built a $10-million, 15,000-square-foot, high-tech manse. If this weren't bitter pill enough for the island's social set to swallow, he razed a 17th century farmstead to build it!)

Although it's a good idea to have a car if you're planning to stay any length of time -- the island is 24 miles long and 10 miles wide -- paved paths make it easy to bike to many of the Vineyard's most popular beaches. Because the island is so big, it offers a wide variety of beach experiences, from pleasant flat swaths of sand packed with families to desolate stretches of dramatic cliff-backed shores.

Although, there are just a few main roads and it is, in fact, easy to get around, it's not a bad idea to get a map. They're

available at the Chamber of Commerce on Beach Road in
downtown Vineyard Haven.

Owen Park Beach
aka **Bayside Beach**
Owen Park Road
Vineyard Haven, MA 02568
508-693-0085

Season: Memorial Day - Labor Day
Hours: 10:00 a.m. - 5:00 p.m.
Parking: Lot
Fees: None
Sand: Soft
Crowd: Mixed
Facilities: Lifeguard, benches, playground, bandstand
Rules/Regulations: No alcohol, unleashed animals, open fires

Directions: From the Steamship Authority Terminal, straight
onto Union Street, right onto Main Street, and right onto
Owen Park Road.

Near the Vineyard Haven ferry dock is this hillside park and
small, sandy beach. See the cedar trees on the park's south
side? Under each one is buried a tiny time capsule with records
of local Civil War heroes. A long stone jetty keeps the surf
here calm and also protects the moored sailboats.

Lake Tashmoo Beach
aka **Herring Creek Beach**
Herring Creek Road
Vineyard Haven, MA 02575
508-693-0085

Season: Memorial Day - Labor Day
Hours: 10:00 a.m. - 5:00 p.m.
Parking: Lot
Fees: None
Sand: Soft
Crowd: Mixed
Facilities: Lifeguard
Rules/Regulations: No alcohol, unleashed animals, open fires

Directions: From the ferry terminal, head to Main Street. Turn right onto Main Street, then left onto Daggett Street and right at the end onto Herring Creek Road (dirt) and follow to the end.

On the northwestern part of the island is a small beach at the Tashmoo jetties, where Tashmoo Lake meets Nantucket Sound via Herring Creek. The lake offers calm, brackish water for swimming. But the creek has swift currents and deep water. From the oceanside portion of the beach, you'll enjoy sweeping views of the Elizabeth Islands and Woods Hole.

Lagoon Bridge Park
Beach Road
Vineyard Haven, MA 02575
508-693-0085

Season: Year-round
Hours: None posted
Parking: Lot
Fees: None
Sand: Soft with stones
Crowd: Mixed
Facilities: None
Rules/Regulations: No alcohol, unleashed animals, open fires

Directions: On Beach Road, near the drawbridge.

This is a quiet place to swim or to watch the harbor activity. Small boats race about near the Vineyard Haven Yacht Club. The lagoon jetty at one end of the bridge can provide good fishing.

Lambert's Cove Beach
Lambert's Cove Road
West Tisbury, MA 02575
508-693-0085

Season: Memorial Day - Labor Day
Hours: 7:00 a.m. - 9:00 p.m.
Parking: Lot, resident sticker required 10:00 a.m. - 5:00 p.m.
Fees: None

Sand: Super soft
Crowd: Mixed
Facilities: Portable restrooms
Rules/Regulations: No alcohol, animals, open fires, vehicles

Directions: From State Road to Lambert's Cove Road to a lot in the woods on the right.

Although this beach is limited to residents and their guests during primary beach-going hours, nonresidents can park here before and after. From the small parking lot along the roadside, it's a pleasant 10-minute walk through oak woodlands on a path of deep, soft sand. Lambert's Cove has perhaps the clearest water and finest sand of any beach on the island's north shore. The crescent-shaped stretch on this wide, inland bay is dune-backed and scattered with stones and shells.

Special Notes: Look for town band concerts every other Sunday evening throughout the summer. Also, the annual Tisbury Street Fair -- a huge block party with food, games and entertainment -- takes place in July. Call 508-693-0064.

Long Point Wildlife Refuge Beach
West Tisbury Road
West Tisbury, MA 02539
508-693-3678 or 508-693-7392

Season: June 15 - September 15
Hours: 9:00 a.m. - 5:00 p.m. (everyone is shooed off by 6:00 p.m.)
Parking: Lot, limited to 100 cars
Fees: $3 per person 18 and over; also nonmembers $6 per car
Sand: Soft
Crowd: Families
Facilities: Restrooms, fresh water
Rules/Regulations: No alcohol, animals, open fires

Directions: From West Tisbury Road to Waldmans Bottom Road. Watch for signs. There's another entrance on Deep Bottom Road, which is also off West Tisbury Road.

This 633-acre refuge is managed by the Trustees of Reservations. The property includes a half mile of open beach, in addition to pine and oak woods and rolling, brush-covered dunes. Over the dunes, just behind the beach area, is Great Pond, which has safe freshwater swimming. Guided tours of the refuge, as well as canoe tours of Great Pond, are available every weekend.

"It's the best beach on the island because it gives the whole south shore experience without the crowds."
Chris Egan, Martha's Vineyard

Special Notes: The Trustees of Reservations manages nearly 4,000 acres on Martha's Vineyard alone. Throughout Massachusetts, it manages property at 76 locations. For membership information, write 572 Essex Street, Beverly, MA 01915-1530, or call 508-921-1944.

Menemsha Town Beach
Dutchers Dock
Chilmark, MA 02535
508-693-0085

Season: Memorial Day - Labor Day
Hours: Sunrise - sunset
Parking: Lot
Fees: None
Sand: Soft with stones
Crowd: Families
Facilities: Lifeguard (9:00 a.m. - 5:00 p.m.); restrooms, snack bars, bicycle rack, public telephone are nearby
Rules/Regulations: No fires, litter, animals, climbing on cliffs, hard surfboards, windsurfers; beach parties and clam bakes allowed with permit

Directions: From State Road to North Road, right to Dutchers Dock.

This scenic harbor beach is on the western side of Martha's Vineyard and is in the midst of the island's only real fishing village. The surf is calm, which is nice for younger kids. But parents should be aware that the beach drops quickly into the water (some of the coldest on the island). Fishing is great from the jetties, and the sunsets are beautiful. A sculpture of a fisherman with spear and swordfish sits in the dunes beside the parking lot: It was created for the town's 300th birthday in 1994.

"Wonderful area to watch fishermen, go fishing, catch crabs, and quahogs, if you have a license."
    Audrey MacKnight, Keene, NH

Special Notes: One of the island's best loved restaurants is right near this beach. The Home Port is an old-fashioned dining hall set right on Vineyard Sound. Consider sampling the Home Port Shore Dinner, complete with lobster, corn on the cob, a stuffed quahog, steamed mussels, and broth. Or get take-out and picnic on the beach. Call 508-645-2679.

Squibnocket Beach
Chilmark, MA 02535
508-693-0085

Season: June 1 - September 30
Hours: None posted
Parking: Lot, Chilmark resident sticker required (The beach is also open to B&B and inn guests staying in Chilmark. Stickers are available at town offices.)
Fees: None
Sand: Mostly rocky
Crowd: Families
Facilities: None
Rules/Regulations: No fires, litter, animals, climbing on cliffs, hard surfboards, windsurfers; no nonresidents allowed during beach season, including bicyclists and walkers

Directions: This beach is difficult to get to, as it's unmarked and accessed via several dirt roads. The turnoff is on State Road across from Menemsha Pond. But your best bet is to ask specific directions at the Chilmark General Store.

Ever-changing is the best way to describe this narrow beach with just 280 feet of sand. Sometimes the shore is rocky, and at other times, powdery soft. Water is shallow. In fact, this beach is so shallow that in early Island days rescue boats could be launched and landed from here during storms. (Rescuers could step in and out of boats without being over their heads in heavy surf.)

Lucy Vincent Beach
Chilmark, MA 02535
508-693-0085

Season: June 1 - September 30
Hours: 7:00 a.m. - 9:00 p.m.; no trespassing before or after hours
Parking: Lot, Chilmark resident sticker required (The beach is also open to B&B and inn guests staying in Chilmark. Stickers are available at town offices.)
Fees: None
Sand: Soft
Crowd: Families
Facilities: Lifeguard, portable restrooms
Rules/Regulations: No fires, litter, animals, climbing on cliffs, hard surfboards, windsurfers, nude sunbathing within the first 1500 feet of beach

Directions: Heading south from Chilmark center, follow South Road about .25 mile. Turn left onto a dirt road -- there's a telephone pole there. Follow road until you see signs for parking.

This breathtaking beach faces the open Atlantic. Cliffs rise behind the beach and large rocks sit solidly in the sand and water. Surf varies according to weather conditions, but is usually strong. Young families tend to stay within comfortable walking distance of the entrance. Nude bathers -- yes, it's true, Chilmark is the only town on the island that allows nude sun bathing -- sit off to the left.

"There are always people flying kites and there are lots of families."
Tracy Cavanaugh, Stow, MA

Special Notes: Just because Lucy Vincent allows nude sunbathing, don't think this is a racy spot. It's a traditional family beach, so proper behavior is expected.

Lobsterville Beach
West Basin Road
Gay Head, MA 02535
508-693-0085

Season: Year-round
Hours: Sunrise - sunset
Parking: Limited roadside parking and small lots; one lot requires resident sticker
Fees: None
Sand: Coarse with shells
Crowd: Mixed
Facilities: Boat launch
Rules/Regulations: No alcohol, animals, open fires, vehicles on the beach

Directions: From State Road to Middle Road, straight onto Lobsterville Road, and left onto West Basin Road.

On the North Shore of Gay Head, along Rhode Island Sound, is a 2-mile long secluded beach within 230 acres of fragile dunes and bog. The dunes are gentle and the sand a bit pebbly. Fishermen here are after bluefish and bonito, not lobster!

Moshup Beach

Moshup's Trail
Gay Head, MA 02535
508-627-7141

Season: Year-round
Hours: Sunrise - sunset
Parking: Lot
Fees: $12 per car
Sand: Soft with stones and boulders
Crowd: Mixed
Facilities: None (Take-out food is available at the Lighthouse, and restrooms [$.25 cent fee] are nearby.)
Rules/Regulations: No alcohol, animals, open fires, climbing on clay cliffs

Directions: From State Road to Middle Road to South Road to Moshup's Trail.

Although the parking lot is a 10-minute walk from the beach, there's a convenient drop-off spot. Possibly because of the long walk and the parking fees, this beach is never crowded. The colorful yellow, red, white, and green clay of the famous cliffs (declared a National Landmark in 1966) makes this the most dramatic looking beach on the Vineyard. While there are no lifeguards, sentries make sure rules are followed. Among the biggest no-no's is taking a "clay bath." In years gone by people would come to Gay Head just to experience the restorative effects of rolling around in the mud: They'd slather themselves with clay, bake in the sun, then rinse off in the ocean. Because these cliffs are now endangered, even this can be harmful. Swimmers and waders should be aware of the strong surf and undertow, not to mention the occasional nude swimmer. Amateur archeologists take note: Fossils bones of camels, horses, and whales have been found here.

Special Notes: The Gay Head Lighthouse, one of five on the island, is among the nation's oldest electrified lighthouses. The original Gay Head Light, with prisms made in France, is a highlight of the historical society collection in Edgartown.

Philbin Beach
Gay Head, MA 02535
508-693-0085

Season: Year-round
Hours: Sunrise - sunset
Parking: Lot, resident sticker required
Fees: None
Sand: Soft with stones and boulders
Crowd: Mixed
Facilities: Public telephone
Rules/Regulations: No alcohol, animals, open fires; no non-residents allowed, including bicyclists and walkers

Directions: Off Moshup's Trail, look for sign and parking lot.

This 7-acre area beach between Moshup and South Beach doesn't have great cliffs . Rather, the hills and dunes are rolling and gentle. Water conditions, however, are strong.

South Beach
aka **Katama Beach**
Katama Road
Edgartown, MA 02539
508-693-0085

Season: May - September
Hours: Sunrise - midnight
Parking: Small lot, also lot in Edgartown center with trolley service ($3 round-trip for trolley)
Fees: None
Sand: Soft
Crowd: Mixed
Facilities: Lifeguard, portable restrooms, changing rooms
Rules/Regulations: No alcohol, animals, open fires; permitted off-road vehicles allowed no farther than Norton Point

Directions: From Main Street near Inner Harbor, to South Water Street (Katama Road). Parking is available at Triangle Parking on the outskirts of Edgartown. It's well marked with signs everywhere. About every 15 minutes the South Beach trolley picks up bathers here and at the Edgartown Visitors Center. It runs from June 16 through Labor Day.

This 3-mile barrier beach area along Norton Point is considered a Vineyard classic. Read: It's crowded. The sand is fine, the waves are strong, and the winds steady. While the waves are great for body surfing, the undertow is persistent. Swimmers should use caution. For those willing to walk the distance, there's calm water in Katama Bay. If you keep walking, you'll eventually walk right onto Chappaquiddick. Over the years sand has built up and thus connected the island to this beach.

"Definitely "Party Central."
    Lara Connolly, Amherst, NH

Chappy Point Beach
Chappaquiddick Road
Edgartown, MA 02539
508-693-0085

Season: Year-round
Hours: Sunrise - midnight
Parking: Small lot
Fees: None
Sand: Soft
Crowd: Mixed
Facilities: None
Rules/Regulations: No alcohol, animals, open fires

Directions: On Chappaquiddick Road near the ferry dock. Ferry charges from Edgartown are $4.50 for a car and driver, $3.50 for a motorcycle and rider, $2.50 for bicycle and rider, $1 per person.

Adjacent to the ferry slip on Chappaquiddick, this small beach has long been used by the public, but only recently purchased by the town. It looks across the harbor toward the lighthouse, and abuts the Chappaquiddick Beach Club, whose colorful pavilions add some whimsy to the scene.

East Beach
Wasque Road
Edgartown, MA 02539
508-627-7689

Season: May - September
Hours: 9:00 a.m. - 6:00 p.m.
Parking: Lot
Fees: $3 per car, also $3 per person, no charge for children 12 and under
Sand: Soft
Crowd: Mixed
Facilities: Portable restrooms, bicycle rack, public telephone
Rules/Regulations: No uncontrolled animals, open fires, wind surfing

Directions: From the Chappaquiddick ferry ($4.50 for a car and driver, $3.50 for a motorcycle and rider, $2.50 for bicycle and rider, $1 per person), past the "Blow Your Bugle" sign at Five Corners, straight to the end of Wasque Road.

This beautiful and remote barrier beach on the east end of Chappaquiddick sits amidst the Cape Pogue Wildlife Refuge (509 acres) and Wasque Reservation (200 acres). (The Trustees of Reservations manages both sanctuaries.) The area is isolated, but accessible through Wasque Reservation both by foot and with recreational vehicles with permits. The long boardwalk from Wasque makes the walk through the marsh to the beach quiet effortless, and is a pleasure in itself. A sign warns swimmers about dangerous water conditions, which include steep beach embankments, fast-changing ocean currents, and shifting winds.

Lighthouse and Fuller Street Beaches

North Water Street
Edgartown, MA 02539
508-693-0085

Season: Year-round
Hours: Sunrise - sunset
Parking: Limited roadside
Fees: None
Sand: Soft
Crowd: Mixed
Facilities: None
Rules/Regulations: No alcohol, animals, open fires

Directions: From North Water Street, follow the Lighthouse Walkway.

At Starbuck's Neck, right near the center of town, this harbor beach enjoys great views of the Edgartown Lighthouse. The original lighthouse was built on a man-made island in the harbor. Over the years, sand filled in the separation, and now the lighthouse is on shore. Just beyond it is a section of sand known locally as Fuller Street Beach. Beautiful homes back this beach, which is on the arm of Eel Pond.

Bend-in-the-Road Beach

Beach Road
Edgartown, MA 02539
508-693-0085

Season: May - September
Hours: 10:00 a.m. - 5:00 p.m.
Parking: Roadside
Fees: None
Sand: Soft with stones
Crowd: Mixed
Facilities: Lifeguard, benches, bicycle rack, picnic tables
Rules/Regulations: No alcohol, unrestrained animals

Directions: On Beach Road, right near the town center.

Joseph A. Sylvia State Beach runs into this beach at its southern end, where there is -- you guessed it -- a bend in the road. The swimming area is roped off. If you're staying in Edgartown or Oak Bluffs this beach makes a nice, easy bike ride: There's a safe, paved bicycle path alongside Beach Road.

Joseph Silva State Beach
aka **Oak Bluffs State Beach**
Beach Road
Oak Bluffs, MA 02557
508-693-0085

Season: Year-round
Hours: None posted
Parking: Lot and roadside
Fees: None
Sand: Soft with stones
Crowd: Families
Facilities: Ice cream vendor
Rules/Regulations: No animals, open fires, vehicles

Directions: Along Beach Road between Oak Bluffs and Edgartown.

This beach too is easy to reach by bike, thanks to the paved path along Beach Road. Because of such easy access, this long, narrow stretch, which is backed by low dunes, is quite popular. The Nantucket Sound water is shallow and warm. Brisk winds can provide a challenge to windsurfers. Behind the beach is a bird sanctuary and Sengekontacket Pond.

Special Notes: Lobster lovers may want to visit the State Lobster Hatchery on Shirley Road (off County Road) in Oak Bluffs. Female lobsters with eggs are brought here, and their young are later released into the sea. Call 508-693-0060.

Oak Bluffs Town Beach
Beach Road
Oak Bluffs, MA 02557
508-693-0085

Season: May - September
Hours: 9:00 a.m. - 6:00 p.m.
Parking: Roadside, 2-hour limit
Fees: None
Sand: Soft with pebbles
Crowd: Families
Facilities: Lifeguard; rest rooms, public telephone, food nearby
Rules/Regulations: No alcohol, unleashed animals, open fires

Directions: Right on Beach Road, near the Oak Bluffs ferry.

Here's a beach with calm, warm, shallow water that is divided by the wharf for the Oak Bluffs ferry. With views of the mainland and the town's colorful gingerbread cottages, Oak Bluffs is a popular spot for residents and day-trippers alike.

Special Notes: The Flying Horses Carousel, the oldest continuously operated platform carousel in the U.S., will send you spinning for just $1. (The hair on the wooden horses is actual horse hair, and look at what you see when you gaze into your horse's eyes -- a miniature painting of a carousel horse!) Located at 33 Circuit Avenue, Oak Bluffs. Call 508-693-9481.

If you're interested in getting a peek inside one of Oak Bluff's gingerbread houses, head to the Cottage Museum, 1 Trinity Park. It's open Monday through Saturday between 10:30 a.m. and 3:30 p.m.

Eastville Point Beach

Beach Road
Oak Bluffs, MA 02568
508-693-0085

Season: Year-round
Hours: None posted
Parking: Lot
Fees: None
Sand: Soft with stones
Crowd: Mixed
Facilities: None
Rules/Regulations: No alcohol, unleashed animals, open fires

Directions: At the bridge between Oak Bluffs and Vineyard Haven.

This small, county-run beach affords great views of the harbor. It's a perfect perch for boat lovers.

Special Notes: If you're here in mid August, try not to miss Illumination Night in Oak Bluffs. For one night only, the houses in "Cottage City" are lit by Japanese lanterns. The date is never announced far in advance to prevent crowds.

NANTUCKET, MASSACHUSETTS

Jetties Beach, Nantucket

Despite its relative inaccessibility -- it takes nearly two hours to reach by boat -- Nantucket enjoys an international reputation for its muted beauty, stalwart architecture, and serene beaches. Located 30 miles off Cape Cod's coast, and just 14 x 3 miles around, Nantucket seems a brave outpost in the midst of a hungry sea. Each year, little by little, but nonetheless inexorably, the ocean claims a bit more of the island's shore. Its south coast has lost a half mile since colonial times, and some experts believe it will be completely submerged in 600 years.

Undeterred by its ominous fate, visitors continue to flock here. In summer, its population swells from 7,000 to nearly 40,000. So far Nantucket has managed to comfortably accommodate its visitors. But if you plan on coming in season, be sure to make plans well in advance. And think about leaving your car behind. You can get around by bike or use the island's reliable taxi and shuttle services.

Children's Beach
Harbor View Way
Nantucket, MA 02554
508-228-0925

Season: 2nd weekend in June - Labor Day
Hours: 9:00 a.m. - 5:00 p.m.
Parking: Limited roadside, 2-hour limit
Fees: None
Sand: Soft
Crowd: Families
Facilities: Lifeguard, restrooms, snack bar, playground, public telephone, bicycle rack, boat launch
Rules/Regulations: No alcohol, animals, fishing

Directions: From Steamboat Wharf, right onto South Beach Street (if walking, right onto Harbor View Way -- a one way street), right onto Easton Street and right onto Harbor View Way.

Because it's an easy walk from town and the waters are gentle, this beach is a family favorite. Enjoy views of Brant Point from the small rectangle of sand. White buoys separate the swimming area from the harbor. Behind the short sea wall is a grassy park with an old fashioned playground.

Special Notes: For a sandwich, try Henry's Sandwich Shop near Steamboat Wharf at 2 Broad Street. The place is decidedly un-gourmet, but the homemade rolls are delicious. Open 9:00 a.m. to 10:00 p.m. Call 508-228-0123.

Brant Point Beach

Easton Street
Nantucket, MA 02554
508-228-0925

Season: Year-round
Hours: None
Parking: Limited
Fees: None
Sand: Coarse
Crowd: Mixed
Facilities: None
Rules/Regulations: No alcohol, animals, fishing

Directions: From Steamboat Wharf, right onto South Beach Street, right onto Easton Street to the end. The beach is to the left of the lighthouse.

A little further away, but still an easy walk from the wharf, this is a great spot for watching harbor traffic. In fact, because there is so much harbor traffic, not to mention a strong current, it's rarely used for swimming. Still, this narrow strip is a pleasant spot for reading and sunning.

Jetties Beach
Bathing Beach Road
Nantucket, MA 02554
508-228-0925

Season: 2nd weekend in June - Labor Day
Hours: 9:00 a.m. - 5:00 p.m.
Parking: Lot
Fees: None
Sand: Soft
Crowd: Families
Facilities: Lifeguard, restrooms, bath house, restaurant, general store, playground, tennis and volleyball courts, public telephone
Rules/Regulations: No alcohol, animals, fishing

Directions: From Steamboat Wharf, right onto South Beach Street to North Beach Street. Turn right onto Bathing Beach Road and follow to the beach.

This beach gets its name from its many jetties, including the long jetty that marks the harbor opening. Located on the north shore, its calm waters, playground, and swimming lessons make it popular with young families. Umbrellas and chairs, as well as windsurfing, sailboat, and kayak equipment, are available to rent. (Lessons are available too.) Although you could walk from town, Barrett's Tours has bus service on the half hour in summer. Four-wheel drive vehicles aren't allowed between May 31 and September 30.

Special Notes: The annual Sand Castle and Sculpture Day is held on this beach in mid August. Preregistration is required. Call 508-228-1700.

In the whaling era, many of Nantucket's businesses were run by women: Most men spent one to five years at sea -- at a time.

Dionis Beach

Dionis Road
Nantucket, MA 02554
508-228-0925

Season: 2nd weekend in June - Labor Day
Hours: 9:00 a.m. - 5:00 p.m.
Parking: Lot
Fees: None
Sand: Soft
Crowd: Families
Facilities: Lifeguard, restrooms
Rules/Regulations: No alcohol, animals, floats, off-road vehicles

Directions: Take Eel Point Road to Dionis Road.

Located on the sheltered north shore, this beach has dunes, rocks, and unusually calm waters. A boardwalk extends through the grassy dunes, which have been undergoing an extensive preservation project. The water contains a fair amount of seaweed, and a sand bar extends out a good distance.

Madaket Beach

Madaket Road
Nantucket, MA 02554
508-228-0925

Season: 2nd weekend in June - Labor Day
Hours: 9:00 a.m. - 5:00 p.m.
Parking: Lot
Fees: None
Sand: Soft
Crowd: Mixed
Facilities: Lifeguard, restrooms, bath house, fishing, general store, restaurant, bicycle racks
Rules/Regulations: No alcohol, animals, floats; off-road vehicles are permitted within posted areas on Smith's Point

Directions: From Main Street to Madaket Road.

This west-facing beach on the south shore has clean white sand and lovely homes along the dunes. Although the swimming may be a little rough, surfers find conditions just right. The water drops quickly at first, but there is a sand bar. Accessed from town via a 5-mile bike path, this is a great spot to watch the sun set.

Special Notes: Beach vehicle permits are available at the Nantucket Police Station on South Water Street from 8:00 a.m. to 12:00 p.m. Call 508-228-1212.

Cisco Beach
Hummock Pond Road
Nantucket, MA 02554
508-228-0925

Season: 2nd weekend in June - Labor Day
Hours: 9:00 a.m. - 5:00 p.m.
Parking: Lot
Fees: None
Sand: Soft
Crowd: Mixed
Facilities: Lifeguard, fishing
Rules/Regulations: No alcohol, animals, floats

Directions: From town, follow Main Street to Madaket Road, left onto Winn Street, right onto Milk Street and straight onto Hummock Pond Road to the end (about 4 miles from the village).

Perfect for strollers, you can walk for miles on this sandy south shore beach. Experienced surfers and body boarders enjoy the strong waves here. Novices and swimmers should pay attention to the undertow. Unfortunately, no bus service is available.

"This is a popular spot for kite flying because it's so windy."
Mary Hampton, Malden, MA

In 1659, Thomas Mayhew, who previously secured royal-patent and Indian sachem-rights, sold Nantucket island to nine men for £30 plus two beaver hats.

Surfside Beach
Surfside Road
Nantucket, MA 02554
508-228-0925

Season: 2nd weekend in June - Labor Day
Hours: 9:00 a.m. - 5:00 p.m.
Parking: Lot
Fees: None
Sand: Soft
Crowd: Mixed
Facilities: Lifeguards, restrooms, bath house, snack bar, playground, fishing, public telephone
Rules/Regulations: No alcohol, animals, floats; off-road vehicles, which can enter the shore here, are not allowed between 9:00 a.m. and 5:00 p.m.

Directions: From Main Street to Pleasant Street. Turn right onto Atlantic Avenue and pick up Surfside Road (the bike path begins here).

Holding true to its name, this large and popular beach on the south shore has the island's best surfing. Nonsurfers enjoy the sand, dunes, and people watching. The waves are larger here than at 'Sconset, but the current is weaker. Surfside is adjacent to additional beaches, neither of which has facilities. Fishermen's Beach is lovely and wide, perfect for beach games and kite flying; further out, Nobadeer is near the airport. If you're car-less, Barrett's shuttle bus leaves the Federal Street stop on the hour ($3 per round trip). A 2.5-mile bike path goes here too.

"I enjoy the wide expanse of the ocean and huge waves."
Lewis Williams, Boston, MA

Siasconset Beach
(pronounced and known as 'Sconset)
Siasconset Road
Nantucket, MA 02554
508-228-0925

Season: 2nd weekend in June - Labor Day

Hours: 9:00 a.m. - 5:00 p.m.
Parking: Lot, but not nearby
Fees: None
Sand: Soft
Crowd: Families
Facilities: Lifeguard, restrooms
Rules/Regulations: No alcohol, animals, floats

Directions: From the rotary circle outside of town to the end of Milestone Road to Gully Road, to Siasconset Road.

An old-time vacation area, this beautiful, long strip of beach -- the only one on the eastern shore -- is known for its strong undertows and riptides. At high tide the water breaches Sesachacha Pond and leaves behind some interesting sea life for strollers to explore at low tide. If you'd like a hike (about two miles), turn left on the beach and walk beyond Sankaty Light to Quidnet. At 10-minutes past the hour, Barrett's shuttle bus leaves the village for this beach. You can also bike here along a path: It's about 6 miles from town.

"You can watch the airplanes coming to the airport, but I prefer to watch the grasses move on the dunes."
Mary Lou Mislak, Ludlow, MA

Francis Street Beach
aka South Beach
Francis Street
Nantucket, MA 02554
508-228-0925

Season: 2nd weekend in June - Labor Day
Hours: None posted
Parking: None
Fees: None
Sand: Soft
Crowd: Mixed
Facilities: Playground, restrooms, kayak rentals
Rules/Regulations: No alcohol, animals, floats

Directions: From the village, follow Candle Street to Washington Street to the corner of Francis Street and Washington Street Extension.

Although the tip of Francis Street houses a small harbor beach, the main attraction is the kayak rentals. Nature lovers should consider kayaking across the harbor to Coatue. This 1,127-acre undeveloped barrier beach is regulated by the Trustees of Reservations and the National Conservation Foundation.

Special Notes: For information on kayak rentals and guided tours, call Sea Nantucket at 508-228-7499.

RHODE ISLAND

Second Beach, Middletown

Rhode Island may be the smallest state in the nation, but its beaches are second to none. From Newport's fabled shores, where the moneyed set still congregates, to the majestic blufflined beaches of Block Island, Rhode Island's oceanfront is distinctive. In fact, the Nature Conservancy, the world's largest nonprofit organization dedicated to protecting rare plants, animals, and natural communities, recently named Block Island as one of the 12 Last Great Places.

Fred Benson Town Beach
(Pavilion Beach, Crescent Beach)
Corn Neck Road
Block Island, RI 02807
401-466-2611

Season: Mid June - mid September
Hours: None posted
Parking: Lot
Fees: None
Sand: Soft
Crowd: Families
Facilities: Lifeguard (9:00 a.m. - 5:00 p.m. weekdays, til 6:00 p.m. weekends), restrooms, bath house, lockers, snack bar, picnic tables, chair and umbrella rentals

Rules/Regulations: No alcohol, unrestrained animals, fires without permit, sleeping on the beach between 8:00 p.m. and 8:00 a.m., walking on dunes, driving on the beach without permit, mopeds on trails or dirt roads

Directions: From the Old Harbor Wharf on Water Street to Dodge Street. Turn right onto Corn Neck Road.

Just north of the ferry dock in Old Harbor, Fred Benson is part of a broad and sandy 3-mile sweep that holds a total of four beaches and is collectively known as Crescent Beach. (The other three beaches are Clay Head, Mansion, and Scotch.) Because Benson has full facilities and is centrally located, it's popular and becomes crowded during peak periods. The surf is gentle, with no undertow. The beach drops gradually into the water before it drops quite suddenly into deeper reaches, as do all Block Island beaches. At one time this was a state beach, but now the town of New Shoreham -- otherwise known as Block Island -- operates it.

"Nice sand and great for walking... it's the classic curved beach."
Diana Tyler, Hebron, CT

Special Notes: The Old Harbor area is the island's nerve central with shops, restaurants, and a few grand Victorian-era hotels. Ferries arrive here regularly from Point Judith, Providence, and Newport, Rhode Island, and New London, Connecticut. Call 401-783-4613 or 203-442-9553. The ferry from Montauk, New York, arrives in New Harbor. Call 516-668-214 .

Scotch Beach
Corn Neck Road
Block Island, RI 02807
401-466-2982

Season: Year-round
Hours: None posted
Parking: Small lot
Fees: None
Sand: Soft
Crowd: Mixed
Facilities: None

Rules/Regulations: No alcohol, unrestrained animals, fires without permit, sleeping on the beach between 8:00 p.m. and 8:00 a.m., walking on dunes, driving on the beach without permit, mopeds on trails or dirt roads

Directions: From the Old Harbor Wharf on Water Street to Dodge Street. Turn right onto Corn Neck Road. The beach is across from the entrance to Mosquito Beach on Great Salt Pond.

In between Town Beach and Mansion Beach, it shares the same moderate surf and sand. Scotch is allegedly where the locals catch their sun.

Special Notes: Kite flying and beaches seem to go hand-in-hand, and the Block Island Kite Company will help you find the right model. Open daily from 9:00 a.m. to 6:00 p.m., the store sponsors the island's annual Kite Festival held in mid September. Call 401-466-2033.

Mansion Beach

Corn Neck Road
Block Island, RI 02807
401-466-2982

Season: Year-round
Hours: None posted
Parking: Small lot
Fees: None
Sand: Soft
Crowd: Mixed
Facilities: None
Rules/Regulations: No alcohol, unrestrained animals, fires without permit, sleeping on the beach between 8:00 p.m. and 8:00 a.m., walking on dunes, driving on the beach without permit, mopeds on trails or dirt roads

Directions: From the Old Harbor Wharf on Water Street to Dodge Street. Turn right onto Corn Neck Road.

Part of Crescent Beach, this sits near the ruins of the former Searles Mansion. (Only a stone foundation remains of this circa 1888, 18-room "cottage.") The surf is moderate -- greater than at both Scotch and Town Beach. The water is shallow for quite a distance, and there are tidal pools to explore at low tide.

Clay Head Beach
Corn Neck Road
Block Island, RI 02807
401-466-2982

Season: Year-round
Hours: None posted
Parking: Small lot
Fees: None
Sand: Soft, some rocks
Crowd: Mixed
Facilities: None
Rules/Regulations: No alcohol, unrestrained animals, fires without permit, sleeping on the beach between 8:00 p.m. and 8:00 a.m., walking on dunes, driving on the beach without permit, mopeds on trails or dirt roads

Directions: From the Old Harbor Wharf on Water Street to Dodge Street. Turn right onto Corn Neck Road.

The northern-most of the beaches that make up Crescent Beach, this one sits under the Clay Head bluffs. The Clay Head Nature Trail leads from here and meanders along the shore for almost a mile. It ends at Settler's Rock and Sandy Point Beach.

Special Notes: At Littlefield Bee Farm, across from the Clay Head Trail, you can learn how honey and beeswax are processed. Call 401-466-5364.

Sandy Point Beach
Corn Neck Road
Block Island, RI 02807
401-466-2982

Season: Year-round
Hours: None posted
Parking: Lot
Fees: None

Sand: Soft
Crowd: Mixed
Facilities: Restrooms (open summer and "shoulder season")
Rules/Regulations: No alcohol, unrestrained animals, fires without permit, sleeping on the beach between 8:00 p.m. and 8:00 a.m., walking on dunes, driving on the beach without permit, mopeds on trails or dirt roads

Directions: From the Old Harbor Wharf on Water Street to Dodge Street. Turn right onto Corn Neck Road to the end.

This beach is home to North Light, which is the oldest lighthouse setting on the island. The current lighthouse, which is made of granite, is the fourth one to stand on the point. Located at Cow Cove, the beach is within a 28-acre wildlife preserve. One of the preserve's interesting features is Settler's Rock, a monument erected in 1911 on the spot where the first white settlers landed with cattle in 1661. The surf and currents are extremely strong and swimming is ill-advised.

Special Notes: North Light and the National Wildlife Sanctuary are open daily. Call 401-466-3201.

West Beach
West Beach Road
Block Island, RI 02807
401-466-2982

Season: Year-round
Hours: None posted
Parking: Small lot
Fees: None
Sand: Soft with rocks
Crowd: Mixed
Facilities: None
Rules/Regulations: No alcohol, unrestrained animals, fires without permit, sleeping on the beach between 8:00 p.m. and 8:00 a.m., walking on dunes, driving on the beach without permit, mopeds on trails or dirt roads

Directions: From the Old Harbor Wharf on Water Street, to Dodge Street, and right on Corn Neck Road. Watch for a narrow sand road on the left (after Mansion Beach Road on the right) which is West Beach Road.

Designated by the community as "open space," and part of the Wildlife Refuge, this beach has an untouched feel even though it's not far from the town landfill.

Charlestown Beach

Coast Guard Road
Block Island, RI 02807
401-466-2982

Season: Year-round
Hours: None posted
Parking: Small lot
Fees: None
Sand: Soft
Crowd: Mixed
Facilities: None
Rules/Regulations: No alcohol, unrestrained animals, fires without permit, sleeping on the beach between 8:00 p.m. and 8:00 a.m., walking on dunes, driving on the beach without permit, mopeds on trails or dirt roads.

Directions: From the Old Harbor Wharf on Water Street to Dodge Street to Ocean Avenue. Go straight at the intersection to reach West Side Road and watch for Coast Guard Road, a sand road on the right.

Located in Dead Man's Cove on the island's western side, this beach extends to the channel jetty for Great Salt Pond. Because it faces west, it's a perfect place to watch the sunset, or to check out the ferries arriving from Montauk, New York. Fishing is popular off the jetty.

Special Notes: Rustic Rides Farm is the place to go if you'd like to rent a horse for a sunset trot. It also offers pony rides for youngsters. Located on West Side Road, hours are 8:00 a.m. to 7:00 p.m. Reservations are required. Call 401-466-5060.

Black Rock Beach

Cooneymus Road
Block Island, RI 02807
401-466-2982

Season: Year-round
Hours: None posted
Parking: Small Lot
Fees: None
Sand: Soft with stones
Crowd: Mixed
Facilities: Bicycle rack
Rules/Regulations: No alcohol, unrestrained animals, fires without permit, sleeping on the beach between 8:00 p.m. and 8:00 a.m., walking on dunes, driving on the beach without permit, mopeds on trails or dirt roads

Directions: From the Old Harbor Wharf on Old Town Road, left onto Center Road. At Isaacs Corner turn right onto Cooneymus Road. Watch for the narrow sand road on the left near Rodman's Hollow, a wildlife refuge.

Be prepared to walk about a mile on a narrow sand trail, through scrub growth and field, to reach this beach. Surf is rough and there's an undertow, as well as swift tidal currents. Expert surfers might want to give it a try. Sand and stones and some especially large boulders make up the remote shoreline. Low tide exposes the giant black rock, for which the beach is named. Rodman's Hollow and Lewis-Dickens Farm, both wildlife refuges, are managed by the Rhode Island Audubon Society and the Nature Conservancy.

"My husband caught a seventy pound striped bass from the shore here, the largest caught in Rhode Island."
    Kathy Szabo, Block Island, RI

Vail Beach
Mohegan Trail
Block Island, RI 02807
401-466-2982

Season: Year-round
Hours: None posted
Parking: Small lot
Fees: None
Sand: Soft with rocks
Crowd: Mixed
Facilities: None

Rules/Regulations: No alcohol, unrestrained animals, fires without permit, sleeping on the beach between 8:00 p.m. and 8:00 a.m., walking on dunes, driving on the beach without permit, mopeds on trails or dirt roads

Directions: From the Old Harbor Wharf to Spring Street, which becomes Southeast Light Road, then Mohegan Trail. Left at the sharp corner onto a sand road, left at the fork to a small parking area.

Under a canopy of scrub-growth branches, a narrow and overgrown path descends a valley to a remote rock-strewn beach. Listen carefully and you'll hear the rocks turn under the force of the waves. It's no wonder they're worn smooth. Because of the long walk down the obscure path, not many people visit here.

Mohegan Beach
Southeast Light Road
Block Island, RI 02807
401-466-2982

Season: Year-round
Hours: None posted
Parking: Small lot
Fees: None
Sand: Soft with stones
Crowd: Mixed
Facilities: Bicycle rack
Rules/Regulations: No alcohol, unrestrained animals, fires without permit, sleeping on the beach between 8:00 p.m. and 8:00 a.m., walking on dunes, driving on the beach without permit, mopeds on trails or dirt roads

Directions: From the Old Harbor Wharf on Water Street to Spring Street which changes to Southeast Light Road, just beyond the Southeast Lighthouse.

Arguably one of the most majestic beaches in New England, it sits under bluffs that rise 200 feet above the beach. They face the ocean squarely, and appear in mock defiance of the water's strength and erosive powers. A 150-step stairway descends one of the bluffs and leads to this wonderful stretch of soft sand that's strewn with melon-size rocks.

"We enjoy the seclusion and snorkeling in the clean water."
Ron Almeida, Narragansett, RI

Special Notes: The Southeast Lighthouse, a great brick
structure, is the tallest lighthouse in New England. It was
recently moved back 245 feet to protect it from erosion, or
worse, falling into the ocean. Open July through September
from 10:00 a.m. to 4:00 p.m. Call 401-466-5200.

Pebbly Beach
Spring Street
Block Island, RI 02807
401-466-2982

Season: Year-round
Hours: None posted
Parking: Limited
Fees: None
Sand: Soft with stones
Crowd: Mixed
Facilities: None
Rules/Regulations: No alcohol, unrestrained animals, fires
without permit, sleeping on the beach between 8:00 p.m. and
8:00 a.m., walking on dunes, driving on the beach without
permit, mopeds on trails or dirt roads

Directions: From the Old Harbor Wharf, south on Spring
Street near St. Andrew's Church.

A jetty protects this beach, located on the southeast shore.
Popular with beachcombers, you'll find an interesting
selection of stones, shells, and sea glass. It's not a far walk from
the ferry landing in Old Harbor.

Ballard's Beach
Water Street
Block Island, RI 02807
401-466-2982

Season: Year-round
Hours: None posted
Parking: Small lot, municipal parking nearby

Fees: None
Sand: Soft
Crowd: Families
Facilities: Lifeguard
Rules/Regulations: No unrestrained animals, fires without permit, sleeping on the beach between 8:00 p.m. and 8:00 a.m., walking on dunes, driving on the beach without permit, mopeds on trails or dirt roads

Directions: From the Old Harbor Wharf to Water Street, behind Ballard's Restaurant.

Although privately owned, this half-mile long beach is open to the public. It sits behind Ballard's Restaurant (401-466-2231), near the old harbor jetty. The central location, wonderful sand, and great surf make it a popular island beach.

Special Notes: If you've always wanted to try parasailing, your trip to Block Island may be the time. Trips depart daily from Old Harbor Dock near Ballard's. No experience is necessary and there's no age limit. Call Block Island Parasail at 401-466-2474.

Napatree Point Beach and Conservation Area
Watch Hill Road
Westerly (Watch Hill), RI 02891
401-596-7761

Season: Year-round
Hours: None posted
Parking: Limited roadside with 2-hour limit; municipal lot at nearby yacht club, and several small privately-owned lots that typically charge $10 per day
Fees: None
Sand: Soft
Crowd: Mixed
Facilities: None
Rules/Regulations: No swimming, picnics, or containers

Directions: From Route 1A (Beach Street) in Westerly to the end of Watch Hill Road.

Due to the tourist congestion in popular Watch Hill and the very limited parking, it's not easy to enter this unimproved barrier beach. However, if you persevere, you'll find it's worth the effort. This area is privately owned but open to the public. Because it's under such stringent conservation restrictions, it lacks the crowd you'd expect at a spot with such beautiful dunes and sand. Anything but quietly tip-toeing along the water's edge is firmly discouraged. If you walk a half-mile out to the point you'll find the ruins of a fort built during the Spanish American War.

"Very isolated and quiet because of the difficulty in getting here."
Bill Tyler, Hebron, CT

Special Notes: The Chorus of Westerly performs a festive Summer Pops concert in nearby Wilcox Park, usually on the third Saturday in June. People bring blankets and picnics, although there are plenty of food vendors. Come for the afternoon open chorus rehearsal or wait until 6:30 p.m. when local talent (singers, dancers, jazz musicians) perform. The 200-member chorus of children and adults is backed by a 65-piece orchestra. Concerts start at 8:00 p.m. and culminate with a fireworks display to the sound of the 1812 Overture and the Star Spangled Banner. Call 401-596-8663.

Watch Hill Beach
Bay Street
Westerly (Watch Hill), RI 02891
401-596-7761

Season: Mid June - Sunday following Labor Day
Hours: 10:00 a.m. - 6:00 p.m.
Parking: Limited roadside with 2-hour limit; municipal lot at nearby yacht club, and several small privately-owned lots that typically charge $10 per day
Fees: $5 per person, $.75 for children under 12
Sand: Soft
Crowd: Families
Facilities: Restrooms, bath house, snack bars, restaurants and shops nearby
Rules/Regulations: No alcohol, animals, glass, fires, grills

Directions: From Route 1A (Beach Street) in Westerly to the end of Watch Hill Road to Bay Street.

Watch Hill is one of the country's oldest -- and wealthiest -- seaside resort communities and is still thriving. The small but popular, privately operated beach is situated beside the Flying Horse Carousel, before Napatree Point. (The beach admission fee gives you free access to the carousel.) The sand is soft, the water clean, and the surf moderate.

Special Notes: The Flying Horse Carousel was built in 1879. Each horse was hand-carved from a single block of wood and wears a leather saddle. The eyes are agate, and the tails and manes are actual horse hair. When in operation, the horses swing out from a center frame. Only children whose feet can't touch the floor may ride. Open June 15 to Labor Day, 1:00 p.m. to 9:00 p.m. on weekdays, 11:00 a.m. to 9:00 p.m. weekends and holidays.

East Beach
Ocean Drive
Westerly (Watch Hill), RI 02891
401-596-7761

Season: Year-round
Hours: Sunrise - sunset
Parking: Limited roadside with 2-hour limit; municipal lot at nearby yacht club, and several small privately-owned lots that typically charge $10 per day
Fees: None
Sand: Soft
Crowd: Mixed
Facilities: None
Rules/Regulations: No alcohol, animals, glass, fires, grills, coolers

Directions: From Route 1A (Beach Street) in Westerly to Watch Hill Road. At the carousel, turn left onto Ocean Drive to the access pathway located at Larkin and Bluff Roads.

Due to the limited public access, and some unfriendly oceanfront homeowners, not many people frequent this beach. It stretches from the Watch Hill lighthouse to beyond the huge Ocean House Hotel. You are within your rights if you stay below the high water line and only go above it at the access point.

Misquamicut Fire District Beach and Windjammer Family Beach

Atlantic Avenue
Westerly, RI 02891
401-596-7761

Season: Memorial Day - Labor Day
Hours: Sunrise - sunset
Parking: Lot for residents near beach, commercial lots nearby
Fees: None
Sand: Soft
Crowd: Families
Facilities: Lifeguard (usually), restrooms
Rules/Regulations: No alcohol, animals, glass, fires, grills, coolers

Directions: From Route 1A (Beach Street) north of Watch Hill to Winnapaug Road to Atlantic Avenue.

Along the Misquamicut area of Westerly are access points and resident parking. There are faint rumors that more beach will be made available to nonresidents.

Misquamicut State Beach

Atlantic Avenue
Westerly, RI 02891
401-277-2632

Season: Memorial Day - 3rd Saturday in June, weekends only; then daily until Labor Day
Hours: 9:00 a.m. - 6:00 p.m.
Parking: Large lot
Fees: Residents, $4 per car weekdays, $5 weekends, $25 per season; nonresidents, $8 weekdays, $10 weekends, $50 per season; busses $40; private lots nearby $5 weekdays, $8 weekends and holidays
Sand: Super soft
Crowd: Mixed
Facilities: Lifeguards, restrooms, bath house, snack bars, picnic tables, gift shop, public telephones, water bubbler
Rules/Regulations: No alcohol, pets, floats, volleyball; board and body surfing in designated areas only

Directions: From Route 1A (Shore Road) north of Watch Hill to Winnapaug Street, and left onto Atlantic Avenue.

Rhode Island's largest state beach is 7 miles long. It's beautiful and popular. A boardwalk leads from the parking lot to fine sand that drops off gradually into the Atlantic Ocean. Great waves abound. But in August, watch out for red seaweed.

Special Notes: The Water Wizz amusement area has six huge water slides for adults and children. Four are serpentine shaped, two are at a 45-degree angle. Open from Memorial Day to Labor Day (weekends only until mid June) from 10:00 a.m. to 6:30 p.m. Call 401-322-0520. Also, the Atlantic Beach Park and Galaxy Roller Rink open, daily 9:00 a.m. to 8:00 p.m. from Memorial Day to Labor Day. Call 401-322-0504.

"A lot of nightlife and excitement for younger people."
Karen Wilcoxon, Torrington, CT

Dunes Park Beach
Atlantic Avenue
Westerly, RI 02891
401-322-1487

Season: Memorial Day - Labor Day
Hours: 8:30 a.m. - 5:30 p.m.
Parking: Lot
Fees: $10 per car, $5 for seniors Monday - Friday; $2 for walk-ins
Sand: Coarse
Crowd: Families
Facilities: Restrooms, bath house
Rules/Regulations: No alcohol, animals, fires, glass

Directions: From Route 1A to Dunes Corner Road, right onto Atlantic Avenue.

Located just north of the town beach (where parking is available for residents only), this beach is accessed only via the private parking lot. Be sure you're off the beach by 5:30 p.m., because gates lock promptly. The beach has some surf but little undertow and drops gradually into the water.

Quonochontaug Barrier Beach

Dunes Corner Road
Westerly, RI 02891
401-322-1487

Season: Mid June - mid September
Hours: 7:00 a.m. - 6:00 p.m.
Parking: Lots, resident sticker required; other limited roadside parking for nonresidents can be found before the Yacht Club by the chainlink fence
Fees: None
Sand: Soft
Crowd: Mixed
Facilities: Portable restrooms
Rules/Regulations: No camping or fires

Directions: From Route 1A to Dunes Corner Road, along the coast to the Weekapaug Yacht Club.

Be aware that regular security checks are made at the resident lot for illegal (nonresident) cars. Narrow boardwalks carry you over the medium-sized dunes to a secluded beach. Although you can see houses off in the distance, you feel far from civilization.

Blue Shutters Town Beach

aka **Sam Ferretti Memorial**
East Beach Road
Charlestown, RI 02813
401-364-1206

Season: Memorial Day - the 3rd weekend in June, weekends only; then daily to Labor Day
Hours: 9:00 a.m. - 9:00 p.m.
Parking: Lot
Fees: $8 per car weekdays, $10 weekends and holidays, half price after 3:00 p.m.
Sand: Soft
Crowd: Mixed
Facilities: Lifeguard (9:00 a.m. - 5:00 p.m.), restrooms, bath house, snack bar, public telephone, bicycle rack, picnic tables
Rules/Regulations: No alcohol, animals

Directions: From Route 1 to East Beach Road.

The town maintains this short strip. High piles of boulders separate the beach from the parking area and road. Private beaches sit on the periphery. Waves are strong and the drop into the ocean is sharp. Behind the dunes is Ninigret Pond. The sandy area by the pond is a good spot for children to play.

East Beach
in Ninigret Conservation Area
East Beach Road
Charlestown, RI 02813
401-322-0450

Season: Memorial Day - Labor Day
Hours: Sunrise - sunset
Parking: Small lot
Fees: Residents, $4 per car weekdays, $8 weekends; nonresidents, $5 weekdays, $10 weekends
Sand: Soft with stones
Crowd: Mixed
Facilities: Lifeguard (8:00 a.m. - 6:00 p.m.), portable restrooms, camping
Rules/Regulations: No alcohol, animals, fires; four-wheel drive vehicles with permits allowed

Directions: From Route 1 to East Beach Road, past Blue Shutters Town Beach to the end.

This beautiful barrier beach is a carefully managed conservation area with few facilities. (The ruinous 1938 hurricane destroyed the houses that had been here.) Parents of young children should be aware that the beach drops off quickly into the water. At high tide, much of this 3.5- mile long beach is under water, leaving only dune grass. Behind the dunes is Ninigret Pond. Camping is available for self-contained units only. Call 401-322-0450.

"Less pollution, less people, good waves, and very clean."
Gary DeCavage, Prospect, CT

Special Notes: Permits for four-wheel drive vehicles are available at Burlingame State Park. Call 401-322-7337/7994.

👓

Charlestown Town Beach

Charlestown Beach Road
Charlestown, RI 02813
401-364-1208

Season: Memorial Day - the 3rd weekend in June, weekends only; then daily to Labor Day
Hours: 9:00 a.m. - 9:00 p.m.
Parking: Lot
Fees: $6 per car weekdays, $8 weekends and holidays
Sand: Soft, some stones
Crowd: Families
Facilities: Lifeguard (9:00 a.m. - 5:00 p.m.), restrooms, bath house, bicycle rack, volleyball nets
Rules/Regulations: No alcohol, animals

Directions: From Route 1 to Route 1A (Mill Pond Road) to Matunuck School Road, right onto Charlestown Beach Road.

This beach mirrors Ninigret Conservation area in size and shape, but aesthetically it's the reverse -- surrounded by a residential area rather than preserved space. The beach has dunes, high waves, and strong surf.

"On a clear day you see Block Island -- and dream of the island life."
Robert John, Oakland, RI

Special Notes: Explore the extensive neighboring Ninigret Pond and National Wildlife Refuge shores by kayak. Rentals, instruction, and guided tours are available from the Narragansett Kayak Company. Call 401-364-2000.

Charlestown Breachway State Park

Charlestown Breach Road
Charlestown, RI 02813
401-322-8910 or 401-364-7000 (summer)

Season: Memorial Day - Labor Day
Hours: 9:00 a.m. - 6:00 p.m.
Parking: Lot

Fees: Residents, $4 per car weekdays, $5 weekends, $40 per season; nonresidents, $8 weekdays, $10 weekends, $50 per season; busses $40
Sand: Soft
Crowd: Mixed
Facilities: Lifeguard, restrooms, bath house, public telephone, camping
Rules/Regulations: No alcohol, animals, floats

Directions: From Route 1 to Route 1A (Mill Pond Road) to Matunuck School Road, right onto Charlestown Breach Road.

On a clear day Block Island is visible from this relatively undeveloped, peaceful beach within this 62-acre park. The surf is strong and so are the currents around the rock jetty that was built where the breach opened Ninigret Pond to the ocean. Camping is available for self-contained trailers only. Call 401-364-7000.

"Next time we come here we'll bring our boat and explore the pond at the breach."
John Zadroga, Foxboro, MA

Green Hill Beach
Green Hill Road
South Kingstown (Green Hill), RI 02879
401-789-9301

Season: Year-round
Hours: None posted
Parking: None
Fees: None
Sand: Soft
Crowd: Families
Facilities: Portable restrooms
Rules/Regulations: No alcohol, unleashed animals, fires

Directions: From Route 1 to Green Hill Road.

Public access is at the end of the road, but there's no parking. Beachgoers should remember to stay below the high water line on the beach to avoid private property. At high tide this sandy beach drops quickly into the water. Swimmers should also be aware of the strong surf and undertow. Experienced surfers, however, like the power of these waters.

Moonstone Beach
Moonstone Beach Road
South Kingstown, RI 02879
401-364-9124

Season: Year-round
Hours: 1/2 hour before sunrise - 1/2 hour after sunset
Parking: Limited roadside for residents
Fees: None
Sand: Soft
Crowd: Mixed
Facilities: None
Rules/Regulations: No alcohol, unleashed animals, fires, kites, dune trespassing

Directions: From Route 1 to the end of Moonstone Beach Road.

For years this was a clothing-optional beach. That changed when the plight of the piping plover became known and the endangered bird needed extra protection for its nesting territory. Today, the beach is set aside as an "Environmental Education Area" and signs warn, "no sunbathing." The beach is part of the 640-acre Trusthom Pond National Wildlife Refuge and was the unfortunate scene of an oil spill in January 1996.

Roy Carpenter's Beach
Cards Pond Road
South Kingstown (Matunuck), RI 02879
401-789-9070/789-9301

Season: Memorial Day - Labor Day
Hours: 7:00 a.m. - 10:30 p.m.
Parking: Lot
Fees: $7 per car weekdays, $10 weekends (between 9:30 a.m. - 4:00 p.m.)
Sand: Soft
Crowd: Families

Facilities: Lifeguard (9:00 a.m. - 5:00 p.m.), restrooms, snack bar at convenience store, public telephones
Rules/Regulations: No alcohol, ball playing, fires/grills, animals, floats

Directions: From Route 1 to Matunuck Beach Road, right onto Cards Pond Road, and left into the vacation community.

This is a vacation neighborhood, made up of many well-kept small cottages with narrow access lanes running between them. The sandy beach drops gradually into water that has moderate surf and no undertow. Conditions vary with the weather: sometimes the beach has both sand and stones, sometimes mostly sand, and sometimes mostly stone.

Special Notes: Theater lovers should check out Theatre-by-the-Sea, 364 Cards Pond Road, Matunuck, RI 401-782-8587. The stage is inside a restored barn.

South Kingstown Town Beach
Matunuck Beach Road
South Kingstown, RI 02879
401-789-9070/789-9301

Season: Memorial Day- to the 3rd weekend in June, weekends; then daily to Labor Day
Hours: Residents: 6:00 a.m. - 9:00 p.m., nonresidents 7:00 a.m. - 8:00 p.m.
Parking: Lot
Fees: Nonresidents, $10 per car
Sand: Soft
Crowd: Families
Facilities: Lifeguards (9:00 a.m. to 6:00 p.m.), restrooms, showers, pavilion, picnic tables, grills, bicycle rack, volleyball court, playground
Rules/Regulations: No alcohol, animals, open fires, floats (unless beach captain says otherwise), glass

Directions: From Route 1 to Matunuck Beach Road.

This is an unusually well-kept town beach which sports a new raised boardwalk. The spacious gazebos with benches are a nice respite if you want to get out of the sun.

Mary Carpenter's Beach
at Carpenter's Beach Meadow
East Matunuck Road
South Kingstown, RI 02881
401-789-9070/789-9301

Season: Year-round
Hours: Sunrise - sunset
Parking: Lots
Fees: $5 per car
Sand: Soft
Crowd: Mixed
Facilities: Restrooms, bath house with showers; nearby snack bars and shops
Rules/Regulations: No alcohol, animals, fires, ball playing, floats

Directions: From Route 1 to East Matunuck Road, past the town beach.

This stretch is packed with vacation residences and a few shops. The only public access is near the neighboring South Kingstown Town Beach.

Matunuck Point State Beach
aka Deep Hole Beach
Matunuck Beach Road
South Kingstown, RI 02879
401-789-9070/789-9301

Season: Year-round
Hours: 5:00 a.m. - 1/2 hour after sunset
Parking: Small lot
Fees: None
Sand: Coarse
Crowd: Mixed
Facilities: None
Rules/Regulations: No alcohol, animals

Directions: From Route 1 to Matunuck Beach Road.

You may wonder where all the people are if the lot is full, but the beach empty. Look way out beyond the breaking waves and you'll spot the surfers waiting for just the right ride. Surf aficionados claim this beach offers one of the best point and reef surfing breaks on the East Coast.

East Matunuck State Beach
aka **Daniel O'Brien State Beach**
Succotash Road
South Kingstown, RI 02879
401-789-8585/401-783-2058

Season: Memorial Day - Labor Day
Hours: 9:00 a.m. - 6:00 p.m.
Parking: Lot
Fees: Residents, $4 per car weekdays, $5 weekends, $40 per season; nonresidents, $8 weekdays, $10 weekends, $50 per season; busses $40
Sand: Coarse
Crowd: Teens
Facilities: Lifeguard, restrooms, bath house, snack bar, picnic tables, water bubbler, bicycle rack
Rules/Regulations: No alcohol, animals, floats

Directions: From Route 1 to Succotash Road.

This white sandy barrier beach is within a 102-acre park. The beach drops gradually into the strong surf with great waves. Risk-taking surfers will be disappointed that surfing is not allowed. Bathers are treated to a parade of ships as they come and go from the piers at Point Judith Pond, including the ferry to Block Island.

"Nice waves. The surf here is exciting and rough. This is a great beach for adults."
Mary McHale, Coventry, RI

Special Notes: Seafood lovers will want to finish their day at the beach at Cap'n Jacks (706 Succotash Rd.). Just .25 miles from East Matunuck, it's famous for its fish and chips and clambake dinners. No tiny clam shack this, the dining room seats 300! Call 401-789-4556.

Salty Brine State Beach

aka formerly Galilee State Beach
Great Island Road
Narragansett, RI 02882
401-789-3563

Season: Memorial Day - Labor Day
Hours: 9:00 a.m. - 6:00 p.m.
Parking: State beach lot and private lots
Fees: State Lot: residents, $4 per car weekdays, $5 weekends, $25 per season; nonresidents, $8 weekdays, $10 weekends, $50 per season; busses $40; private lots: $5 per car
Sand: Soft
Crowd: Families
Facilities: Lifeguard, restrooms, outside showers, picnic tables, water bubbler
Rules/Regulations: No alcohol, animals, floats, volleyball

Directions: From Route 1 to Route 108 (Point Judith Road). Turn right onto Galilee Escape Road, then left onto Great Island Road.

If it's a bustling atmosphere you're looking for, this beach is it. Located in a section of town known as Galilee, there are many shops and restaurants, as well as docks that harbor cruise boats and ferries. A jetty protects the 150-foot long stretch from the harbor, so the surf is gentle.

Roger Wheeler State Park Beach

aka Sand Hill Cove Beach
Galilee Escape Road
Narragansett (Galilee), RI 02882
401-789-3563

Season: 1st weekend in May - Memorial Day, weekends only; then daily until Labor Day
Hours: 9:00 a.m. - 6:00 p.m.
Parking: Lot
Fees: Residents, $4 per car weekdays, $5 weekends, $25 per season; nonresidents $8 weekdays, $10 weekends, $50 per season; busses $40
Sand: Soft with shells
Crowd: Families

Facilities: Lifeguard, restrooms, bath house, picnic table, bicycle rack, public telephone, viewing machine, old-fashioned tot swings, water bubbler, surf chair

Rules/Regulations: No alcohol, animals, fires, surfing

Directions: From Route 1 to Route 108 (Point Judith Road) to Sand Hill Cove Road on the left just beyond the Galilee Escape Road.

A jetty keeps the waters of this beach calm, so it's a favorite with young families. The beach drops gradually into the water, but it can be a long walk out to deeper water. Swimming lessons are offered. If you want a bit of history, listen to the loudspeaker of the tour boats as they cruise by.

"The waves don't knock you over but you have *fun in them. We also like watching the boats go by."*
George Pike, Warwick, RI

Special Notes: A "Surf Chair," a beach accessible wheelchair, is available here and at Scarborough State Beach. As funding permits, more will be purchased for other state beaches. The chairs are available to use at no cost but arrangements should be made prior to the user's visit.

Scarborough State Beach

Ocean Road
Narragansett, RI 02882
401-789-8013

Season: 1st weekend in May - Memorial Day, weekends only; then daily until Labor Day

Hours: 9:00 a.m. - 6:00 p.m.

Parking: Lot

Fees: Residents, $4 per car weekdays, $5 weekends, $25 per season; nonresidents $8 weekdays, $10 weekends, $50 per season; busses $40

Sand: Soft

Crowd: Mixed

Facilities: Lifeguard (9:00 a.m. - 6:00 p.m.), restrooms, bath house, snack bar, pavilion with observation deck, gift shop, public telephones, water bubbler, surf chair (beach-accessible wheelchair)

Rules/Regulations: No alcohol, animals, fires or grills, glass, floats, volleyball; surfing and body boarding allowed in designated areas

Directions: From Route 1 to Route 108 and left onto Ocean Road.

This beach, perhaps Rhode Island's most popular, now includes the former Lido and Olivo's beaches. The consolidation makes it 3,000 feet long. A stone pavilion and its observation tower were recently restored. Surf is moderate but sometimes there's a strong undertow. The northern end of the beach is mostly rocks.

"I met my husband at this beach."
    Mary Alice Gasboro, Providence, RI

Dodsworth Beach
Ocean Road
Narragansett, RI 02882
401-783-3563

Season: Year-round
Hours: Sunrise - sunset
Parking: None
Fees: None
Sand: Soft
Crowd: Mixed
Facilities: None
Rules/Regulations: No alcohol

Directions: From Route 1 to Route 108, left onto Burnside Avenue to Ocean Road.

This quiet beach reaches out to rocky Black Point, which has been preserved by the state. Most of the people who come here live in the homes across Ocean Road. The dunes are low, covered with grass, and barely provide visual cover from the road.

Because of its nearness, the moon has twice the effect on the ocean's tides as the sun.

Narragansett Town Beach

Ocean Road
Narragansett, RI 02882
401-783-3563

Season: Memorial Day - Labor Day
Hours: 9:00 a.m. - 6:00 p.m.
Parking: Lot
Fees: $5 per car plus $4 for adults, $3 for teens 12-17; no charge for children under 12
Sand: Soft
Crowd: Teens
Facilities: Lifeguard, restrooms, bath house, snack bar
Rules/Regulations: No alcohol, dogs; volleyball allowed in evenings only

Directions: From Route 1 to Route 1A (Ocean Road) across from the entrance to the Canonchet Farm.

In the late 1800s, this area was home to a popular casino. A fire at the turn of the century destroyed all but a pair of architectural towers. These restored towers are now the centerpiece of the Narragansett Towers, a condominium development, which is visible from the beach. The large, crescent-shaped stretch is a favorite, and the lots fill up quickly. The waves, which come in at an angle, are sizable but gentle, and the beach drops off gradually. A good spot for the novice surfer or body boarder. On Wednesdays, pros give free lessons at 12:00 p.m. For details, call Watershed Sports at 401-789-1954. Lockers ($150/$250 per season resident and nonresident) and changing rooms ($350/$550) can be rented on a seasonal basis. For information, call the Narragansett Parks and Recreation Department at 401-789-1044.

Special Notes: The New England Morey Boogie Challenge (a body board competition) is held in early July. Call 401-789-3399. For surf conditions in the Narragansett Bay area, call 401-789-1954.

North Kingstown Town Beach

Beach Street
North Kingstown, RI 02852
401-294-3331

Season: Memorial Day - Labor Day
Hours: 9:00 a.m. - 9:00 p.m.
Parking: Limited, residents only
Fees: None
Sand: Coarse
Crowd: Families
Facilities: Lifeguard (9:00 a.m. - 5:00 p.m.), restrooms, snack bar, shaded picnic tables, grills, playground, bicycle rack, containers for recycling aluminum
Rules/Regulations: No alcohol, animals, balls, boating, snorkels/face masks/scuba gear

Directions: From Route 1 to Route 1A to Beach Street.

This narrow town beach is a short walk from the little known but quaint Wickford historic district, a part of North Kingstown that has many well-preserved 18th and 19th century homes. While the beach is for residents, anyone can walk in. The sand is somewhat gravelley; a tree-shaded lawn sits behind, and might be a better spot to spread your blanket. Views of the State Marine Base are to the north.

Mackerel Cove Beach and Jamestown Town Beach
Beavertail Road
Jamestown, RI 02835
401-423-7260

Season: Mid June - Labor Day
Hours: 9:00 a.m. - 5:00 p.m.
Parking: Lot
Fees: $10 per car
Sand: Coarse
Crowd: Families
Facilities: Lifeguard (10:00 a.m. - 5:00 p.m.), restrooms, snack vendors
Rules/Regulations: No alcohol, dogs, boats, fires, ball playing, floats, snorkel/face masks/scuba gear
Directions: From Route 138 in Jamestown, go south on North Road to Beavertail Road.

The only public swimming beach in Jamestown sits along this narrow strip of land that faces scenic Mackerel Cove. Dutch

Island Harbor is to the rear. The gentle waves break evenly along the nearly mile-long beach. Due to its location at the end of a long, thin bay, litter and algae in the water is sometimes a problem.

Special Notes: If the kids get tired of the surf and sand, head to the large wooden playground next to the Jamestown public library. Open daily 7:00 a.m. to 9:00 p.m.

Beavertail State Park

Beavertail Road
Jamestown, RI 02835
401-884-2010/277-2632

Season: Year-round
Hours: Sunrise - sunset
Parking: Lots
Fees: None
Sand: Soft
Crowd: Mixed
Facilities: Portable restrooms
Rules/Regulations: No alcohol

Directions: From Route 138 in Jamestown, south on North Road to the end of Beavertail Road.

Although swimming isn't encouraged here, this point has an exciting rocky coastline to explore. The park consists of 153 acres around the Beavertail Lighthouse, now a museum. The coast has seaweed-covered ledges, strong surf, and tiny sandy coves. The scene -- waves crashing on the rocks, boats cruising the bay, and fishermen casting from the scenic overlooks – is mesmerizing. The Beavertail Lighthouse Museum is open daily from 10:00 a.m. to 4:00 p.m. between June 22 and Labor Day, and 12:00 p.m. to 3:00 p.m., after Memorial Day and from Labor Day to Columbus Day. Donations are appreciated. Call 401-423-3270.

Special Notes: The Fool's Rules Regatta is held in mid August. This annual "sailboat" race is one in which true sailboats are not allowed. Participants must construct their "vessels" at the park, between 9:00 a.m. and 11:00 a.m. on race day. Call 401-423-1492.

Sandy Point Beach

Ives Road
Warwick, RI 02887
401-738-2000, ext. 6806

Season: Year-round
Hours: Sunrise - sunset
Parking: Limited roadside
Fees: None
Sand: Coarse
Crowd: Mixed
Facilities: None
Rules/Regulations: No alcohol

Directions: From Route 1, past Goddard Memorial State Park to the end of Ives Road.

A quiet neighborhood beach, it's got lovely open views toward Warwick Neck, Narragansett Bay, and the Narragansett Bay Estuarine Sanctuary on Prudence Island. People fish from the jetty that faces toward the Warwick Neck Lighthouse.

Goddard State Park

Ives Road
Warwick, RI 02887
401-884-9620 (beach)/884-2010 (park)

Season: Year-round
Hours: 6:00 a.m. - 11:00 p.m.
Parking: Lot
Fees: Residents, $2 per car, $1 for seniors 65 and over; nonresidents, $4 per car, $2 for seniors 65 and over
Sand: Soft
Crowd: Families
Facilities: Lifeguards (9:00 a.m. - 6:00 p.m.), restrooms, showers, snack bar, picnic tables, benches, boat ramp, fishing, water bubbler
Rules/Regulations: No alcohol, pets, floats, volleyball

Directions: From Route 1 to Ives Road.

All of Goddard Park is beautiful and well-groomed. The beach reaches from Sally Rock to Long Point on Greenwich Bay. Unfortunately, water quality is questionable after periods of heavy rain. But Goddard's 489 acres offer more activities than just swimming. Facilities include a 9-hole golf course, walking paths, horseback riding trails (18 miles), and a carousel which has been renovated for use as a performing arts center. Extra fees are imposed to use some facilities -- even the picnic tables. There are 384 of them: They must be reserved and the charge is $2.

Warwick City Park Beach

Asylum Road
Warwick, RI 02887
401-738-2000, ext. 6806

Season: Memorial Day - mid June, weekends only; then daily to Labor Day
Hours: 7:00 a.m. - 9:00 p.m.
Parking: Lot
Fees: None
Sand: Soft
Crowd: Families
Facilities: Lifeguard (10:00 a.m. - 6:00 p.m.), restrooms, picnic tables, playground, bicycle paths and rack, ball fields (by permit)
Rules/Regulations: No alcohol, unrestrained animals, open fires, boat launching

Directions: From I-95, across Route 1 on Route 117 (Warwick Avenue) to Buttonwoods Avenue (at Almacs). Turn left onto Asylum Road to City Park's entranceway.

There isn't much sand at this town beach, and sometimes there are high amounts of algae in the shallow water. But the view of Greenwich Bay is pleasant. At low tide you can walk way, way out. This and other Warwick beaches are becoming better known to nonresidents and at this writing city officials were considering establishing entrance fees.

Special Notes: Rocky Point Park, one of the largest amusement areas in New England, closed its doors at the end of 1995 -- after 155 years in business. Many will miss the park's

Rocky Point Shore Dinner Hall, known as "the world's largest dinning room." It was famous for clam cakes and chowder.

Oakland Beach
Oakland Beach Avenue
Warwick, RI 02887
401-738-2000, ext. 6806

Season: Memorial Day - mid June, weekends only; then daily to Labor Day
Hours: 7:00 a.m. - 9:00 p.m.
Parking: Lot
Fees: None
Sand: Coarse
Crowd: Families
Facilities: Lifeguard (10:00 a.m. - 6:00 p.m.), restrooms, fishing, ball park, public telephone; nearby restaurant and snack bar
Rules/Regulations: No alcohol, unrestrained animals, open fires, boat launching

Directions: From I-95, cross Route 1 onto Route 117 (West Shore Road) to Oakland Beach Avenue.

There are several distinct beach areas here, separated by jetties and a stone sea wall. The two primary beaches sit on either side of the long parking lot. The beach to your right is a walk, but is larger than the one at the far left. Both have inlets from which small boats sail. In the distance you can see the bridges for Jamestown and Newport. Years back, folks from Providence used to flock here by trolley.

Special Notes: The Oakland Beach Festival is held here in mid August. It includes music, crafts, and a flea market. Call 401-737-2904.

Connimicut Beach
West Point Road
Warwick, RI 02887
401-738-2000, ext. 6806

Season: Memorial Day - mid June, weekends only; then daily to Labor Day
Hours: 7:00 a.m. - 9:00 p.m.
Parking: Lot
Fees: None
Sand: Coarse with shells
Crowd: Mixed
Facilities: Lifeguard (10:00 a.m. - 6:00 p.m.), portable restrooms, snack truck, playground, boat launch
Rules/Regulations: No alcohol, unrestrained animals, open fires, boat launching

Directions: From Route 117 to Bush Avenue. Left onto Symonds Avenue, and right onto West Point Road to the end.

Water shoes are as important as your beach chair and bathing suit when you come here. The barnacles on the rocks in the water are quite sharp. Despite this, Connimicut is a lovely long, narrow beach. At the far end of the point is a grassy park with views of a small lighthouse, Prudence Island, and the Jamestown Bridge. If you look to the north, you can see the State House dome.

Barrington Town Beach
Bay Road
Barrington, RI 02806
401-247-1925

Season: First weekend of summer - Labor Day
Hours: Sunrise - 9:00 p.m.
Parking: Lot for residents only
Fees: None
Sand: Coarse with shells
Crowd: Mixed
Facilities: Lifeguard, restrooms
Rules/Regulations: No alcohol, animals

Directions: From Route 114 to Rumstick Road at the sharp bend in the road. Turn right at the stop sign onto Nayatt Road, then left onto Bay Road.

While the parking lot is for residents only, walkers and bicyclists are welcome. The beach, in a quiet suburban neighborhood, is long and has wide open ocean views. Because of its location -- in a curve of the upper bay -- the water is generally calm. But swimmers should be aware that water quality may be poor after heavy storms.

Special Notes: If you can't bear the thought of cooking when you get home, try Wallis Seafood. It offers oven-ready seafood dinners, prepared from freshly caught fish and lobster. The market is conveniently located on Maple Avenue (at lights), off Route 114. Call 401-245-6666. Closed Mondays.

Bristol Town Beach
Route 114
Bristol, RI 02809
401-253-1611/253-7000 ext. 54

Season: Memorial Day until the 3rd Monday in June, weekends only; daily until mid August; then weekends only again from mid August to Labor Day
Hours: 8:00 a.m. - 10:00 p.m.
Parking: Lot
Fees: Residents, $2 per car weekdays, $3 weekends, nonresidents; $3 weekdays, $5 weekends
Sand: Coarse with shells
Crowd: Families
Facilities: Lifeguards (10:00 a.m. - 5:00 p.m.), restrooms, snack bar, tennis and basketball courts, bicycle rack, benches, water bubbler
Rules/Regulations: No alcohol, unleashed dogs, clamming, surfing within the marked swim area, card playing/gambling, floats, horseback riding, fires

Directions: From Route 114 to the Colt State Park entrance road.

The town recreation area and beach is located just outside Colt State Park. Be sure to bring beach shoes to protect your feet from the rocks and shells on the beach and in the water. However, this is a nice place to spread a blanket and enjoy the sun or go beachcombing. The town has tried to bring in some softer sand, and hopefully this will continue. But unfortunately, the currents seem to be washing the new sand away.

Special Notes: The ferry to Prudence Island leaves from the Church Street wharf in Bristol. Prudence Island is somewhat smaller than Jamestown but much less developed. South Prudence Bay Island Park is on the southern end and Narragansett Bay Estuarine Sanctuary is to the north. It's a fun place to explore by bicycle, and there are several undeveloped beaches. For ferry information, call 401-253-9808.

Island Park Town Beach and Teddy's State Beach

Park Avenue
Portsmouth, RI 02871
401-683-3255

Season: Year-round
Hours: Sunrise - sunset
Parking: Limited
Fees: None
Sand: Soft
Crowd: Mixed
Facilities: None
Rules/Regulations: No alcohol, animals

Directions: From Route 114 to Boyd's Lane, cross routes 24 and 138 and turn onto Park Avenue.

Two beaches sit at this small area at the end of the Sakonnet River. The surf is gentle with no undertow, and the beaches drop off gradually into the water. From here you can watch the boating activity at Stone Bridge Marina and look out to Gould Island. At one time the state staffed and groomed Teddy's Beach. Reductions in funding moved their focus elsewhere, a change that disappointed many area residents.

Special Notes: Flo's Drive-In has been here for ages. It's a simple clam shack with a reputation for great fried clams and a saltwater view. (You sit outside on picnic tables.) Flo's has a new, second location with an expanded menu across from First Beach in Middletown. No phone.

Block Island was created 400 centuries ago by the same glacier that formed Martha's Vineyard and Nantucket.

Sandy Point Beach

Sandy Point Road
Portsmouth, RI 02871
401-683-3255

Season: Memorial Day - Labor Day
Hours: 9:00 a.m. - 9:00 p.m.
Parking: Lot
Fees: Nonresidents, $5 weekdays, $10 weekends
Sand: Coarse
Crowd: Families
Facilities: Lifeguards (9:00 a.m. - 5:00 p.m.), restrooms, indoor and outdoor showers, bicycle rack, picnic tables, grills, boat launch
Rules/Regulations: No alcohol, animals, cooking on the beach, floats

Directions: From Route 138 to Sandy Point Road in East Portsmouth.

The beach drops gently from its pebbly shoreline into gentle surf along the Sakonnet River. Because there is no undertow, families enjoy it. Also, beginner wind surfers find this is a great place to pick up some skill. The beach looks across to Fogland Point in Tiverton. The fragile low dunes are fenced off to help them rebuild.

"It's quiet and rarely crowded; a family beach."
Joyce Mitchell, Portsmouth, NH

Special Notes: With 80 sculptured trees and shrubs, Green Animals Topiary Gardens will change forever your concept of landscape. Plan for at least an hour's visit to the grounds, which are open daily between May 1 and October 31 from 10:00 a.m. to 5:00 p.m. Call 401-847-1000.

Kings Park Beach

Wellington Avenue
Newport, RI 02840
401-849-8098

Season: Memorial Day - Labor Day
Hours: 9:30 a.m. - 5:30 p.m.

Parking: Roadside
Fees: None
Sand: Coarse
Crowd: Families
Facilities: Lifeguard, restrooms, picnic tables, boat launch, playground, carousel, snack bar
Rules/Regulations: No alcohol

Directions: From Route 138 to Route 238 (Farewell Street) to Thames Street, continuing straight at the intersection with West Memorial Boulevard in Newport Harbor onto (lower) Thames Street. Turn right onto Wellington Avenue to the beach.

If you hanker to leave the city streets behind for a while, this park may not suit you. Located in busy, tourist (dare we say, infested) downtown Newport, it's a hectic place. Water quality may be a problem, especially after heavy rainstorms. The slim beach area has a mixture of sand and stones.

Fort Adams State Park

Harrison Avenue
Newport, RI 02840
401-849-8098

Season: Memorial Day - Labor Day
Hours: 6:00 a.m. - 11:00 p.m.
Parking: Lot
Fees: Residents, $4 per car weekdays, $5 weekends, $25 per season; nonresidents, $8 weekdays, $10 weekends, $50 per season; busses $40
Sand: Soft
Crowd: Families
Facilities: Lifeguard (10:00 a.m. - 6:00 p.m.), restrooms, outdoor showers, snack bar, picnic tables, grills, boat launch, fishing piers, soccer and rugby fields, water bubbler
Rules/Regulations: No alcohol, animals, floats

Directions: Same as Kings Park: At the end of Wellington Avenue, left onto Halidon Avenue, then right onto Harrison Avenue to just beyond Hammersmith Road.

You'll feel that you've left busy Newport behind as you enter this 21-acre state park -- until you spot the harbor -- there are more boats than swimmers. The parking lot is a hike from the beach but there's a drop-off area. This small, sandy, man-made beach sits within a rocky cove with gentle water. The fort, built for the War of 1812, is open to the public for guided tours. Sailing lessons and sailboat rentals, as well as harbor tours, are available. Call 401-849-8385.

Special Notes: Guided tours of many Newport mansions are also available. If you decide to visit only one, make sure it's The Breakers on Ochre Point Avenue (401/847-1000). It took only two years to construct this 70-room palace. Among its most impressive rooms is the grand salon with its gold-inlaid ceilings: It was completely constructed in France, and then dismantled and rebuilt by the same French artisans in Newport.

Brenton Point State Park

Ocean Avenue
Newport, RI 02840
401-847-2400/277-2632

Season: Memorial Day - Labor Day
Hours: 6:00 a.m. - 11:00 p.m.
Parking: Lots
Fees: None
Sand: Soft with rocks
Crowd: Mixed
Facilities: Restrooms, benches, water bubbler
Rules/Regulations: No alcohol

Directions: Same as for Fort Adams: Continue onto Harrison Avenue, turn right onto Ridge Road to Ocean Avenue.

This is not a swimming beach, but a beautiful rocky coastline park. It's a wonderful place to walk, take in the salty air, and admire the power of the ocean. Think about bringing a kite; there's a large grassy lawn -- perfect for launching into flight.

Special Notes: Kayak, sailboat, and other boat rentals, as well as parasail tours, are available from Adventure Sports, 2 Bowen's Landing, Newport, RI 02840. Call 401-849-4820.

Gooseberry Beach

Ocean Avenue
Newport, RI 02840
401-849-5344

Season: Memorial Day - Labor Day
Hours: 9:00 a.m. - 6:00 p.m.
Parking: Small lot
Fees: $12 per car, $1 per bicycle, $3 per motorcycle (for both residents and nonresidents), $2 for nonresident walk-ins
Sand: Soft
Crowd: Mixed
Facilities: Lifeguards, portable restrooms, outdoor shower, snack bar, bicycle rack, lockers
Rules/Regulations: No alcohol, animals, balls, floats

Directions: Either continue along Ocean Avenue from Brenton Point State Park or arrive on Ocean Avenue by turning onto Bellevue Avenue from Route 138A.

This small private beach admits the public. The sand, banked by small dunes, drops gently into a compact bay with interesting rock ledges throughout.

Reject Beach

aka **People's Beach at Bailey**
Ocean Avenue
Newport, RI 02840
401-849-8098

Season: Year-round
Hours: None posted
Parking: None
Fees: None
Sand: Soft
Crowd: Mixed
Facilities: None
Rules/Regulations: No alcohol, animals, balls, floats

Directions: Either continue along Ocean Avenue from Brenton Point State Park or arrive on Ocean Avenue by turning onto Bellevue Avenue from Route 138A.

The unknown public side of Bailey Beach, better known as the exclusive Sprouting Rock Beach Association (SRBA), is on the eastern end of the Cliff Walk. Once thought to be private, in the 1950s it was learned that a portion of the beach had been actually set aside for public use. For years, only the locals knew about it. Now you do. If you're staying in town, you can bike or walk here since there's no parking.

Special Notes: If you want to stretch your legs, walk at least some of the 3-mile Cliff Walk, which takes you past the back lawns of Newport's grandest seaside mansions, including The Breakers. You can reach it from many of the side roads that run from famous Bellevue Avenue.

First Beach
aka **Easton's Beach**
Newport, RI 02840
401-486-9600

Season: 3rd weekend in May - June 15, weekends only; then daily until Labor Day
Hours: 9:00 a.m. - 6:00 p.m.
Parking: Lot and 3-hour roadside parking
Fees: $10 per car weekdays, $15 weekends
Sand: Soft
Crowd: Families
Facilities: Lifeguard, restrooms, bath house, snack bars, picnic tables, pavilion, public telephones, miniature golf, kiddie amusements, including an enclosed carousel
Rules/Regulations: No alcohol, jet skis

Directions: From Route 138 to Route 138A, Memorial Boulevard, right onto the Newport/Middletown line near Easton's Pond.

Three beaches in this area are named First, Second, and Third. First is almost a mile long and is near the beginning of the Cliff Walk, which takes you behind many of Newport's famous "cottages." It has fine gray sand in a large bay-like area. Areas are set aside for surfing and body boarding. Waves break both left and right a distance from the beach. The only drawback is that seaweed can be a problem in late summer.

Special Notes: Special events on Tuesday evenings include concerts at 6:30 p.m. On Thursday evening there are children's shows.

Atlantic Beach

Purgatory Road
Middletown, RI 02840
401-847-1993

Season: Memorial Day - Labor Day
Hours: 10:00 a.m. - 4:00 p.m.
Parking: Lot
Fees: $5 per car
Sand: Soft
Crowd: Mixed
Facilities: Lifeguard, restrooms, restaurant, snack bar
Rules/Regulations: No alcohol, jet skis, animals during the day

Directions: Route 138 to Route 138A (Aquidneck Avenue) to Purgatory Road.

This small, sandy beach is actually an extension of Newport's First Beach and it's got the same great sand and waves. It's managed by the Atlantic Beach Club.

Second Beach

aka **Sachuest Beach**
Sachuest Point Road
Middletown, RI 02840
401-847-1993

Season: Memorial Day - Labor Day
Hours: 8:00 a.m. - 8:00 p.m.
Parking: Lots, gates lock at 8:00 p.m.
Fees: $10 per car weekdays, $15 per car weekends and holidays
Sand: Soft
Crowd: Mixed
Facilities: Lifeguard (8:00 a.m. - 6:00 p.m.), restrooms and portable toilets, bath house, snack bar, picnic tables, pavilion, fishing, bicycle rack

Rules/Regulations: No alcohol, animals during the day, jet skis, fires or grills, surfing except for designated areas

Directions: From Route 138 to Route 138A. At the intersection with Memorial Boulevard and Purgatory Road, turn left onto Purgatory Road to Hanging Rock Road, then straight onto Sachuest Point Road.

This 1.5-mile long beach has some small dunes, but perhaps its most interesting feature is the rock ledge found on the western end. The sand is soft and gray, and the waves are good for surfing. (To get the latest on surf conditions, call 401-846-4485.) Purgatory Chasm, at the western end, is a narrow split in the rock ledges that drops 160 feet and has a scenic overlook. At the other end is Sachuest Point Park, a 242-acre wildlife preserve where visitors are welcome daily from sunrise to sunset. Call 401-364-9124 to learn about special programming.

"I come to watch my daughter surf."
　　　　Helen O'Neill, Fort Myers, FL

Third, Navy, and Peabody Beaches
Third Beach Road
Middletown, RI 02878
401-847-1993

Season: Memorial Day - Labor Day
Hours: 8:00 a.m. - 6:00 p.m.
Parking: Lots
Fees: $10 per car weekdays, $15 weekends and holidays; Peabody parking is $15 per car every day
Sand: Soft
Crowd: Families
Facilities: Varies by section. Includes restrooms, portable toilets, bath houses, boat ramp and picnic tables to far right, snack bar to far left at Peabody Beach
Rules/Regulations: No alcohol, animals during the day, jet skis, fires or grills, surfing except for designated areas

Directions: From Route 138 to Route 138A. At the intersection with Memorial Boulevard and Purgatory Road, turn left onto Purgatory Road to Hanging Rock Road, then straight onto Sachuest Point Road. Turn left onto Third Beach Road.

Third Beach comprises three sections: on the right, adjacent to the Sachuest Point National Wildlife Refuge, is the town beach and boat launch. Navy, also managed by the town, sits in the middle, and Peabody, privately operated, is to the left. The water in this bay-like beach is calm, the sand is soft and gray, and the view of small boats on the Sakonnet River and the Little Compton coastline is scenic. Markers delineate the swimming area. During the summer of 1995, a Blacktail Gull from Asia visited here: This bird had never been spotted before on the Eastern U.S. Coast, so its arrival brought curious birders from afar.

"Not many tourists come here."
Eban Horton, Middletown, RI

Special Notes: The Newport Equestrian Center at 287 Third Beach Road offers shore and trail rides. Call for reservations, 401-848-5440/847-7022.

Grinnell's Beach
Route 177
Tiverton, RI 02878
401-625-6786

Season: Memorial Day - Labor Day
Hours: Sunrise - 1/2 hour after sunset
Parking: Lot; gate closes 1/2 hour after sunset
Fees: $5 per car
Sand: Coarse
Crowd: Teens
Facilities: Lifeguards (9:00 a.m. - 4:00 p.m.), restrooms, outside showers, playground, picnic tables, surf fishing, public telephone
Rules/Regulations: No alcohol, unleashed dogs, open fires, floats

Directions: Off Route 177, near the junction of Route 138.

The small 150-foot sandy beach leads gradually into gentle, but sometimes murky, water. However, it must be healthy enough: The Rhode Island Department of Environmental

Management has transplanted thousands of pounds of quahogs offshore so they might purify themselves in the clean waters. Unfortunately the view is marred by a nearby gas station and old bridge. The Red Cross offers swimming lessons here.

Special Notes: Mykonos Restaurant, across the street, has great Greek food, in addition to sandwiches and hamburgers. Call 401-625-5780.

Sapowet Beach
Neck Road
Tiverton, RI 02878
401-625-6786

Season: Memorial Day - Labor Day
Hours: Sunrise - sunset
Parking: Lot
Fees: None
Sand: Soft
Crowd: Mixed
Facilities: None
Rules/Regulations: No alcohol, unleashed dogs

Directions: From Route 77 (Main Road) to Sapowet Avenue, left onto Neck Road.

People come to this primitive beach primarily to fish, but also to enjoy the water, especially at low tide. It is at the edge of the Sapowet Management area, which is protected marshland.

Fogland Beach
Fogland Point
Tiverton, RI 02878
401-625-6786

Season: Memorial Day - Labor Day
Hours: Sunrise - 1/2 hour after sunset
Parking: Lot
Fees: $5 per car
Sand: Soft with stones
Crowd: Families
Facilities: Lifeguards, portable restrooms, swings, picnic tables

Rules/Regulations: No alcohol, unleashed animals, open fires, floats
Directions: From Route 77 onto Fogland Road to Fogland Point.

This beach sits primarily on the southern side of the Fogland Peninsula. It looks directly across to Sandy Point Beach in Portsmouth. A nice family beach, you'll enjoy watching windsurfers who are out in force if conditions are right. (Note to the windsurfers: The southern exposure is more challenging.)

Special Notes: For interesting sandwiches and gourmet food, head to the Provender bakery and deli on Route 77. Call 401-624-8084.

👓 Little Compton Town Beach
aka **South Shore Beach**
South Shore Road
Little Compton, RI 02837
401-635-8529/635-4400

Season: Weekend following Memorial Day - Labor Day
Hours: Sunrise - sunset
Parking: Lot
Fees: Nonresidents, $9 per car weekdays, $13 weekends and holidays
Sand: Soft with stones and shells
Crowd: Families
Facilities: Lifeguards (9:00 a.m. - 5:00 p.m.), portable restrooms
Rules/Regulations: No alcohol, animals, open fires, glass, jet skis, unsupervised children under age 12; surfing in designated areas only

Directions: From Route 77 onto Commons Road. Right at Wilber General Merchandise, left at the end of Brownell Road. After approximately .5 miles, turn right, just before the left-hand bend in the road (no sign). The beach is at the end of South Shore Road.

Although not the easiest beach to find, it's well worth the effort. On the way there you'll drive by handsome homes, many antiques, that give you the feeling you've stepped back in time. Situated on the east side of Little Compton, the beach is long, narrow, and sandy. This beach is an amazing example of how the shore recovers from storm damage: Hurricane Bob deposited a slope of fist-sized rocks and took away all the sand. Now, several years later, the sand has returned.

Special Notes: Can you be in Little Compton without having a cone at Gray's Ice Cream? Open from 6:30 a.m. to 10:00 p.m., it's located at the intersection of routes 77 and 179 in Tiverton. Call 401-624-4500.

Goosewing Beach
South Shore Road
Little Compton, RI 02837
401-635-4400

Season: Year-round
Hours: Sunrise - sunset
Parking: At Little Compton Town Beach
Fees: Nonresidents, $9 per car weekdays, $13 weekends and holidays
Sand: Soft with stones and shells
Crowd: Mixed
Facilities: None
Rules/Regulations: No alcohol, animals, open fires, glass, jet skis, children under age 12

Directions: From Route 77 onto Commons Road. Right at Wilber General Merchandise, left at the end of Brownell Road. After approximately .5 mile, turn right, just before the left-hand bend in the road (no sign). The beach is at the end of South Shore Road.

For years this was a private beach. Then it was managed by the Nature Conservancy and now by the town. Little Compton Beach and Goosewing Beach, both barrier beaches, sit side-by-side, sharing the same bay near Quick Sand Pond on Rhode Island Sound. While it's not difficult to reach one beach from the other -- you just cross a small, quiet inlet -- there is talk about building a bridge. Many locals consider this rural gem their favorite "secret" beach.

Special Notes: Gray is a long-time name here. Gray's Store was built in 1788 and is one of the country's oldest continuously operating stores. For a sampling of rural New England, this is a must visit. The store boasts its original soda fountain, aged cheddar cheese, penny candy, and more. Call 401-635-4566.

CONNECTICUT

Hammonasset Beach State Park, Madison

When most New Englanders think about the beach, Connecticut isn't the first state that comes to mind. Most of Connecticut's beaches aren't tourist attractions, and the residents like it that way. Witness the town of Greenwich's strict policy: Nonresidents -- unless they're accompanied by a local -- can't even walk or bike onto a Greenwich beach, let alone find parking.

That said, such tony suburbs as Darien and Westport do open up their beaches to the public -- and even allow nonresidents to park in lots. In addition, Connecticut has some impressive state parks. Most residents agree that among the best is Rocky Neck. This 710-acre park has a picturesque mile-long beach and an enclosed picnic shelter with more than 800 tables.

Byram Park Beach
Rich Avenue
Greenwich, CT 06831
203-622-7817

Season: Memorial Day - Labor Day
Hours: 10:00 a.m. - 6:00 p.m. (facilities); park closes 20 minutes before sunset
Parking: Lot for residents only

Fees: Residents' guests pay $3 on weekdays, $5 on weekends and holidays; no nonresident walk-ins
Sand: Soft with rocks and shells
Crowd: Mixed
Facilities: Lifeguard, restrooms, bath house, snack bar, playground, playing fields, picnic tables, grills, swimming pool, bicycle rack, boat launch
Rules/Regulations: No alcohol, animals, feeding of wildlife

Directions: From I-95, exit 2, to Delavan Avenue. At the lights, continue straight onto Rich Avenue. The entrance is on the right.

Depending on your perspective, New England's public beaches begin or end here. The region's southern-most beaches are located in exclusive communities and are incredibly congested -- a stark contrast to their northern counterparts. Residents are grateful for, and protective of, this park's natural setting, with woods and hills and a limited portion of shoreline. Though the community has had legal challenges to its rules excluding nonresidents from access to the town beaches -- even on foot -- as of this writing the restrictive policy continues. There are two beach areas at this park. They are separated by a neatly constructed stone wall and jetty. Jellyfish, rockweed, horseshoe crabs, and bivalves (mollusks) are not uncommon in these waters. As with all beaches within Long Island Sound, the warm water is calm and has no surf.

Greenwich Point Beach
Tod's Driftway
Greenwich, CT 06870
203-622-7817

Season: Memorial Day - Labor Day
Hours: 10:00 a.m. - 6:00 p.m. (facilities); park closes 20 minutes after sunset
Parking: Lot for residents only
Fees: Residents' guests pay $3 on weekdays, $5 on weekends; no nonresident walk-ins
Sand: Soft
Crowd: Mixed
Facilities: Lifeguard, restrooms, bath house, picnic area, snack bar, overnight camping
Rules/Regulations: No alcohol, animals

Directions: From I-95, exit 5, to Route 1 N (Putnam Avenue). Right at traffic lights (note sign directing toward Civic Center), through the village area, onto Sound Beach Avenue. At the end, turn right onto Shore Road, then straight onto Tod's Driftway.

The drive out to this barrier beach through impressive Old Greenwich neighborhoods is a pleasure. But unless you're a resident or traveling with a resident, it's a wasted journey, as the gatekeepers do their job well. The park is surrounded by water on all sides and also has an area of woods and marshland.

West Beach

Shippan Avenue
Stamford, CT 06903
203-977-4692

Season: Memorial Day - Labor Day
Hours: Sunrise - 10:00 p.m.
Parking: Lot, resident sticker required
Fees: None
Sand: Coarse with shells
Crowd: Mixed
Facilities: Lifeguard, restrooms, snack bar, boat ramp, playing fields
Rules/Regulations: No alcohol after 9:00 p.m.

Directions: From I-95, exit 8, onto Elm Street. Right onto Shippan Avenue, turn left at the lights (this is still Shippan Avenue), then left into the park.

Westcott Cove is in plain view from this beach, which sits in front of an open-field park. Although open to the public, there's no parking for nonresidents. Unless you're staying in the area and can come on bike or by foot, you're out of luck.

Special Notes: Hop aboard an 80-foot, three-masted schooner for a 3-hour, hands-on eco-cruise of Long Island Sound. Available at Yacht Haven West Marina. For information and reservations, call 203-323-1978.

Cummings Park

Shippan Avenue
Stamford, CT 06903
207-977-4692

Season: Memorial Day - Labor Day
Hours: 5:30 a.m. - midnight
Parking: Lot, resident sticker required
Fees: None
Sand: Coarse with shells and rocks
Crowd: Mixed
Facilities: Lifeguard, restrooms, playground, snack bar, picnic tables, ball field, tennis, fishing, benches
Rules/Regulations: No alcohol after 9:00 p.m.

Directions: From Route 1, exit 8, onto Elm Street. Right on Shippan Avenue, and left into the park (before lights).

Like West Beach, this park is also on Westcott Cove. Popular with joggers, walkers, tennis players, sunbathers, and anglers, it's always busy. An extensive road system runs through woods and fields. The beach is broken by several small jetties and one large one that runs beside the water channel.

Cove Island Park

Weed Avenue
Stamford, CT 06903
203-977-4692

Season: Memorial Day - Labor Day
Hours: 5:30 a.m. - one hour after sunset
Parking: Lot, resident sticker required
Fees: None
Sand: Coarse with shells
Crowd: Families
Facilities: Lifeguard, restrooms, playground, snack bar, sail boat launch, picnic area, ball field, tennis, basketball, fishing
Rules/Regulations: No alcohol after 9:00 p.m., motors on boats

Directions: From I-95, exit 8, onto Elm Street. At the intersection with Shippan Avenue, turn left onto Cove Road and follow to Weed Avenue to end.

Well-organized. That's the best description for this island park, which is accessible via a short walking bridge. Everything is orderly and labeled, including specific lanes on paved pathways (with arrows for proper direction) to accommodate bicyclists and skaters. The system works well and there is something for everyone, including beautiful crescent-shaped beaches on Cove Harbor.

"We have the most beautiful coastline all year long. I love to walk here."

Sandie DeFilippis, Stamford, CT

Weed Beach Park

Nearwater Lane
Darien, CT 06820
203-656-7325

Season: Memorial Day - Labor Day
Hours: 9:00 a.m. - 8:00 p.m.
Parking: Lot
Fees: Nonresidents, $10 per car
Sand: Coarse with shells
Crowd: Mixed
Facilities: Lifeguard, restrooms, bath house, bicycle rack, benches, tennis courts, public telephone, picnic area, playground
Rules/Regulations: No animals, glass, alcohol without a permit

Directions: From I-95, exit 9, onto Boston Post Road. Right onto Nearwater Lane (at lights) and right into park.

This 22-acre harbor park, which looks into Cove Harbor and across to Cove Island Park, has two sandy beaches that are divided by a smooth, low rock ledge. A special area is available for wind surfing. For information on one-week windsurfing sessions, call 203-852-1857.

Special Notes: Summer evening concerts are held here. Call the parks department for information, 203-656-7325.

Pear Tree Point Beach
Pear Tree Point Road
Darien, CT 06820
203-656-7325

Season: Memorial Day - Labor Day
Hours: 9:00 a.m. - 8:00 p.m.
Parking: Lot
Fees: Nonresidents, $10 per car
Sand: Soft with shells
Crowd: Mixed
Facilities: Lifeguard, restrooms, bath house, picnic tables, grills, snack bar, boat launch, bicycle rack, benches, telephone
Rules/Regulations: No animals, glass, alcohol without a permit

Directions: From I-95, exit 9, to Route 1 (Boston Post Road). Turn right onto Rings End Road. After crossing over a bridge, turn right, and then right again at the fork onto Pear Tree Point Road.

At the mouth of the Darien Goodwives River, this park encompasses 6.9 acres. You'll find two designated swimming areas that are divided by a wooded rocky point of land. A gazebo, located on the point, is a pleasant spot from which to watch the bay's boat activity.

Calf Pasture Beach
Beach Road
Norwalk, CT 06854
203-854-7806

Season: Memorial Day - Labor Day
Hours: 7:00 a.m. - 1:00 a.m. (no one admitted after midnight)
Parking: Lot
Fees: Nonresidents, $15 per car
Sand: Coarse
Crowd: Mixed
Facilities: Lifeguard (10:00 a.m. - 6:00 p.m.), restrooms, snack bar, benches, fishing pier, picnic tables, small boat ramps, swings

Rules/Regulations: No animals, flying objects (such as balls, Frisbees), fires, glass, walking out onto the jetties, beer kegs without permit

Directions: From I-95, exit 16, East Avenue. Follow the blue signs to the beach area. You'll turn left onto Cemetery Road, right onto Gregory Boulevard, left onto Marvin Street, and right onto Beach Road.

The beach at this 33-acre mainland park is long and narrow, and is separated from the parking area by a border of trees. Calf Pasture Point Park looks (not surprisingly) out to Calf Pasture Island, as well as out to Sheep Rock Island. Also visible is Sheffield Island where there is a picnic and camping area for those with their own boat. (Or you can catch the ferry from Hope Dock.) Windsurfing rentals and lessons are available (203-852-1857). Concerts on the beach are randomly scheduled throughout the summer.

"The Sound is a great place to sail."
      Anita Coffee, Norwalk, CT

Special Notes: SoNo (South Norwalk) is a neighborhood of restored buildings along the Norwalk River with shops, galleries, restaurants, and an IMAX movie theater at the Maritime Center aquarium. Take I-95, Exit 14 N or 15 S. Also, the Norwalk Seaport Association offers half-hour narrated cruises to historic Sheffield Island from Hope Dock. For cruise information, call 203-838-9444.

Shady Beach
Canfield Road
Norwalk, CT 06854
203-838-7531, ext. 306

Season: Memorial Day - Labor Day
Hours: 8:00 a.m. - 8:00 p.m.
Parking: Lot, resident sticker required
Fees: None
Sand: Coarse
Crowd: Mixed
Facilities: Lifeguard, restrooms, picnic tables
Rules/Regulations: No animals

Directions: From I-95, exit 16, onto East Avenue. Follow blue signs. You'll turn left on Cemetery Road, right on Gregory Boulevard, left on Marvin Street, right onto Beach Road and left onto Canfield Road just before Calf Pasture Beach.

Appropriately named for its wooded surroundings, Shady Beach shares the same shoreline as Calf Pasture Beach. While the parking lot is for town residents with permits only, you can park at Calf Pasture and walk over.

Compo Beach
Compo Beach Road
Westport, CT 06880
203-226-8311

Season: Memorial Day - Labor Day
Hours: 4:00 a.m. - midnight
Parking: Lot
Fees: Residents, $20 per season for those with cars registered in Westport, $115 per season for those with cars registered outside of Westport; nonresidents, $10 weekdays, $25 weekends and holidays
Sand: Coarse with shells
Crowd: Mixed
Facilities: Lifeguard (10:00 a.m. - 6:00 p.m.), restrooms, bath house, tables with grills, covered brick pavilion at snack bar (closes at sunset), covered wooden pavilion near playground (closes at sunset), basketball court, public telephone
Rules/Regulations: No alcohol without permit in park or at South Beach picnic area between 6:00 p.m. and 6:00 a.m., animals in most areas, fires, glass, scuba diving without permit, skateboards

Directions: From I-95, exit 17, north on Saugatuck Road, sharp right onto Riverside Avenue, and left onto Bridge Street. Turn right onto Compo Road. After the golf course, Compo Road turns to the right. If you are dropping someone off, there is a pull-in area just beyond the park entrance (but the road becomes one-way here and you won't be able to leave the same way you arrived).

At this popular spot, lots fill up quickly during peak summer weekends. The views of Saugatuck Bay and Long Island Sound are expansive. Parents with children will appreciate an impressive wooden playground.

"It's great for walking, Rollerblading, people watching, and just contemplating life."
      Jocelyn Ragonesi, Westport, CT

Special Notes: Interested in trying sailing, canoeing, rowing, or windsurfing? The Longshore Sailing School, 260 South Compo Rd., offers lessons and rentals between June and August. Call 203-226-4646.

Old Mill Beach
Old Mill Beach Road
Westport, CT 06880
203-226-8311

Season: Saturday before Memorial Day - Labor Day
Hours: 6:00 a.m. - midnight
Parking: Lot, resident sticker required
Fees: $20 per season for town residents with cars registered in Westport, $115 per season for town residents with cars registered outside of Westport
Sand: Coarse
Crowd: Mixed
Facilities: None
Rules/Regulations: No alcohol between 6:00 p.m. and 6:00 a.m., glass

Directions: From I-95, exit 17, north on Saugatuck Road, sharp right onto Riverside Avenue, left onto Bridge Street, and right onto Compo Road. Just beyond the golf course, Compo Road turns to the right. Pass Compo Beach onto Hills Point Road (which is one-way for a short distance), and right into the parking area for Old Mill Beach.

This is a very small beach within Compo Cove and part of a neighborhood.

> Ever notice broken shells along beachside streets? Seagulls drop clams on the road to break their shells so they can eat their soft bodies.

Sherwood Island State Beach

Sherwood Island Connector
Westport, CT 06436
203-226-6983

Season: Memorial Day - end of September
Hours: 8:00 a.m. - sunset
Parking: Lots
Fees: State residents, $5 per car weekdays and $7 weekends;
nonresidents, $8 per car daily
Sand: Sand with pebbles
Crowd: Families
Facilities: Lifeguard, restrooms, snack bar, fishing, field sports,
scuba diving
Rules/Regulations: No alcohol, animals, glass, dogs, fires,
floats other than Coast Guard-approved life preservers

Directions: From I-95, exit 18, to the end of the Sherwood
Island Connector.

The two beaches at this 234-acre state park total 1.5 miles and
are known as East Beach and West Beach. West Beach, to the
right as you enter, feels intimate because it comprises several
crescent-shaped stretches that are separated from one another
by substantial jetties. East Beach has a more spacious feeling.
Between the two beaches is the snack bar with facilities and a
covered pavilion (the roof serves as a deck) and viewing
machines. Although the surf is gentle, the drop into the water
is a little steeper than at other Westport beaches. An
unexpected treat during nonpeak days might be watching
members of a local radio-controlled airplane club put their
planes through their paces at a nearby miniature "flying field."

*"You smell wonderful aromas of the world as families prepare
their picnic meals here."*
Margaret Hennesy, Milford, CT

Burying Hill Beach

Beachside Avenue
Westport, CT 06436
203-226-8311

Season: Saturday before Memorial Day - Labor Day

Hours: 5:00 a.m. - 10:00 p.m.
Parking: Roadside
Fees: State residents, $6 per car weekdays, $9 weekends; nonresidents, $8 per car weekdays, and $13 weekends
Sand: Stones
Crowd: Mixed
Facilities: Lifeguard
Rules/Regulations: No alcohol between 6:00 p.m. and 6:00 a.m., glass

Directions: From I-95, exit 18 N, to Green Farms Road. Turn right onto Morningside Drive, then left onto Beachside Avenue.

This rocky beach is favored by fishermen and walkers. It's about a mile long and has nice views of Long Island Sound. Sherwood Island State Beach is just to the south on the other side of the canal.

"It's a good walk from one side to the other."
Barbara Myers, Westport, CT

Sasco Beach
Sasco Beach Road
Fairfield, CT 06430
203-256-3010

Season: Memorial Day - Labor Day
Hours: Sunrise - 11:00 p.m.
Parking: Lot, resident sticker required
Fees: $10 for seasonal resident sticker
Sand: Coarse
Crowd: Mixed
Facilities: Lifeguard, restrooms, snack bar
Rules/Regulations: No alcohol, unrestrained animals, glass, open fires, swimming to or from boats, unaccompanied children under 8, diving, floats (except at the westerly side of the jetty), scuba diving

Directions: From I-95, exit 19, to Route 1. Just beyond Southport Harbor, turn right onto Sasco Hill Road to the end.

The beach is long and open, although there is some grass on the right-hand end. Permits for Fairfield beaches are issued at Jennings and Penfield Pavilion.

South Pine Creek Beach
South Pine Creek Road
Fairfield, CT 06430
203-256-3010

Season: Memorial Day - Labor Day
Hours: Sunrise - 11:00 p.m.
Parking: Limited lot and roadside, resident sticker required
Fees: $10 for seasonal resident sticker
Sand: Coarse
Crowd: Mixed
Facilities: Lifeguard (10:00 a.m. - 6:00 p.m.), restrooms, snack bar
Rules/Regulations: No alcohol, unrestrained animals, glass, open fires, swimming to or from boats, unaccompanied children under 8, diving, floats, scuba diving

Directions: From I-95, exit 19, to Route 1. Right onto South Pine Creek Road.

This is a very small beach and is used primarily by people in the neighborhood. Although there are dunes and a rustic wooden boardwalk, an apartment building next to the beach detracts significantly from the ambiance.

Penfield Pavilion Beach
Fairfield Beach Road
Fairfield, CT 06430
203-256-3010

Season: Memorial Day - Labor Day
Hours: Sunrise - 11:00 p.m.
Parking: Lot
Fees: Nonresidents, $10 per car weekdays, $15 weekends, $50 per season; sticker required for residents
Sand: Coarse
Crowd: Mixed

Facilities: Lifeguard (10:00 a.m. - 6:00 p.m.), restrooms, snack bar

Rules/Regulations: No alcohol, unrestrained animals, glass, open fires, swimming to or from boats, unaccompanied children under 8, diving, floats, scuba diving

Directions: From I-95, exit 22, onto Round Hill Road. Cross Route 1 onto Beach Road and turn right onto Fairfield Beach Road. The beach is across from Penfield Road.

There is a large pavilion at this long, sandy beach and the view is wide open to Long Island Sound.

Jennings Beach

South Benson Road
Fairfield, CT 06430
203-256-3010

Season: Memorial Day - Labor Day
Hours: Sunrise - 11:00 p.m.
Parking: Lot
Fees: Nonresidents, $10 per car weekdays, $15 weekends, $50 per season; sticker required for residents
Sand: Coarse
Crowd: Mixed
Facilities: Lifeguard (10:00 a.m. - 11:00 p.m.), restrooms, boat launch, playground
Rules/Regulations: No alcohol, unrestrained animals, glass, open fires, swimming to or from boats, unaccompanied children under 8, diving, floats, scuba diving

Directions: From I-95, exit 22, to the end of Beach Road at South Benson Road near the old town hall building.

To the left of Penfield Pavilion Beach is a small beach along the Sound. Because of its close proximity to Penfield, people travel back and forth between the two.

Seaside Park

Barnum Drive
Bridgeport, CT 06602
203-576-7233

Season: Year-round
Hours: Sunrise - sunset
Parking: Lot
Fees: $10 per car
Sand: Coarse
Crowd: Mixed
Facilities: Restrooms, bath house, snack bar, picnic tables
Rules/Regulations: No alcohol, animals, fires

Directions: From I-95, exit 27. After going under I-95 take a left onto South Avenue, then left onto Park Avenue. Go straight under the Perry Arch to Seaside Park.

Not far from the University of Bridgeport, the narrow and sandy barrier beach is almost a mile long. A stone jetty leads to a wooded island, which is home to a small lighthouse. The drop into the Sound is gentle and the sand bars that form at low tide are fun for little ones. But it's a long walk out to deep water if you want to swim.

Circus master P.T. Barnum was once mayor of this city. He gave 200 acres for this park, which was designed by Frederick Law Olmstead (who also designed New York's Central Park), and a statue of Barnum was placed here in his honor.

Special Notes: Circus junkies shouldn't miss the Barnum Museum, 820 Main Ave. (I-95, exit 27). Museum fees are $5 for adults, $3 for children ages 4-18. Call 203-331-9881. Also, the Barnum Festival, held July 4th weekend, includes a huge circus parade, band contests, and fireworks at Seaside Park. Call 800-866-7925 for festival information.

Long Beach
Oak Bluff Drive
Stratford, CT 06497
203-385-4052

Season: Third weekend in June - Labor Day
Hours: Sunrise - sunset
Parking: Lot
Fees: Nonresidents, $10 per day per car, $100 per season (sold at Recreation Office); sticker required for residents
Sand: Coarse with shells

Crowd: Mixed
Facilities: Lifeguard (10:00 a.m. - 5:00 p.m.), portable restrooms
Rules/Regulations: No alcohol, animals, floats

Directions: From I-95, exit 30 N, to Lordship Boulevard. Turn right at the light and head to airport. At stop sign turn right onto Oak Bluff Drive.

Adjacent to the McKinney Wildlife Refuge, this is a natural, undeveloped beach. Although it has fewer amenities than Stratford's other beach (Short), it has better swimming. It's on the Sound rather than on a bay.

Short Beach Park

Short Beach Road
Stratford, CT 06497
203-385-4052

Season: Third weekend in June - Labor Day
Hours: 6:00 a.m. - midnight
Parking: Lot
Fees: Nonresidents, $3 per car; sticker required for residents
Sand: Coarse with shells
Crowd: Families
Facilities: Lifeguard, restrooms, snack bar, picnic area, ball fields, playground, tennis court, golf course, fishing, hiking/bicycling trails
Rules/Regulations: No animals, floats, alcohol except in picnic area

Directions: From I-95, exit 30 N, to the end of Lordship Boulevard. Turn right onto Main Street then watch for a fork in the road. Turn left onto Short Beach Road to the park.

This wonderful 30-acre community park was created out of property that was once thought to be an eyesore -- the local landfill. Although the setting is lovely, swimmers should note that because this is a bay beach you have to walk way out to reach deep water at low tide.

Walnut Beach
Viscount Drive
Milford, CT 06460
203-783-3280

Season: Memorial Day - Labor Day
Hours: Sunrise - 10:00 p.m.
Parking: Lot
Fees: Nonresidents $5 per car; sticker required for residents
Sand: Coarse
Crowd: Mixed
Facilities: Lifeguard, restrooms (11:00 a.m. - 3:00 p.m.
Memorial Day to July 1; 10:00 a.m. - 4:00 p.m. July through
Labor Day), designated beach volleyball areas
Rules/Regulations: No alcohol, animals, floats, fires without a
permit

Directions: From I-95, exit 34, to Route 1. Turn right onto
Meadows End Road, straight onto Pumpkin Delight Road,
straight onto Monroe Street and left onto Viscount Drive.

A number of raised wooden steps and bridges provide access
over low dunes to this narrow beach. Many local
organizations have had a part in transforming this once
undeveloped shore into something people can enjoy: The Boy
Scouts, for example, planted dune grass and beach roses. The
dense marsh behind is set aside for conservation.

"Until recently this was private, now there's a lot going on here."
Margaret Hennesy, Milford, CT

Special Notes: An 890-acre National Wildlife Refuge is not far
from here. It runs along the shore and includes beach and mud
flats. From Viscount Road, turn left at the end of Seaview
Avenue. It's open year-round and there are no fees.

Silver Sands State Park
Nettleton Road
Milford, CT 06460
203-783-3280

Season: Memorial Day - Labor Day
Hours: Sunrise - midnight

Parking: Lot
Fees: None
Sand: Coarse with shells
Crowd: Mixed
Facilities: Lifeguards (11:00 a.m. - 3:00 p.m. Memorial Day to July 1; 10:00 a.m. - 4:00 p.m. July through Labor Day)
Rules/Regulations: No alcohol, animals, floats, fires without permit

Directions: From I-95, exit 34, to Route 1 N. Turn right onto Meadows End Road (lights), straight onto Pumpkin Delight Road, left onto Nettleton Road and follow the road through the marsh to the water's edge. The unnamed park is on the right. (In the future, Silver Sands Beach Road, which has been built, but is not open to through traffic, will lead directly to the beach.)

Perhaps someday there will be a wonderful state park at this run-down beach. It's on the maps and there's even been a specific road constructed. But for more than 20 years there's been lots of talk and no action. Currently, there is just a rough dirt pot-holed roadway along a length of beach, but you can see the potential for something nice. At low tide, the wooded Charles Island (where Captain Kidd is said to have buried treasure!) is accessible. Strong swimmers may feel comfortable walking there at low tide, but it is not recommended that nonswimmers chance the changing tides.

Gulf Beach
Gulf Street
Milford, CT 06460
203-783-3280

Season: Memorial Day - Labor Day
Hours: Sunrise - 10:00 p.m.
Parking: Lots
Fees: Nonresidents, $5 per car, sticker required for residents
Sand: Coarse with shells and rocks
Crowd: Mixed
Facilities: Lifeguard, restrooms, snack bar (11:00 a.m. - 3:00 p.m. Memorial Day to July 1; 10:00 a.m. - 4:00 p.m. July through Labor Day), picnic tables, public telephone, ice machine, fishing pier with access for the handicapped

Rules/Regulations: No alcohol, animals, floats, fires without permit

Directions: From I-95, exit 37, to Wheelers Farm Road. Turn left onto Route 1 and right onto High Street. At the intersection with Cherry Street, continue straight onto Gulf Street.

Because this beach is so rocky, it's best enjoyed from its long wooden pier. The large deck at the end of the pier attracts fishermen. It's also a great spot for watching the sun set.

Special Notes: Free concerts are held on the town green (Broad Street) on Friday evenings in July and August. Call 203-878-0681

Bradley Point Park and West Haven Promenade

Captain Thomas Boulevard
West Haven, CT 06516
203-937-3651

Season: Memorial Day - Labor Day
Hours: Sunrise - sunset
Parking: Lot
Fees: Nonresidents, $10 per car, $5 per car after 4:00 p.m.
Sand: Soft
Crowd: Families
Facilities: Lifeguard (10:15 a.m. - 4:00 p.m.), portable restrooms
Rules/Regulations: No alcohol, open fires, floats

Directions: From I-95, exit 42, to Route 162. At the sharp bend, head straight onto Kelsey Avenue, then right onto Captain Thomas Boulevard.

The elbow that curves from Long Island Sound into the Quinnipiac River basin is a perfect location for a greenbelt of beach access. Paved walkways extend along the shore between roads and homes. While people do flock to the beach, they also come to bike, walk, run, and just enjoy the scenery.

Special Notes: On Friday evenings in July and August, free concerts are held at the bandstand on Center Green. They start at 7:00. For information, call 203-937-3510.

Oak Street Beach

Oak Street
West Haven, CT 06516
203-937-3651

Season: Memorial Day - Labor Day
Hours: Sunrise - sunset
Parking: Lot
Fees: Nonresidents, $10 per car, $5 per car after 4:00 p.m.
Sand: Soft
Crowd: Families
Facilities: Lifeguard (10:15 a.m. - 4:00 p.m.), portable restrooms
Rules/Regulations: No alcohol, open fires, floats

Directions: From I-95, exit 42, to Route 162. At the sharp bend, head straight onto Kelsey Avenue, then left onto Savin Avenue and right onto Oak Street before Savin Rock Park.

The beach is separated from its neighbors by a rock ledge. But it's quite similar to Bradley Point and Morse Beach.

Morse Beach, East Avenue Beach, Peck Beach

Beach Street
West Haven, CT 06516
203-937-3651

Season: Memorial Day - Labor Day
Hours: Sunrise - sunset
Parking: Lot
Fees: Nonresidents, $10 per car, $5 per car after 4:00 p.m.
Sand: Soft
Crowd: Families
Facilities: Lifeguard (10:15 a.m. - 4:00 p.m.), portable restrooms
Rules/Regulations: No alcohol, open fires, floats

Directions: From I-95, exit 42, to Route 162. Follow Route 162 E to Main Street. At the end, turn right onto Beach Street and pass just beyond Sandy Point.

A portion of this beach, which extends from Oak Street to Third Avenue Extension, has recently undergone a reclamation project. At East Avenue and Peck, there's new soft sand. The other side, as of this writing, is still coarse with rocks. The beaches are divided by cement piers and rocky barriers.

Sandy Point Beach
Beach Street
West Haven, CT 06516
203-937-3651

Season: Memorial Day weekend - Labor Day
Hours: Sunrise - sunset
Parking: Lot
Fees: Nonresidents, $10 per car, $5 per car after 4 p.m.
Sand: Soft
Crowd: Mixed
Facilities: Lifeguard (10:15 a.m. to 4:00 p.m.), portable restrooms
Rules/Regulations: No alcohol, open fires, floats

Directions: From I-95, exit 42, to Route 162. Follow Route 162 E to Main Street. At the end, turn right onto Beach Street.

This long, skinny, finger-like beach points into New Haven Harbor. In early summer this is a popular nesting spot for birds. Visitors are urged not to disturb them.

Lighthouse Point Park
Woodward Avenue
New Haven, CT 06515
203-787-8005

Season: Memorial Day - Labor Day
Hours: Sunrise - sunset
Parking: Lot
Fees: $2 per car weekdays, $3 per car weekends and holidays; $25 for seasonal residents pass, $50 for nonresidents
Sand: Rocky with shells

Crowd: Mixed
Facilities: Lifeguard, restrooms, bath house, snack bar, boat launch and rentals, pavilion, picnic tables, playground, fishing
Rules/Regulations: No open fires, animals on beach; leashed-animals allowed in park grounds; alcohol permitted, but beer and wine only

Directions: From I-95, exit 50 N, right onto Townsend Avenue. Or, exit 51 S, to Route 1 to Townsend Avenue. Right onto Lighthouse Road.

The pavilion and antique carousel are just two of the reasons children love to come to this 82-acre park on Long Island Sound. (The carousel is open Tuesday through Friday 3:00 p.m. to 7:00 p.m., Saturday and Sunday 11:00 a.m. to 7:00 p.m. The cost is $.50 per ride). There is also a marine animal touch tank. Black Rock Fort (Revolutionary War) and Fort Nathan Hale (Civil War) have been reconstructed and have excellent views of the New Haven Harbor. There is no charge.

Special Notes: An interesting sidetrip is West Rock Ridge State Park, which surrounds a 428-foot high rock that can be reached by car. There is also a nature center next door. Call 203-787-8016.

Hammonasset Beach State Park
Hammonasset Connector
Madison, CT 06443
203-245-2785

Season: Memorial Day - Labor Day
Hours: Sunrise - sunset
Parking: Lots
Fees: Residents, $5 per car weekdays and $7 weekends; nonresidents, $8 per car weekdays and $12 weekends
Sand: Coarse with broken shells
Crowd: Families
Facilities: Lifeguard, restrooms, bath house, food, picnic area (bring your own grill), bicycle racks, fishing, camping, interpretive programs, public telephone
Rules/Regulations: No alcohol, animals, glass, fires, non-Coast Guard approved floats

Directions: From I-95, exit 62, follow the Hammonasset Connector to end.

Three beaches, West Beach, East Beach, and Meigs Point, run along the 2 miles of waterfront at this 900-acre park. (It's the state's largest shoreline park.) The sand and stone beaches are shallow and have sand bars you can drop off of quite suddenly. The water is somewhat murky, but reportedly clean. West Beach has more sand than East. There are boardwalks, several jetties, a scenic section of rocky coast, and an observation platform (at Meigs Point), as well as picnic pavilions, a bike path, and a nature center with hiking trails. The campground has 541 mostly open sites.

Special Notes: The Madison Historical Society holds an antique show on the town green the third Saturday in August.

Clinton Town Beach
Waterside Lane
Clinton, CT 06413
860-669-6901

Season: Memorial Day - Labor Day
Hours: 9:00 a.m. - 5:00 p.m.
Parking: Lot
Fees: Nonresidents, $7 per car
Sand: Coarse
Crowd: Families
Facilities: Lifeguard, restrooms, snack bar, playground, picnic tables, picnic pavilion
Rules/Regulations: No dogs

Directions: I-95, exit 63, to Route 81 S. Turn left onto Main Street. Go .5 miles, then turn right onto Waterside Lane. (Don't follow signs to "Clinton Beaches" as they direct only to private, residential beaches.)

This friendly beach has pleasant views of Clinton Harbor and Hammonasset Beach State Park. Kids love to play in the water here and explore the edges of the salt marsh. It's possible to walk way out at low tide.

Special Notes: Clinton is known as the "Bluefish Capital." Every August, on the town dock, Clinton celebrates with a 3-

day festival of entertainment, crafts, and food. Admission is $1 for anyone over 12. Call 860-669-0301.

Harvey's Beach
Great Hammock Road
Old Saybrook, CT 06475
860-388-3557

Season: Memorial Day - Labor Day
Hours: 10:00 a.m. - 4:00 p.m., to 4:30 p.m. on weekends
Parking: Lot
Fees: $6 per car and driver, plus $.50 per person
Sand: Coarse
Crowd: Families
Facilities: Restrooms, outside shower, snack bar, picnic tables, playground
Rules/Regulations: No alcohol, animals, glass

Directions: From I-95, exit 67, to Route 154 (Great Hammock Road). Look carefully, because the entrance sign is off the road and easy to miss.

This is a small beach with a big view. There's some marsh grass in the center of the water, but at low tide you can walk way out from the beach, almost touching the boats passing by.

Special Notes: An annual arts and crafts show of juried artists is held on the town green (Main Street) the last weekend in July. Call 860-388-3266.

Old Saybrook Beach
Great Hammock Road
Old Saybrook, CT 06475
860-388-3557

Season: Memorial Day - Labor Day
Hours: 10:00 a.m. - 4:30 p.m.
Parking: Lot, resident permit required
Fees: None
Sand: Coarse
Crowd: Families
Facilities: Lifeguard, restrooms, pavilion, benches

Rules/Regulations: No alcohol, animals

Directions: From I-95, exit 67, to Route 154 (Great Hammock Road).

Although anyone can enter this beach, which is very close to Harvey's Beach, the small parking lot is for residents only. A picnic pavilion stands at the entrance, and traditional beach cottages flank the back.

"It is clean, quiet, and easily accessible."
Carol Sandler, Orange, CT

Sound View Beach
Hartford Avenue
Old Lyme, CT 06371
860-434-1605

Season: Year-round
Hours: None posted
Parking: Limited roadside (2-hour limit), many small lots within the nearby neighborhood
Fees: $3 - $5 per car depending on the lot
Sand: Soft
Crowd: Young
Facilities: Restrooms, picnic table
Rules/Regulations: No coolers, animals

Directions: From I-95, exit 70, to Route 156 (Shore Road) to Hartford Avenue.

It's been called "Main Street USA," and the road that leads to this beach is a busy stretch crammed with shops, snack bars, and stands. The beach itself is crowded, and the cement boardwalk is the place where teens go to see and be seen.

"There's a sea of people."
Matt Petz, Woodstock, CT

Special Notes: Lyme's Annual Midsummer Festival is held the first Friday evening and Saturday in August. Thirteen area organizations join together to help celebrate the area's culture with concerts, entertainment, and demonstrations. Art sales are also held at the Florence Griswold Museum, the Lyme Art Association, and the Academy of Fine Arts. Call 860-434-5232.

Rocky Neck State Park

Giants Neck Road
Niantic, CT 06357
860-739-5471

Season: Memorial Day - Labor Day (weekends only mid April - Memorial Day)
Hours: 8:00 a.m. - sunset
Parking: Lot
Fees: State residents, $5 per car weekdays and $8 weekends; nonresidents, $7 per car weekdays and $12 weekends; preseason, state residents $5 per car, $7 per car nonresidents
Sand: Soft
Crowd: Families
Facilities: Restrooms, bath house, snack bar, picnic tables, fishing, camping, viewing machines
Rules/Regulations: No alcohol, animals, glass

Directions: From I-95, exit 72, follow the connector south. Turn left onto Route 156 (West Main Street). The park is on the right on Giants Neck Road.

Many say this 710-acre park has the best beach in the state. It's almost a mile long, with warm, shallow water and a sand bar. There's no undertow. To reach the beach from the parking lot, you walk through a short tunnel under the Amtrak lines. A jetty on the south side is a good spot for fishing and exploring, as is the beach area beyond, although there's no swimming there. Up on the hill is a splendid cobblestone building that serves as a picnic shelter. Inside are row upon row of picnic tables -- total capacity is 800.

"Kids have a really great time here. The sand is soft and ripply under your feet."
     Joanne Wadleigh, New London, CT

Special Notes: North of the park is the Millstone Information & Science Center, with exhibits on the Millstone Nuclear Power Station, nuclear energy, as well as other energy sources. There are also computer games, a marine aquarium, and multimedia shows. Summer hours are Monday-Tuesday 9:00

a.m. to 4:00 p.m., Wednesday-Friday 9:00 a.m. to 7:00 p.m.,
Saturday and Sunday 12:00 p.m. to 7:00 p.m. Free. Call 860-
444-4234.

Harkness Memorial State Park
Great Neck Road
Waterford, CT 06385
203-443-5725

Season: Year-round
Hours: 8:00 a.m. - 5:00 p.m.
Parking: Lot
Fees: State residents, $4 per car weekdays, $5 weekends;
nonresidents, $5 weekdays, $8 weekends
Sand: Soft
Crowd: Mixed
Facilities: Restrooms, picnic facilities, fishing
Rules/Regulations: No animals

Directions: From I-95, exit 83, or Route 1 to Route 213, Great
Neck Road.

Although swimming is not allowed, this large Long Island
Sound beach at Goshen Point has rich, white sand, just right
for walking and fishing. The park's facilities for the
handicapped were the first of their kind in the country. On
the park grounds is the 42-room Harkness Mansion with
sweeping lawns and formal gardens.

*"We appreciate Harkness and the beautiful handicapped area for
the blind to experience nature walks."*
Betty Sweeney, Waterford, CT

Ocean Beach Park
Ocean Avenue
New London, CT 06320
860-447-3031 or 800-510-7263

Season: Memorial Day - Labor Day
Hours: 9:00 a.m. - 10:00 p.m.
Parking: Lot

Fees: $10 per car or $2 per hour, $3 maximum after 6:00 p.m.; $2 for walk-ins, $1 for children and seniors
Sand: Soft
Crowd: Mixed
Facilities: Lifeguard, restrooms, bath house, snack bar, arcade including water slide and miniature golf, paddle boats (portions of arcade are open year-round)
Rules/Regulations: No alcohol, animals (except for seeing-eye dogs), bicycles, skateboards, in-line skates; grilling allowed

Directions: From I-95, exit 75 N or 83 S, to Williams Street. Left onto Hempstead Street, right onto Truman Street, right onto Bank Street, and left onto Ocean Avenue, Route 213.

Close to a mile long, this sandy beach has clean water and a gentle surf. One of the largest recreation parks in the area, diversions include a triple water slide, miniature golf, boating, and arcades. An Olympic-size freshwater pool is available for those who prefer their swimming water chlorinated ($2 for adults, $1 for children, $2.50 and $2 weekends and holidays).

Esker Point Beach
Marsh Road
Groton, CT 06340
860-441-6777

Season: Memorial Day - Labor Day
Hours: Sunrise - sunset
Parking: Lot
Fees: $1 per car
Sand: Coarse
Crowd: Families
Facilities: Lifeguard, restrooms, snack bar, grills, picnic tables(facilities 10:00 a.m. - 4:00 p.m.)
Rules/Regulations: No alcohol, animals, glass

Directions: From I-95 to Route 1 to Route 215 (Groton Long Point). Turn right onto Marsh Road (at the bend in the road).

Although this beach is scenic, the shallow swimming area is thick with seaweed. Have lunch at the picnic tables in the wooded and grassy grove. Afterward maybe you can pick up a game of volleyball -- nets are all set up.

Special Notes: If you've never been on board a submarine, a visit to the *USS Nautilus* is a must. Free. Call 800-343-0079.

Bluff Point Coastal Reserve State Park

Depot Street
Groton, CT 06340
no phone

Season: Year-round
Hours: 8:00 a.m. - sunset
Parking: Lot
Fees: None
Sand: Very coarse
Crowd: Families
Facilities: None
Rules/Regulations: No animals

Directions: From I-95 to Route 117 S to Route 1. Head south on North Road to Depot Street.

This 800-acre park points into Long Island Sound. Trails lead walkers and bicyclists about a mile and a half through the woods to the end of the peninsula. The mile-long tombolo (a sand bar that connects an island to the mainland) ends at Bushy Point, a rocky island. While swimming is not encouraged, this is a lovely, undeveloped park with a tidal salt marsh, some rocky shoreline, and woods.

Williams Beach Park

Harry Austin Road
Mystic, CT 06355
860-536-3575

Season: Mid June - Labor Day
Hours: 10:00 a.m. -sunset
Parking: Lot
Fees: $4 per car, $2 for walk-ins, $1 for children to 17
Sand: Coarse
Crowd: Families
Facilities: Lifeguard (weekends 10:00 a.m. - 4:30 p.m.), restrooms, covered picnic tables, playground, grills
Rules/Regulations: No alcohol, animals

Directions: From I-95, exit 90, to Route 1 N. Right onto
Masons Island Road, then right onto Harry Austin Road.
If you need a change from the hustle and bustle of Mystic's
shops and museums, try this small community beach. Be
aware that although the water is gentle, the drop is somewhat
steep. Children will love the swings in the park.

Special Notes: A sea shanty festival is held here in mid June,
as are occasional free concerts.

duBois Beach
Water Street
Stonington, CT 06378
860-535-2476

Season: Memorial Day - Labor Day
Hours: 10:00 a.m. - 5:00 p.m.
Parking: Lot
Fees: $5 per family or $2 per person weekdays; $6 per family
or $3 per person weekends
Sand: Coarse
Crowd: Families
Facilities: Lifeguards, portable restrooms
Rules/Regulations: No alcohol, animals, glass, fires, floats

Directions: From I-95 to North Water Street to Water Street.
Park at point.

This beach is at the first protected harbor in Long Island
Sound, an active sailing port with views to Napatree Point in
Watch Hill, Rhode Island, and Montauck Point in Long
Island. Sand has been brought in to refurbish this small beach,
which sits across from a historic lighthouse. Breakwaters
provide calm water. History buffs take note: This area was
attacked by the British in 1812, when Commander Thomas
Hardy brought five warships into the harbor.

Special Notes: Climb the circular stone steps of the Old
Lighthouse Museum tower and you'll have lovely views, not
only of Connecticut but also of Rhode Island and New York.
Exhibits include a history of the community (it was settled in
1649), the China Trade, and pre-1835 pottery. Located at 7
Water St., the museum is open daily during July and August,
and Tuesday through Sunday in May, June, September,

October, and November. Hours are 11:00 a.m. - 5:30 p.m. Admission is $3 for adults, $1 for children 6-12. Call 860-535-2440.

If you're looking for a casual meal after a day at the beach, head to Skipper's Dock (66 Water St., 860-535-2000). Sit on a picnic bench by the harbor and enjoy a bowl of bouillabaisse or some grilled haddock.

QUICK REFERENCE INDEX

Following are some of the best beaches for:

fishing

Ballston, Truro, MA, 208

Charlestown, Block
    Island, RI, 253

Colony, Kennebunkport,
    ME, 26

Gulf, Milford, 310

Harkness Memorial State
    Park, Waterford, CT,
    319

Lobsterville, Gay Head,
    MA, 231

Menemsha Town,
    Chilmark, MA, 229

Popham Beach State Park,
    Phippsburg, ME, 42

Rockland Point Beach,
    Rockland, ME, 47

Rocky Neck State Park,
    Niantic, 318

Sapowet, Tiverton, RI,
    290

Sea, Roque Bluffs, ME, 56

White Crest, Wellfleet,
    MA, 202

bringing the children

Appanagansett Park,
    Dartmouth, MA, 118

Bicentennial Park,
    Hampton, NH, 63

Children's, Nantucket,
    MA, 240

Clinton Town, Clinton,
    315

Compo, Westport, CT,
    301

Crane's Beach
    Reservation, Ipswich,
    MA, 96

Crescent Beach State
    Park, Cape Elizabeth,
    ME, 36

Cummings Park,
    Stamford, CT, 297

Deveraux, Marblehead,
    MA, 78

First, Newport, RI, 286

Fogland, Tiverton, RI,
    290

Forest River Park, Salem,
    MA, 79

Fort Adams State Park,
    Newport, RI, 283

Fred Benson Town (and
    Pavilion, Crescent),
    Block Island, RI, 248

Goddard State Park,
    Warwick, RI, 276

Grays, Kingston, MA, 129

Hammonasset Beach State
    Park, Madison, CT, 314

Hen's Cove, Bourne, MA,
    145

Hingham Bathing,
    Hingham, MA, 140

Jetties, Nantucket, MA,
    242

Lighthouse Point Park,
    New Haven, CT, 315

Lynch Park, Beverly, MA,
    83

New Castle, New Castle,
    NH, 70

Owen Park, Tisbury,
    MA, 226

Oyster Pond, Chatham, MA, 189

Paine's Creek, West Brewster, MA, 220

Parkers River South, South Yarmouth, MA, 167

Pemaquid Beach Park, Bristol, ME, 44

Pleasure Bay, Boston, MA, 107

Rocky Beach at City Park, Belfast, ME, 51

Rocky Neck, Niantic, CT, 318

Roger Wheeler State Park, Narragansett, RI, 270

Seaside Park, Bridgeport, CT, 306

Sherwood Island State Forest, Westport, CT, 303

Skaket, Orleans, MA, 194

South Kingstown Town, South Kingstown, RI, 267

Surf Drive, Falmouth, MA, 151

Thomas Point, Brunswick, ME, 40

Veterans Park, Barnstable, MA, 162

Walker Park, Rockport, ME, 48

Wallis Sands, Rye, NH, 68

Warwick City Park, Warwick, RI, 277

Watch Hill, Westerly, RI, 258

Wingaersheek, Gloucester, MA, 91

Weed Beach Park, Darien, CT, 298

people watching

Atlantic, Westerly, RI, 287

Ballard's, Block Island, RI, 256

Cahoon Hollow, Wellfleet, MA, 202

Compo, Westport, CT, 301

Cove Island, Stamford, CT, 297

Craigville, Barnstable, MA, 158

Crane's Beach Reservation, Ipswich, MA, 96

Deveraux, Marblehead, MA, 78

First, Newport, RI, 286

Fred Benson Town (and Pavilion, Crescent), Block Island, RI, 248

Good Harbor, Gloucester, MA, 90

Hampton Central State, Hampton, NH, 61

Herring Cove, Provincetown, MA, 215

Joseph Sylva State, Oak Bluffs, MA, 237

Long Sands, York, ME, 18

Misquamicut State, Westerly, RI, 260

Nahant, Nahant, MA, 75

Nantasket, Hull, MA, 138

Narragansett Town, Narragansett, RI, 273

Nauset, Orleans, MA, 192,

Ocean Beach Park, New London, CT, 319

Ogunquit, Ogunquit, ME, 20

Old Orchard, Old Orchard, ME, 33

Revere, Revere, MA, 113

Salisbury, Salisbury, MA, 101

Scarborough State, Narragansett, RI, 271

Short Sands, York, ME, 18

Singing, Manchester by-the-sea, MA, 84

Sound View, Old Lyme, CT, 317

South, Edgartown, MA, 233

Surfside, Nantucket, MA, 245

West Dennis, West Dennis, MA, 170

Willow, Salem, MA, 81

Wingaersheek, Gloucester, MA, 91

windsurfing

Burton Baker, Wellfleet, MA, 207

Calf Pasture, Norwalk, CT, 299

Fogland, Tiverton, RI, 290

Fort Foster State Park, Kittery, ME, 15

Horseneck Beach State Reservation, Westport, MA, 116

Indian Neck, Wellfleet, MA, 207

Joseph Sylvia State, Oak Bluffs, MA, 237

Little Harbor, Wareham, MA, 125

Nahant, Nahant, MA, 75

Nauset, Orleans, MA, 192

Sea Point, Kittery, ME, 16

Weed Beach Park, Darien, CT, 298

West Dennis, West Dennis, MA, 170

surfing

Black Rock, Block Island, RI, 253

Cisco, Nantucket, MA, 244

Coast Guard, Eastham, MA, 194

First, Newport, RI, 286

Gooch's, Kennebunk, ME, 26

Green Hill, South Kingstown, RI, 265

Head of the Meadow, Truro, MA, 210

Lond Sands, York, ME, 18

Longnook, Truro, MA, 209

Madaket, Nantucket, MA, 243

Matunuck Point State, South Kingstown, RI, 268

Narragansett State, Narragansett, RI, 273

Narragansett Town, Narragansett, RI, 273

Nauset, Orleans, MA, 192

North Beach State Park, Hampton, NH, 62

Old Orchard, Old Orchard, ME, 33

Pine Point, Scarborough, ME, 34

Scarborough Beach Park, Scarborough, ME, 35

Second, Middletown, RI, 287

Surfside, Nantucket, MA, 245

York Harbor, York, ME, 17

ELLEN'S PICKS
an unabashedly subjective list

Black Rock, Block Island, RI, 253

Charlestown Breachway State Park, 264 Charlestown, RI, 264

Compo, Westport, CT, 301

Cove Island Park, Stamford, CT, 297

Crane's Beach Reservation, Ipswich, MA, 96

Deveraux, Marblehead, MA, 78

Drakes Island, Wells, ME, 22

East, Edgartown, MA, 235

Ferry (and Western), Scarborough, ME, 31

First Encounter, Eastham, MA, 199

Half Mile (at Reid State Park), Georgetown, ME, 42

Halibut Point Reservation, Rockport, MA, 95

Hammonasset Beach State Park, Madison, 314

Horseneck Beach State Reservation, Westport, MA, 116

Jasper, Machias, ME, 57

Little Compton Town, Little Compton, RI, 291

Marconi, Wellfleet, MA, 200

Plymouth, Plymouth, MA, 127

Popham Beach State Park, Phippsburg, ME, 42

Race Point, Provincetown, MA, 214

Rexhame Town, Marshfield, MA, 134

Sandy Neck, Barnstable, MA, 222

Second, Middletown, RI, 287

Sherwood Island State, Westport, CT, 303

Siasconset Beach, Nantucket, MA, 245

South Cape Beach State Park, Mashpee, MA, 154

South Kingstown Town, South Kingstown, RI, 267

Wallis Sands State Park, Rye, NH, 68

West Island Town, Fairhaven, MA, 122

Wingaersheek, Gloucester, MA, 91

GENERAL INDEX

Maine

Bay View, 31
Biddeford Pool, 29
Birch Point State Park, 44
Camden Hills State Park, 49
Camp Ellis, 30
Carrying Place Cove, 58
Cleaves Cove, 27
Colony, 26
Crescent (in Owls Head), 45
Crescent Beach State Park, 36
Drakes Island, 22
Ducktrap, 50
East End, 38
Ferry (and Western), 34
Ferry Beach State Park, 31
Footbridge, 21
Fort Foster Park, 15
Fort Point State Park, 53
Fortune Rocks, 28
Gooch's, 26
Goose Rocks, 27
Half Mile (at Reid State Park), 42
Higgins, 36
Hills, 29
Jasper, 57
Laite Memorial Park, 48
Lamoine (at Lamoine State Park), 55
Laudholm, 23
Lincolnville, 50
Little, 20
Long Sands, 18
Marlboro, 55
Middle, 25

Mile (at Reid State Park), 43
Mother's, 24
Ocean, 32
Ogunquit, 20
Old Orchard, 33
Owls Head Light, 45
Parsons and Crescent Surf, 24
Passaconaway (aka Cape Neddick), 19
Pemaquid Beach Park, 44
Pine Point, 34
Popham Beach State Park, 42
Rockland Point (at Marie H. Reed Memorial Park), 47
Rocky Beach at City Park, 51
Sand, 53
Sandy Beach Park, 46
Sandy Point, 52
Scarborough Beach Park, 35
Sea (at Roque Bluffs State Park), 56
Sea Point and Crescent Beach, 16
Seal Harbor, 54
Seawall (and Small Point), 41
Short Sands, 18
South Lubec, 57
Thomas Point , 40
Walker Park, 48
Wells, 22
Willard, 37
Winslow Memorial Park, 38

Wolfe's Neck State Park, 39

York Harbor, 17

New Hampshire

Bass, 64
Bicentennial Park, 63
Cable Road, 66
Foss, 67
Hampton Central State, 61
Hampton State, 60
Jenness State, 66
New Castle, 70
North Beach State Park, 62
North Hampton, 64
North Side Park, 63
Odiorne Point State Park, 69
Ragged Neck State Park, 67
Sawyers, 65
Seabrook, 60
Wallis Sands State Park, 68
Wallis Sands, 68

North Shore, Massachusetts

Back, 94
Black, 86
Black Rock, 71
Blaney, 76
Canoe, 73
Crane's Beach Reservation, 96
Cressey's, 87
Dane Street, 83
Dead Horse, 81
Deveraux, 78

Forest River Park, 79
Forty Steps, 74
Front, 94
Good Harbor, 90
Grace Oliver, 79
Gray, 86
Half Moon, 88
Halibut Point Reservation, 95
Independence, 82
Long, 92
Lynch, 83
Nahant and Long, 75
Niles, 89
North Plum Island, 99
Old Garden, 93
Parker River National Wildlife Refuge, 99
Pavilion (Gloucester), 88
Pavilion (Ipswich), 97
Pebble, 92
Phillips, 77
Plum Cove, 91
Preston, 77
Rices, 84
Salisbury, 101
Salisbury Beach State Reservation, 100
Sandy, 82
Sandy Point State Reservation, 98
Short, 74
Singing, 84
Tudor, 72
Waikiki, 80
Whales, 76
Wharf, 73
White, 85
Willow, 81
Wingaersheek Beach, 91

Boston and beyond, Massachusetts

Carson, 105
Constitution, 109
Frederick W. Yirrell, Jr., 111
King's, 114
L Street, 106
Lovells, 108
Lynn, 113
M Street, 107
Malibu, 105
Pleasure Bay, 107
Revere, 113
Savin Hill, 104
Short, 112
Simon J. Donovan's, 110
Tenean, 103
Winthrop, 111
Wollaston, 103

South Shore, Massachusetts

Apponagansett Park, 118
Brant Rock, 132
Demarest Lloyd State Park, 117
Dr. O'Toole's Memorial (aka East), 120
Duxbury State Reservation, 132
Duxbury Town, 131
Egypt, 136
Ellison (aka Shipyard Lane), 130
Fort Phoenix State, 121
George Lane, 140
Grays, 129
Hingham Bathing, 140
Horseneck Beach State Reservation, 116
Humarock, 134

Jones Park Town, 119
Little Harbor, 125
Mattapoisett Town, 123
Minot, 137
Nantasket Beach Reservation, 138
Nelson, 129
North Scituate, 137
Onset, 126
Pegotty, 135
Plymouth (aka Long), 127
Pope's, 122
Rexhame Town, 134
Round Hill, 118
Sand Hills, 135
Shell Point, 125
Stephen's Field, 128
Stony, 139
Sunrise, 133
Swifts Neck and Swifts, 124
Veterans of Mattapoisett Memorial Park, 123
Wessagussett, 141
West, 120
West Island Town, 122
Westport Town (aka East Beach), 117
Westport Town, 115
White Horse, 127

Cape Cod, Massachusetts

Atlantic Avenue, 183
Ballston, 208
Bank Street, 184
Barlows Landing, 145
Bass River, 168
Bay View (in Dennis), 178
Bay View (in Yarmouth), 163
Boat Meadow, 200
Breakwater, 218

Bristol, 153
Burton Baker, 207
Cahoon Hollow, 202
Campground, 197
Chapin Memorial, 180
Chapoquoit, 148
Chatham Light, 191
Coast Guard, 194
Cockle Cove, 186
Cold Storage, 176
Colonial Acres, 164
Cooks Brook, 197
Corn Hill, 212
Corporation Road, 178
Craigville, 158
Crosby Landing, 216
Depot Street, 174
Dowses, 158
Duck Harbor, 204
Earle Road, 182
East, 160
East Sandwich, 221
Ellis Landing, 217
Englewood, 164
Falmouth Heights, 152
First Encounter, 199
Fisher, 213
Forest, 186
Glendon Road, 172
Gray Gable, 143
Gray's (aka Bass Hole),
   169
Great Hill, 204
Great Hollow, 212
Grey Neck Road, 181
Haigis, 172
Harborview, 177
Hardings, 188
Head of the Meadows,
   210
Hen's Cove, 145
Herring Cove, 215
Highland, 210
Howe Street, 177
Indian Neck, 207

Inman Road, 175
Kalmus Park, 161
Keyes Memorial, 160
Kingsbury, 198
LeCount Hollow, 201
Linnell's Landing, 217
Longnook, 209
Loop, 157
Marconi, 200
Mashnee Island, 143
Mayflower Public, 179
Mayo, 206
Megansett, 147
Menauhant, 154
Mill Way, 162
Monomoy Island, 189
Monument, 144
Nauset, 192
Nauset Light, 195
Newcomb Hollow, 203
Nobska, 150
North, 192
Old Silver, 147
Oregon, 156
Oyster Pond, 189
Paines Creek, 220
Parker's River South, 167
Pilgrim, 211
Pleasant Bay, 185
Pleasant Road, 181
Point of the Rocks, 218
Powers Landing, 205
Race Point, 214
Raycroft Parkway, 174
Red River, 184
Ridgevale, 187
Robbins Hill, 219
Rock Harbor, 193
Ropes, 157
Ryder, 213
Sagamore, 146
Saint's Landing, 219
Sandy Neck, 222
Scusset, 223
Sea Gull, 165

Sea Street (in Dennis), 173
Sea Street (in East
    Dennis), 175
Sea Street (in Harwich),
    183
Sea View, 166
Skaket, 194
South Beach Island, 190
South Cape Beach State,
    155
South Cape Town, 154
South Middle, 167
South Village Road, 171
Stoney, 149
Sunken Meadow, 196
Surf Drive, 151
Thatcher, 166
The Tides, 152
Thumpertown, 198
Town, 222
Veterans' Park, 162
West Dennis, 170
White Crest, 202
William H. Covell, 159
Windmill, 169
Wood Neck, 149

Martha's Vineyard, Massachusetts

Bend-in-the-Road, 236
Chappy Point, 234
East, 235
Eastville Point, 238
Joseph Silva State (Oak
    Bluffs State), 237
Lagoon Bridge, 227
Lake Tashmoo, 226
Lambert's Cove, 227
Lighthouse (and Fuller
    Street), 236
Lobsterville, 231
Long Point Wildlife
    Refuge, 228
Lucy Vincent, 231
Menemsha Town, 229
Moshup, 232
Oak Bluffs Town, 237
Owen Park, 226
Philbin, 233
South (aka Katama), 233
Squibnocket, 230

Nantucket, Massachusetts

Brant Point, 241
Children's, 240
Cisco, 244
Dionis, 243
Francis Street, 246
Jetties, 242
Madaket, 243
Siasconset, 245
Surfside, 245

Rhode Island

Atlantic, 287
Ballard's, 256
Barrington Town, 279
Beavertail State Park, 275
Black Rock, 253
Blue Shutters Town, 262
Brenton Point State Park,
    284
Bristol Town, 280
Charlestown Breachway
    State Park, 264
Charlestown Town, 264
Charlestown (on Block
    Island), 253
Clay Head, 251
Connimicut, 278
Dodsworth, 272
Dunes Park, 261
East (in Charlestown), 263

East (in Westerly), 259
East Matunuck State
    (Daniel O'brien), 269
First (aka Easton's), 286
Fogland, 290
Fort Adams State Park,
    283
Fred Benson Town (and
    Pavilion, Crescent), 248
Goddard State Park, 276
Gooseberry, 285
Goosewing, 292
Green Hill, 265
Grinnell's, 289
Island Park Town (and
    Teddy's State), 281
Kings Park, 282
Little Compton Town,
    291
Mackeral Cove, (and
    Jamestown Town), 274
Mansion, 250
Mary Carpenter's, 268
Matunuck Point State (aka
    Deep Cove), 268
Misquamicut Fire District
    (and Windjammer
    Family), 260
Misquamicut State, 260
Mohegan, 255
Moonstone, 266
Napatree Point, 257
Narragansett Town, 273
North Kingstown Town,
    274
Oakland, 278
Pebbly, 256
Quonochontaug Barrier,
    262
Reject (aka People's), 285
Roger Wheeler State Park
    (aka Sand Hill Cove),
    270
Roy Carpenter's, 266
Salty Brine State, 270

Sandy Point (in
    Portsmouth), 282
Sandy Point (in
    Warwick), 276
Sandy Point (on Block
    Island), 251
Sapowet, 290
Scarborough State, 271
Scotch, 249
Second, 287
South Kingstown Town,
    267
Third (and Navy,
    Peabody), 288
Vail, 254
Warwick City Park, 277
Watch Hill, 258
West, 252

Connecticut

Bluff Point Coastal
    Reserve State Park, 321
Bradley Point Park, 311
Burying Hill, 303
Byram Park, 294
Calf Pasture, 299
Clinton Town, 315
Compo, 301
Cove Island, 297
Cummings Park, 297
duBois, 322
Esker Point Beach, 320
Greenwich Point, 295
Gulf, 310
Hammonasset Beach State
    Park, 314
Harkness Memorial State
    Park, 319
Harvey's, 316
Jennings, 306
Lighthouse Point, 315
Long, 307

Morse (and East Avenue, Peck), 312
Oak Street, 312
Ocean Beach Park, 319
Old Mill, 302
Old Saybrook, 316
Pear Tree Point, 299
Penfield Pavilion, 305
Rocky Neck State Park, 318
Sandy Point, 313
Sasco, 304

Seaside Park, 306
Shady, 300
Sherwood Island State, 303
Short Beach Park, 308
Silver Sands State, 309
Sound View, 317
South Pine Creek, 305
Walnut, 309
Weed Beach Park, 298
West, 296
Williams Beach Park, 321

ACKNOWLEDGEMENTS

The beach facts, marked by a sun icon and interspersed throughout *The New England Beach Guide,* were gratefully culled from a variety of sources. They include:

The Beachwalker's Guide, 1982, by Edward R. Ricciuti, Curtis Brown Publishers

The National Seashores, The Complete Guide to America's Scenic Coastal Parks, 1994, by Ruthe N. Wolverton, Roberts Rinehart Publishers

A Guide to New England's Landscape, 1977, by Neil Jorgensen, The Globe Pequot Press